DANTE ALIGHIERI

THE CROSSROAD SPIRITUAL LEGACY SERIES
Edited by John Farina

The Rule of Benedict: Insights for the Ages
by Joan Chittister, O.S.B.

Ignatius Loyola: Spiritual Exercises
by Joseph A. Tetlow, S.J.

Francis de Sales: Introduction to the Devout Life
and Treatise on the Love of God
by Wendy M. Wright

Teresa of Avila: Mystical Writings
by Tessa Bielecki

St. Francis of Assisi: Writings for a Gospel Life
by Regis J. Armstrong, O.F.M. Cap.

Augustine: Essential Writings
by Benedict J. Groeschel, C.S.R.

Thomas Aquinas: Spiritual Master
by Robert Barron

Hildegard: Prophet of the Cosmic Christ
by Renate Craine

Karl Rahner: Mystic of Everyday Life
by Harvey D. Egan

C.S. Lewis: Spirituality for Mere Christians
by William Griffin

DANTE ALIGHIERI

DIVINE COMEDY
DIVINE SPIRITUALITY

Robert Royal

A Crossroad Book
The Crossroad Publishing Company
New York

The Crossroad Publishing Company
www.CrossroadPublishing.com

Printed in the United States of America

Library of Congress Cataloging-in-Publication Data

Royal, Robert, 1949–
    Dante Alighieri : Divine comedy, divine spirituality / Robert
Royal.
        p.   cm. — (The Crossroad spiritual legacy series)
    Includes bibliographical references.
    ISBN 0-8245-1604-4 (pbk.)
    1. Dante Alighieri, 1265–1321. Divina commedia. 2. Dante
Alighieri, 1265–1321—Religion. 3. Spirituality in literature.
I. Title. II. Series.
PQ4416.R69   1999
851'.1—dc21   98-46449
                                        CIP

3 4 5 6 7 8 9 15 14 13 12

Contents

List of Illustrations

Acknowledgments

The idea for this book originated with my old friend and general editor of this series, John Farina, who for many years has been a stimulating conversation partner on many topics within and outside the Dantean orbit. He cares, as no one else I have met, for the spiritual legacy of the race at a time when many people are fumbling to regain their spiritual bearings. May his tribe increase.

My family has contributed—directly and indirectly—all along the way. My wife, Veronica, not only patiently endured while I spent what must have seemed unending hours closed in a room with Dante. She also has given proof for decades of forms of love that even Dante, who never had to settle down and raise a family with Beatrice, did not write about. My children, Elizabeth and John Paul, helped in retyping the manuscript, as did my assistant, Jason Boffetti, who also created the diagrams of the various realms that are interspersed in the text.

Finally, I owe it to my brother, the now Rev. Kevin Royal, that I ever got interested in Dante at all. More years ago than either of us cares to remember, he handed me the Ciardi translation of the *Inferno*, which he was reading at a minor seminary. It was Easter vacation, an auspiciously Dantesque season. And what I found in that book over the next few days, like many other things my brother has conveyed to me over the years, changed and continues to change my whole way of looking at the world. I hope that this little work, which owes its existence to these and many other figures who, I am grateful, have shaped my own spiritual pilgrimage, will encourage readers to study Dante himself more closely, one of the West's indisputable spiritual masters.

Foreword

Writing in the fourth century, a North African Christian by the name of Lactantius offered the following definition of virtue. For him, virtue is nothing less than "enduring of evils and labors." How unlike contemporary notions this definition of virtue is and how odd it sounds for us to be told so plainly that the fullness of life can be had only through enduring evils and trials. Yet, despite our inclination to write off Lactantius as an overly pessimistic nay-sayer, we must admit that life does include a large dose of suffering. We can take it well or badly. We can flee it or embrace it, but it will come and find us wherever we hide, and then it will test our mettle. Virtue does involve suffering evils, not simply actualizing ourselves, or conquering our fears, or visualizing success, or learning techniques to cope with stress, or building better "relationships" with members of the opposite sex. There are things in life that simply cannot be so easily manipulated. Situations that don't get better. Unpleasant realities that won't go away. Where do we turn when confronted by them?

We can turn to the externals, to our comforts and our conveniences, to the superficialities of our lives, or we can turn to our depths. Many who have lived before us have learned the hard way that turning to the depths is the way to a fuller life. Their insights have been handed down, often in forms that are now hard to find and harder to read. Their language is archaic. Their morality out of sync with ours. Their clarity, off-putting. Their humility, disconcerting. Yet they are there, waiting quietly to share with us their hard-won wisdom, waiting to dialogue with us as we face situations that are different from those they encountered only in the particulars, not in the essences.

Simply put, that is the reason why Crossroad, I, and a team of well-known scholars and spiritual leaders have joined together to undertake the Spiritual Legacy series. The need for spiritual wisdom is great. Our situation is critical. This then is more than an enterprise in scholarship, more than a literary exercise. It is an effort to convey life.

Certainly the idea of doing editions of the works of spiritual guides from the past is not new. There are a host of books available that do just that. How is the Spiritual Legacy series different?

The uniqueness of this series abides in its content and its style. In content it endeavors to present both texts from the spiritual guide and extensive commentary by a present-day disciple of the sage. It gives the reader the chance to encounter for herself the writings of a spiritual master. Nothing can take the place of that experience. However demanding it might be, whatever efforts it might require, there can be no substitute for it. One, for instance, cannot simply hear a description of the tenth chapter of Augustine's *Confessions*. No commentary, however skilled, can take the place of reading for oneself Augustine's words of unparalleled power: "Late have I loved Thee, O Beauty, so ancient, yet so new!"

While it is true that there is no substitute for encountering the text firsthand, it is also certain that for most people that encounter will be an excursion into a foreign land. Often many centuries and numerous barriers of language, customs, philosophy, and style separate us from the writings of bygone sages. To come to that point where we can understand the horizon of the author, we must be taught something about the historical context, the literary style, and the thought forms of the age, for instance. That is why we have included in this series extensive commentary on the text. That commentary is alternated with the text throughout the books, so that one can be taught, then experience the writings firsthand, over and over as one moves deeper into the text. At that point, the horizon of the reader meets that of the author, aided by the expert guidance of the editor of each book, who suggests not only what the text might mean, but how it might be made part of our lives.

The style of the Spiritual Legacy series is also unique in that it attempts to convey life with a certain degree of sophistication that befits an educated readership. Yet it does not assume that everyone will have a background in the material presented, nor does it purport to offer original or arcane scholarship. The editors' mastery of the texts is in each case complemented by their experience in putting the meaning of the texts into practice and helping others to do so as well. We are trying to present a series of books that will fit somewhere between the scholarly editions that pride themselves on their accuracy and originality and the popular pieces that offer too little substance for the healthy reader.

The series is designed to be used by a broad range of people. For those seekers who wish to journey toward spiritual wholeness as part of a group, the series is ideally suited. The texts presented can be easily divided into sections for discussion by a group meeting, say, on a weekly basis.

For those who are traveling alone, the series is a trustworthy and enjoyable tour book. The direct, simple language of the commentaries frames the memorable words of the classical texts and offers them in an attractive setting for meditation and practical application.

The publisher and editors of the Spiritual Legacy series join me in inviting you to undertake a journey that will take you back to an encounter with ancient wisdom and challenge you to an experience of self-understanding and, at its best, self-transcendence. It is our hope that that experience will help you to grow and to be a source of fresh life for all those around you.

John Farina

Introduction

Christianity recounts the story of salvation in two ways. First, it recalls God's work in history: the creation of the world, the Fall, the history of Israel, Christ's Incarnation and Redemption, the end of the world, and our ultimate destination in the afterlife. All of this explains to us the nature of the universe in which we live, how we are to conduct ourselves, and the final meaning of existence. But there is a second way to repeat the Christian story that, while acknowledging all the universal truths of salvation history, emphasizes the particular pilgrimage that each of us must make in our movement toward God. Indeed, the very notion that we are all pilgrims and wayfarers in this life has been a major theme in Christian thought in every age and an important contribution to the self-understanding of the human race.

Innumerable theologians, homilists, spiritual writers, and poets have taken up the subject of the *itinerarium mentis in Deum*, the soul's journey into God, as St. Bonaventure called it. But perhaps no one has given a more lively, colorful, complete, and moving account of the spiritual pilgrimage than the medieval Catholic poet Dante Alighieri (1265–1321). His long poem *The Divine Comedy* is by universal agreement one of the very great, if not the greatest, Christian literary works. Dante ranks among the giants of world literature, with figures such as Homer, Vergil, Shakespeare, and Goethe. The *Comedy* recounts how, in the middle of his life, the poet finds himself lost in a dark wood of sin and error. In desperation, he seeks to return to the right path and true life in God. His quest takes him through the realms of Hell, Purgatory, and Paradise to the beatific vision. Along the way Dante encounters sinners, penitents, saved souls—some great and well-known figures from history or from his own time, others humble spirits never known beyond the small circle of their friends and acquaintances. Through these encounters, Dante the pilgrim learns about the various aspects of the spiritual life, and Dante the poet writes a drama that he calls a comedy, not in the modern sense of a series of light and amusing episodes but in a deeper way that he read about in classical literature. Some classic writers suggested that the difference between tragedy and comedy is that the former ends in misery, the latter in happiness. Dante could describe the whole spiritual universe as a comedy because, in spite of the many tragic evils and sufferings in our life, the story has a happy ending—if we learn the right lessons and make the right choices. (The adjective "divine" was added by later readers and became standard when the poem was first printed in 1555, almost two and a half centuries after it was written.)

But another dimension of all Dante's work makes it of particular immediacy and significance to modern readers: his vision of romantic love—the love between a man and a woman—as one of the most powerful inducements to come alive to the love of God. Romantic love, as modern poetry, novels, and films attest, often goes wrong. It did in Dante's time as well, and the greatest medieval legends—Lancelot and Guenevere, Tristan and Isolde—recognize as much. All loves present grave risks of failure along with great possibilities of fulfillment. Dante explored, as no one before or since, the full depths and heights to which a different kind of romantic love than our usual fickle variety can lead us.

Dante was born in 1265 amid a medieval world that had behind it over a century of courtly love poetry and troubadour songs expressing the ennobling effects of love and devotion to a lady. His great insight was to see that the richness and power of this poetry could be coupled with the great flowering of theological and spiritual thought during the same period. An old Augustinian theme reminds us that the "order of our loves" (*ordo amoris*) constitutes the Christian life. Dante would show how the love for Beatrice, a young woman in his home city of Florence, led him first to envision and then to encounter the order of loves spread over the entire universe.

It will be helpful to anticipate his journey by examining more precisely the kind of world we are about to enter. Though there have been debates about how orthodox a Catholic Dante was, his universe is indisputably a Christian universe. He took it almost for granted that God was the Creator of the universe and redeemer of the human race. But like everyone who claims to be a believer, it took him a while to come to a recognition of what these large theological concepts meant for him as an individual person. The record he left of how an ordinary, if exceptionally gifted, human soul is moved through the concrete circumstances of his life to the highest realms of spiritual experience holds out a hopeful promise for everyone, however humble, willing to enter into the way.

Midway through the *Purgatory*, the second of the three main divisions of his *Comedy*, Dante—in a characteristically medieval union of form and substance—gives us his central theme at the very center of his poem. The mainspring of the universe as a whole and all its individual parts is a reality both transcendently simple and infinitely complex: Love. In canto 17 of the *Purgatory*, Dante gets a lesson from the Roman poet Vergil, his guide for much of the trip through the other world:

> "Neither Creator nor a creature ever,
> Son," he began, "was destitute of love
> Natural or spiritual; and thou knowest it.
> The natural was ever without error;
> But err the other may by evil object,
> Or by too much, or by too little vigour.
> While in the first it well directed is,
> And in the second moderates itself,
> It cannot be the cause of sinful pleasure;
> But when to ill it turns, and, with more care
> Or lesser than it ought, runs after good,
> 'Gainst the Creator works his own creation.
> Hence thou mayst comprehend that love must be
> The seed within yourselves of every virtue,
> And every act that merits punishment."

This vision differs markedly from our own view that the world is largely made up of meaningless physical processes. Yet it is a claim that any believer in a Creator must take seriously: the Creation itself must somehow be both material, as we experience it every day, and an expression of the divine love mediated through various physical forms.

Natural love, says Dante, must always go the way the Creator intended. By natural love he roughly means the physical tendencies that God has put into all created things—from galaxies to atoms, plants and animals to human beings. The supernatural dimension in the human person, however, who is a compound creature with both a physical and a spiritual dimension, can go awry by choosing evil objects or by pursuing good objects too little or too much. We have learned through developments in science how the physical constitution of our bodies is often marred by both genetic inheritance and accidents. But Dante, who employs the most up-to-date science of his own day, would not think that these instances of damage to what, by nature, should be different invalidated the basic theory. Accidents occur and our bodies show imperfections, but human nature, because of the way we have been put together by God, necessarily resides in free choices and acts of love, however much these may be affected by the circumstances in which we find ourselves.

All those loves are ordered, particularly in the case of the human person, to Love Himself, since it is God in this view whom we are finally seeking amidst our other loves. The very first canto of the Paradise, the third part of Dante's journey to God, begins with this moving description:

> The glory of Him who moveth everything
> > Doth penetrate the universe, and shine
> > In one part more and in another less.

The glory and love that Dante will see in the highest heaven, "The love that moves the sun and other stars," as he will write in his concluding line to his whole work, are to be found everywhere and attract everything toward Himself. In Heaven, Dante will find himself speeding toward God and unable to understand how that can be. Beatrice, the lady who initially drew him into the path that leads toward universal love, explains:

> All things whate'er they be
> > Have order among themselves, and this is form,

That makes the universe resemble God.
Here do the higher creatures see the footprints
  Of the Eternal Power, which is the end
  Whereto is made the law already mentioned.
In the order that I speak of are inclined
  All natures, by their destinies diverse,
  More or less near unto their origin;
Hence they move onward unto ports diverse
  O'er the great sea of being; and each one
  With instinct given it which bears it on.
This bears away the fire towards the moon;
  This is in mortal hearts the motive power
  This binds together and unites the earth. . . .

Thou shouldst not wonder more, if well I judge,
  At thine ascent, than at a rivulet
  From some high mount descending to the lowland.
Marvel it would be in thee, if deprived
  Of hindrance, thou wert seated down below,
  As if on earth the living fire were quiet."

So in Dante's universe we would be naturally speeding toward
our encounter with God if we were not weighed down by false or
disordered loves and the sheer inattention to our deepest being
that makes up so much of human life. Indeed, as Dante sees the
damned in Hell and then begins climbing the mountain of Pur-
gatory, he is told that, arduous as the climb is, once he begins to
find it something he is eager to do, he will know he has really
entered on his way, whatever impediments may remain in him.

It is important to understand that, as these passages show, for
Dante the "Love that moves the Sun and other stars," fits into a
highly hierarchical physical universe. Modern science has left us
with a weakened sense of hierarchies of all kinds. We still speak
of higher and lower animals or of more complex systems that
have evolved from simpler ones. The human brain, for example,
is the most complex object that we know of in the entire universe.
But we lack a powerful and suggestive worldly image for what
Dante took quite for granted: that the cosmos contains an ordered
scale of beings with God at the top as Absolute Being, the angels
next as pure spiritual creatures, man after that as a composite
of a spiritual and physical nature, and below him the various

orders of more or less complex beings such as animals, plants, and minerals.

In addition to that natural hierarchy (natural since all created things by the natures God has given them fit into this scheme), Dante envisions a further ordering that involves the specific qualities of human beings. The human person, who has intellect and will, can choose good or evil. As we have seen in the quotations above, this entails praise or blame and salvation or damnation in the mysterious ways of God's justice. We may hope that God's mercy and grace will save all the creatures that, out of love, he brought into being. But Dante, echoing the Bible itself, wishes us to understand the cosmic significance of our actions and attachments in this world, and he represents them as leading to various places in Hell, Purgatory, and Heaven.

He had a ready-made scientific scheme for doing this. The geocentric system of astronomy, which had been invented by the ancient Greek astronomer Ptolemy and accepted by the classical and medieval worlds, put the Earth at the center of the universe. All the planets, the sun, and what the medievals called the Fixed Stars, Crystalline Heaven, and Empyrean (the Sphere of Fire) revolved around Earth. This was a natural view before scientific research demonstrated that there are other ways of describing the phenomena we see in the sky. It is often claimed that this Greek astronomy, as adopted by Christians, proudly put man at the center of things. This is true in a sense. But we should not read anthropocentrism back into this system. The great ancient philosophers Plato and Aristotle regarded the Good of God, which existed above this world, as the primary reality, and this lower world as derivative from the higher. The Ptolemaic universe, as Christianity recast it, further emphasized the humble position of the earth. In fact, human beings were at the *bottom* of a hierarchy whose highest term lay with God in the heavens.

This astronomy enabled Dante to envision an order of saved souls in various heavens thought of as concentric circles centered on Earth. Taking hints from the Bible and the classical pagan writers, he also imagined circles in Hell that went deeper and deeper into the Earth until they reached the true center, the farthest point away from God, in the person of Lucifer. And between the circles of Heaven and those of Hell, Dante put the mountain of Purgatory. Given the great symmetry that he builds everywhere into his poem, it was only to be expected that he would also divide this mountain into various terraces for the various faults being purged. The result of all this is a universe of love, neatly articulated into three major realms, each of which is further divided into the sins, purgations, or illuminations proper to it. We will look more closely into these cosmological features at the appropriate places.

How did Dante, as an individual man and poet, come to this understanding of the universe as a vast sea of diverse loves tending toward the ultimate Love? The seed for this development was planted quite early. In his first book, *The New Life (La Vita Nuova)*, a brief and visionary autobiography, Dante described his first meeting as a child of nine with Beatrice, who was about the same age. She was dressed in a noble crimson, the color of charity. In a series of brief poems and short prose commentaries, he tells the whole story of how this love for a particular woman in what was then a moderately important commercial city in Europe opened to him the great cosmic mysteries.

The early parts of this little book follow a familiar pattern in Dante's day. Dante begins as a rather typical courtly lover, writing poetry in praise of his ideal lady, who is distant and perfect. When he sees her in the street, his heart is tormented. In the very first poem, he recalls a dream in which Love appeared to him as a joyful Lord carrying the sleeping Beatrice in his arms wrapped in a mantle. Love holds Dante's heart, which is on fire, in his hands, wakes Beatrice and convinces her to eat it, then ascends weeping to Heaven.

As these very first pages of this early work show, Dante began with much larger intuitions about love's nature than the other poets in his day. At first, like them, he describes the emotional turmoil that love brings. No writer has ever put better how dazed and tongue-tied we become, even the most eloquent among us, when we first meet love:

> Whenever and wherever she appeared, in the hope of receiving her miraculous salutation I felt I had not an enemy in the world. Indeed, I glowed with a flame of charity which moved me to forgive all who had ever injured me; and if at that moment someone had asked me a question, about anything,

> my only reply would have been: "Love," with a countenance
> clothed with humility.

Moralists since the beginning of time have warned that there are many ways that this powerful influence can go awry and Dante will show how in the *Inferno*. But Dante claims that Beatrice's effect on him was such that "it did not suffer Love to rule me without the faithful counsel of reason." And in what follows, he convinces us that when we take love rightly, it leads us out to unimagined worlds.

The events that set loose this consuming passion are remarkably few. He did not actually meet Beatrice again after their initial encounter at nine until they both were about eighteen. On that occasion, he saw her wearing a white gown and walking through the street accompanied by two other ladies, and she saluted him. Many of the particulars, including the numerical references to multiples of nine, were part of the symbolic tradition that Dante inherited. And Dante is careful to record the effects of this powerful and mysterious salute on his body and mind.

But one striking difference between Dante and many of his contemporaries was that he soon came to a conscious decision that he should not indulge in the usual complaints. Love keeps telling him enormous truths. For example, in one episode, Love remarks mysteriously, "I am the center of the circle to which all parts of the circumference are in a similar relation; but you are not so." This has obvious theological echoes. Several other episodes suggest an encounter with something that, at this stage in his understanding, Dante is barely able to express. But even more remarkably, a Copernican Revolution in Dante's perspective occurs when some ladies with whom he had been discussing love tell him that, if he really believed what he was saying about the perfection of Beatrice and the nobility she produced in him, he would stop complaining and write in a far different way.

This hit him like a lightning bolt. He says, "Since there is so much joy in words which praise my lady, why have I ever written in any other manner?" Dante resolves to write only in praise of "this gracious being"; a new element had appeared in the literature of love.

After several stumbling efforts to follow this intuition, Dante faces another great test. Beatrice died on June 8, 1290, at the age of twenty-four. Many men have experienced the death of a loved one and have written movingly of the loss and of the hope of being reunited with that person in the next life. But after a complicated series of events during which Dante accuses himself of having been temporarily unfaithful to Beatrice's image, he remarks at the end of his little book that "there appeared to me a marvelous vision in which I saw things which made me decide to write no more of this blessed one until I could do so more worthily." We know that he applied himself to many studies—philosophical, theological, literary—after that. And he predicts, "Thus, if it shall please Him by whom all things live that my life continue for a few years, I hope to compose concerning her what has never been written in rhyme of any woman." That hope was to be fulfilled in the remarkable story of Dante's journey from sin to Heaven under Beatrice's inspiration and guidance in the *Divine Comedy*.

The idea that the love between a man and a woman can be the entry point into a deep encounter with divine love is, of course, perfectly compatible with Christian theology, though it remains a sort of minority position. The more usual path identifies Christian love with asceticism and denial. Even Dante, in his *Purgatory*, will give an exhaustive account of the disciplines and virtues that we must acquire when we are on the way of love inspired by Beatrice. But the way he takes—what the English writer Charles Williams has called the "affirmation of images" as opposed to the "denial of images"—may be a more accessible path for most people. In terms of later spiritual schools, Dante would probably have been more at home in the Marian affirmations of a St. Louis de Montfort than, say, the strict asceticism of a St. John of the Cross.

Without question, seductive dangers lurk in claiming that Love Himself appears in our loves, not the least being that we may try to value our loves, disordered and imperfect as they are, as Love. This is a special danger in the case of passionate romantic love in the modern world, when the perfectly proper assertion that "God is Love" quite often is turned around so that we think "Love (in the sense of our own wayward choosing) is God."

The New Testament presents the fidelity and love between husband and wife as the image of Christ's love for his church. We may feel that sex and passion somehow distract us from the purity and peacefulness that should accompany the highest Christian life. For many people, of course, sex and passion do not have a happy result. But Dante would respond to them that it is not because of any necessary contradiction between human love and divine love. Rather, it is what we have done and misunderstood with regard to human love ever since the Fall—ever since, that is, Eve and Adam, intended by God to be helpers and companions of one another, found themselves ashamed of their nakedness after their sin—placed a division of loves where there had originally been a harmony.

Dante's aims must, therefore, be twofold. He has to explain how his love for Beatrice is ennobling and spiritual, even as it is passionate. And he must show how this personal passion fits in with God's universal scheme of redemption. Nothing of this kind and scope had ever been attempted in the more than twelve Christian centuries that had preceded Dante. We probably have to go all the way back to the Song of Songs in the Old Testament, and that in an allegorical reading, to find the kind of human love as a dimension and image of the divine passion for us that we find explicitly and literally in Dante. Like the Incarnation, this love joins two worlds. And Dante makes sure to tell us what must certainly reflect a profound experience: that "heaven and earth" have put a hand to shaping his "sacred poem" (*il poema sacro*).

This is an important point for understanding Dante's spirituality. For Dante, God leads us not primarily by an abstract set of ideas (as important as those are in bringing body, mind, and spirit into full harmony with the divine) but by particular people and the circumstances in which he has placed us. Dante never neglects this great truth. He viewed the particular details of his life as having universal significance in several mutually reinforcing ways. For many of us, the Christian story is something we believe in rather abstractly; we do not believe we play a high role in it. Yet it has always been the teaching of the church that Jesus would have died on the cross had there only been one human soul that needed saving. So each individual Christian lives a far higher destiny than we usually think. As we shall see when we turn to the first few cantos of the *Comedy*, Dante himself had to overcome some doubts about whether he was worthy of the high Christian honor about to be permitted him in his journey through the other world. But Vergil, the stern voice of reason, perceives that it is cowardice and lack of faith, that Love itself, passed down in Dante's case from Almighty God, to the Virgin, St. Lucy, and Dante's own Beatrice to the more earthy figure of Vergil himself, really and concretely calls us. At Vergil's mention of Beatrice, Dante feels within himself a powerful eagerness to embark, confirming that the first love in the soul is the wellspring out of which the great journey must be undertaken.

Since Dante will use many other autobiographical facts to make his case about the moral, political, and spiritual life, it is worth looking in some detail at what we know about him. He was born in May 1265 in Florence, an important city in the High Middle Ages. It was to become the virtual center of the Italian Renaissance, which formally began shortly after Dante's death. The most familiar names of the Renaissance, Botticelli, Ghirlandaio, Michelangelo, Leonardo da Vinci, the Medici, and many others all had connections with Florence. Some would say, however, that the great cultural flowering of Florence takes its origins from Dante's times. The great painters Cimabue and Giotto were Florentines roughly contemporary with Dante. Boccaccio and other writers slightly younger than Dante's generation remain among the most eminent figures in Italian intellectual life. The city into which Dante was born was in many ways an ideal environment for a poet of genius; it opened up great opportunities without limiting him to a particular school of thought such as already existed in more formally developed intellectual centers.

Dante's family claimed to be descended from ancient Roman nobility who, in a medieval tradition, settled the city after the Roman army defeated Catiline in that region around 62 B.C. Several of his ancestors had been knights or had received honors from the Holy Roman Emperor. By the time Dante was born, the family was living in a more modest fashion than in the past, but he managed to get a good education, to think for himself, and to act as a gentleman. We do not know much about these early years, but it is quite clear that Dante studied rhetoric and Latin literature, a good preparation for public affairs. Later, when he was already a mature man, he tells us, he frequented "the schools of the religious and the disputations of the philosophers." Details of this advanced study are not clear, but we know that Florence was blessed with serious educational establishments: the Franciscans at Santa Croce, the Dominicans at Santa Maria Novella, and the Augustinians at Santo Spirito. And Dante became an ardent student of philosophy after Beatrice's death.

Old noble families like his still dominated the city of Florence. In fact, they were divided into factions that took turns exiling one another and aligning the city with the larger interests of Europe: the emperor or pope. Dante, who by nature was the kind of person who excels in a wide range of activities, incorporates a political dimension—though never merely a partisan one—into his reading of spirits in the *Divine Comedy.* (Heaven and Earth are united in that way as well.) The two large factions in the Florence of Dante's day were the Guelphs, the party of the pope, and the Ghibellines, the party of the emperor. The Ghibellines were composed largely of the old feudal aristocracy, while the Guelphs numbered the lesser urban nobles and artisans.

Like many other young men of his time, Dante did military service, fighting for the commune of Florence as a mounted soldier in 1289 at the battle of Campaldino. In his thirtieth year, in July 1295, he began to be drawn into the political life of Florence and was elected, as a member of the guild of physicians and apothecaries, to the council of the people. He participated in the council that elected the priors, the highest officers in the city government, and belonged to the Council of the Hundred, which controlled finances and other important matters. Florence sent him as ambassador to various cities, including the papal court in Rome, and in the summer of 1300, Dante assumed the priorate, the highest office in Florence, for a two-month term.

During the period of his involvement in Florentine politics, though he was a Guelph who in theory supported the pope against the emperor, Dante became embroiled in attempts by Pope Boniface VIII to achieve political domination over Tuscany. Not only did he and his colleagues have to resist this external threat, but the Black Guelphs (in the growing factionalism that plagued the city, the prominent Guelph families themselves had divided into Whites and Blacks) supported Boniface. Dante, as a White, would learn a lesson about the intrusion of the spiritual power on the temporal power from this whole experience. In his essay *On Monarchy*, he boldly argues that we are created for two perfections: one in this life, which involves political order, and one in the next. "Two suns," he says, the pope and the emperor, are intended to illuminate our two paths to these perfections. This was a daring statement in his day, when it was more usual to speak of the spiritual power as the sun and the secular power as only a moon shining with reflected light. Dante had intuited some of the benefits of the separation of church and state long before that concept became common.

But all this would come, only much later than his days in office. In an attempt to rid the city of strife, Dante counseled banishing the more quarrelsome leaders of both the Blacks and the Whites. Among the latter group was his best friend and fellow poet Guido Cavalcanti, who would die of a fever contracted in exile. Needless to say, both the political ferment and the attempt to deal with it divided the people still further into violently opposed and very dangerous factions.

Dante loved Florence with the same kind of passion he showed toward Beatrice. Since it was impossible to find a neutral corner, he joined the White Guelphs as the closest among available alternatives to a party of tolerance and moderation. He would pay heavily for this loyalty to the city of his birth. Though married to a woman (Gemma) of the Donati family, the leading family in the Black Guelph faction, Dante's political affiliations placed him squarely in the path of Corso Donati, who had been exiled along with many of both factions with Dante's approval. Indeed, Corso had publicly assaulted Dante's friend Guido Cavalcanti, who had, in turn, tried to kill Corso. In light of such passions, it is easy to see why Dante recommended exiling both bands of troublemakers. Corso returned with the occupation of Florence by Charles of Valois, and these events would lead to Dante's exile for the rest of his life.

The details are uncertain, but the best evidence suggests the following scenario. As Charles and his army approached Florence in the fall of 1301, Dante was selected by a special emergency council for a diplomatic mission to the pope. After a short while,

Boniface sent Dante's two colleagues back to tell the Florentines that he only wanted peace. He deliberately kept Dante in Rome, depriving the Whites of a strong voice. When Charles took the city in January of 1302, Dante, still abroad on the ambassadorial mission, was banished for two years and ordered to pay a large fine for a series of trumped-up charges of graft and factional strife. When he failed to show up to defend himself, another judgment was handed down: he was to be burned alive if he were captured by the Commune. So far as we know, he never again set foot in Florence.

By the time of his exile, we may be relatively sure that a few developments had taken place in his artistic, intellectual, and spiritual life. The shift from the standard troubadour's view of love as an affliction to Dante's discovery of love as something ennobling and praiseworthy that led beyond itself toward the infinite was, as we have seen, the major turn and would continue developing. Yet toward the end of the *New Life*, after Beatrice's death, another lady entered his life who briefly made him unfaithful. He returned to his devotion to Beatrice within a short while.

Many commentators have tried to sort out what all this means. The *Vita Nuova* was written not much later than the early 1290s. In the somewhat later *Banquet*, Dante claims that the lady who had made him unfaithful was not a flesh-and-blood woman but the Lady Philosophy, whom a late Roman writer, Boethius, had depicted in his *Consolation of Philosophy*. This explanation is not entirely plausible; the infidelity was probably of a carnal nature. There is also a discernible shift in Dante's work around 1295, the time, as we have seen, when he emerges as a participant in Florentine politics. He writes in a much more strictly philosophical and almost rationalistic vein until the *Comedy*.

In the first few years of exile, he probably began his little treatise *On Vernacular Eloquence*, which makes the case for using the common spoken language of men, women, and children—rather than the learned language of Latin—to write the greatest of literary works. This was a major breakthrough for popular culture, the growth of literature in the modern languages, as well as a step in developing standard Italian. He simultaneously or a little later proposed a commentary on fourteen poems to explain many theological and philosophical points. These were to form the basis for his *Banquet*, which must be a work of exile. As we have seen, 1302 is the date when his exile was proclaimed, and the commentaries on the philosophic poems must have been composed from 1304 to around 1308, when, it appears, Dante abandoned this and other works to take up the *Comedy*.

But what of his personal life during this period of intellectual ferment? It is a testimony to Dante's great sense of mission that he was able to accomplish so much in exile. Banishment probably made it necessary for Dante to become a courtier to various minor nobles. The exiled White Guelphs, by sheer force of circumstance, made temporary political alliance with the Ghibellines. But Dante, who had fought the Ghibelline forces at Campaldino, could not rest content with this compromise. By temperament and political circumstance he was destined to become a party of one.

Where exactly, however, did he go? There has been speculation that he could only have acquired the learning his later work so obviously displays by visiting one or more of the great medieval intellectual centers such as Paris or Oxford. But there is no evidence that he ever crossed the Alps. If he did study at a university during this period—something by no means certain—it would probably have been at Bologna, not far from Florence. In the first few years after the 1302 banishment, we know he was in various cities in Tuscany sympathetic to his political cause. Dante's skills in rhetoric and Latin composition, and his obvious abilities as a politician and diplomat, would have been very useful in any nobleman's court.

But there are at least some signs that he ranged much farther than we can document. He says in the *Banquet*: "I have gone through nearly all the regions to which the Italian tongue extends, a wanderer, almost begging, showing against my will the wound of fortune, often unjustly held against him who is wounded." Where all these regions where Italian is spoken may have been we do not know. We do know, however, that several offers were made to him over the years to return to Florence that would have required a merely formal admission of guilt. But in spite of his heartache in exile, Dante never wavered in his adherence to truth and strict justice. As he would say with a certain bravado in one of his surviving letters when a humiliating offer arrived:

> Not this the way of return to my country, O my father! But if another may hereafter be found by you or any other, which hurts not Dante's fair fame and honor, that will I accept with no lagging feet. If no such path leads back to Florence, then will I never enter Florence more. What then? May I not gaze upon the mirror of the sun and stars wherever I may be? Can I not ponder on the sweetest truths wherever I may be beneath the heaven, but I must first make myself inglorious, nay infamous, before the people and the state of Florence?

We hear in this the true note of Dante's soul. We feel his profound love of his native city—and the love of honor still more.

The experience in exile also shifted Dante's political views. As a Guelph, he had believed that the party's support of the pope kept cities like Florence free of the domination of the German emperor. But the tyrannies of the Black Guelphs led him to reflect more fully on the usurpations that the pope too could perpetrate in the temporal realm. Without exactly becoming a Ghibelline—that would have involved accepting the claims of the old feudal nobles in the Italian city-states—Dante came to see the emperor as a medieval equivalent of the ancient Roman emperor.

God had sent His Son into the world at the height of the old Roman Empire, the "fullness of time," which enabled the early Christians to move quickly into much of the known world. Dante would come to see that a principle of international order, such as the emperor, could actually be a way of furthering the freedom of city-states like Florence. The ancient city-states like Athens and Sparta had constantly feuded with one another, to their detriment. The Italian city-states had done the same. Although the small political communities in both periods allowed for a very high level of citizen participation and the consequent vigor of political life, they could not overcome the basic limitations of small, mutually jealous political entities living in close proximity to one another. A central, but limited power was necessary to unify large territories and keep them from fighting with one another, but also to protect the liberties so jealously guarded by local political powers.

In light of these developments in his thinking, it is not surprising that when Dante came to write the *Comedy*, he chose a figure to guide him through Hell and Purgatory who was the greatest ancient exponent of an ideal Roman Empire, the poet Vergil. To us this may seem an odd choice. The historical Vergil had written the greatest epic in the Latin language, the *Aeneid*, which tells the story of the legendary heroes who escaped from the battle of Troy to found the city of Rome. But little in the historical record leads us to believe that Vergil was a great philosopher or possessed unusual insight into the spiritual world. Dante, however, had inherited the medieval tradition which suggested that Vergil and the other classical poets were sages—competent therefore to deal with the natural perfections as far as the earthly Paradise.

In the sixth book of his *Aeneid*, Vergil's hero, Aeneas, takes a trip through the underworld, which gave Dante many ideas for his *Inferno*. And in one of his *Eclogues*, a set of pastoral poems, Vergil had predicted, just a few years before the birth of Christ, that a child was about to come into the world who would begin a new age for the entire human race. A coincidence, perhaps, but the combination of otherworldly knowledge and prophetic insight with an anticipation of Dante's own view that the Roman emperor was a providential instrument for the good order of both church (checking the temporal usurpations of the popes) and state, made Vergil an ideal guide. For Dante, what we would call politics is an important dimension of spirituality and accompanies him up to all but the very highest reaches of Paradise.

But given Dante's well-known admiration for the "love of wisdom," also called philosophy, why not choose one of the great philosophers of antiquity like Plato or Aristotle, or one of the great philosopher-theologians of the High Middle Ages like Thomas Aquinas or Bonaventure? Had Dante been a professional philosopher, perhaps he would have. But Dante was a poet who saw ideas in their images in the world. Though he incorporated much thought in his poetry and expended a great deal of labor thinking through various issues of ethics, politics, and aesthetics, his vocation was poetry.

Early on in the *Comedy*, Dante tells Vergil that he has learned from the ancient Romans the style that has brought him honor.

We need to understand exactly what that style is. Anyone who knows a little Latin and Italian can compare the two writers and will immediately find that Vergil writes in an intricate, allusive Latin. Dante, by contrast, writes a straightforward, mostly no-frills Italian that gets its grandeur not so much from language as from the subject. That may be primarily what he means by having learned Vergil's style: in his treatise on the vernacular tongue, Dante says that the only themes of the highest poetry are exploits of arms, love, and virtue. His work contains all three.

In a letter to Can Grande della Scala of Verona, one of his patrons in exile, Dante lays out the basic principles that we need to keep in mind while reading a poem like the *Comedy*. The medieval Scripture scholars believed there were four different meanings to be found in the Bible: a literal or historical sense and three additional symbolic or allegorical senses. The literal sense is usually easy to determine and corresponds to the kind of approach we might take to events we see around us in everyday life. The other senses are called allegorical because they see alternative meanings conveyed by the literal sense. Though Scripture obviously emphasized one meaning more than another in different passages—the book of Kings, for example, is meant to be far more literal than the book of Revelation—all interpretation began with careful attention to the letter of the text.

Dante gives an example to Can Grande to illustrate his point. Quoting some verses on the exodus from Psalm 113, Dante goes on to provide additional meanings for the historical event:

> "When Israel came out of Egypt, and the house of Jacob from a people of strange speech, Judea became his sanctification, Israel his power." Now if we attend to the letter alone, the departure of the children of Israel from Egypt in the time of Moses is presented to us: if to the allegorical sense, our redemption wrought by Christ; if to the moral sense, the conversion of the soul from the grief and misery of sin to the state of grace; if to the anagogical sense, the departure of the holy soul from the slavery of this corruption to the liberty of eternal glory. And although these mystic senses have each their special denominations, they may all in general be called allegorical.

Some of the terminology used here is not familiar to modern

readers, but the meanings they point to are the common inheritance of those who read the Bible.

For example, early Christians persecuted by the Roman Empire, American blacks under slavery, and contemporary liberation theologians have read the story of the exodus in an *allegorical sense*, seeing in physical liberation a corresponding spiritual liberation. Christ's redemption of all human beings from the bondage of sin includes both the internal liberation from their own personal faults and the external liberation from wrongs committed by others. The *moral sense* conveys how specifically some of the liberation from sin occurs. And finally, the *anagogical sense* has the most purely mystical meaning in that it shows how God leads our souls (*anagōgē* in Greek means a "leading up") to eternal beatitude.

As is the case with Scripture, Dante's poem will at some times tend more toward the literal, at other times more toward the mystical. When the latter is the case, he often alerts us to pay special attention. But we need to keep another set of considerations in mind. Dante describes a journey through Hell, Purgatory, and Heaven. He believed that those realms or something like them corresponded in some kind of literal sense to reality. Though we do not know what life in the next world is like precisely, we should not make the mistake of thinking that, for Dante, everything he writes is merely symbolic. There are too many indications in Scripture and the great classical thinkers that the afterlife is not merely a great blur or realm of light or psychological projection. The articulations and hierarchies Dante introduces are meant to correspond to something we should find in reality.

In our day, various psychological theories might try to substitute themselves for spiritual facts. Freudians, for example, may see in the exaltation of love the kind of sublimation of libido that Freud thought took place in the creation of civilization. There is a kernel of truth to the Freudian view, but it does sheer reductive violence to the riches of the *Comedy*. Similarly, Jungians may read the more mythological side of the *Comedy* as an instance of universal themes of descent into the underworld and rebirth into psychological wholeness. Jung was more conscious of and sympathetic toward the wider realities of the spirit. A Jungian approach to the *Comedy*, therefore, has its uses, but ultimately cannot tell us much about the reality that either does or does not underlie the allegory. Theology, not psychology, must do that.

Did Dante, then, actually make the journey he describes? As we shall see in the opening of the *Inferno*, he believed that St. Paul and Aeneas had journeyed to the other world while still alive. But he also knew that he was not in the same league with such religious and historical giants. In discussing his doubts with Vergil and his proper concern that neither he nor anyone else would consider him worthy of such an honor, Dante is given the classical Christian answer to all such doubts: God has willed this, do not draw back. Perhaps that is why in the same epistle to Can Grande that we quoted above, Dante says that those who doubt he traveled from Earth to Heaven should read St. Augustine, the medieval theologian Richard of St. Victor, and St. Bernard of Clairvaux, all of whom show that, at times, it happens. So the literal meaning of his poem may indeed be about a journey that Dante somehow took beyond our usual world.

But there is another meaning to the whole poem that becomes clear the moment we think about it. Dante's overall theme is the love that pervades the universe and how we mortal beings either find harmony in that order of love or, by opposing God's Love, damage the creation, ourselves, and others around us. So the journey through the other world has crucial importance for this world—further evidence of Dante's belief that the true order of loves unites heaven and earth.

As Dante tells Can Grande, the second purpose of his work is to show how "man, as by good or ill deserts, in the exercise of his freedom of choice, becomes liable to rewarding or punishing justice." This sounds a bit narrowly moralistic, but we must always keep in mind that for Dante moral meanings are only one of the three allegorical meanings set in the great sea of being.

The present volume is intended to be a help toward understanding Dante as a spiritual guide and will move rather freely among the several senses. It follows the format established for the previous volumes in the Spiritual Legacy series in providing a commentary, primarily on the *Divine Comedy*, explaining some of the spiritual insights and philosophical wisdom to be encountered in an eminent figure of Christian culture. Many lengthy and detailed volumes have been written on every facet of Dante's vision. This book can only briefly lead the reader through a poem Dante intended to be both a description of a spiritual pilgrimage and, in the reading, a kind of spiritual pilgrimage itself. As such, the whole poem deserves to be read: a select bibliography at the end of this text suggests reading for those who wish to journey further.

Though our method here may seem to do violence to Dante's poetry, the approach was Dante's own. He wrote commentaries on his earlier poetry to explicate its moral and spiritual meanings, meanings he believed were quite detachable from the poetic form in which they were embodied. In fact, he claims that it would be an embarrassment for a serious poet to be unable to say what a passage of his poetry meant. This easy separability of meaning from the shape in which it is presented is not the usual modern aesthetic. But one of the values of encountering Dante's work is that it asks us to rethink issues like these that had a different meaning for him than they do for us. We may read the *Comedy* for its literary beauties at times, but if that is all we do, we are making an idol of Dante's work in a way that was not his intention.

About the text and translation: The *Comedy* consists of 100 *cantos* of about 150 lines each divided into three *cantiche*: *Inferno*, *Purgatory*, and *Paradise*. An introductory canto opens the *Inferno*, making 34 in that section rather than the 33 for the other two. Dante carefully calculated every detail of his great poem so that it would reach the beatific vision just as he concluded the one-hundredth canto. In addition, he has woven into the whole structure a reflection of the trinitarian origin of the universe. The lines rhyme in what is called *terza rima*, alternating lines rhyme with one another three times, after which a new rhyme is introduced and repeated three times to be replaced yet again all the way through the one hundred cantos.

To get a clearer idea of this, let us look at a passage from Lawrence Binyon's translation of the *Comedy*, which heroically preserves the original form in English, a language relatively poor in rhymes. The famous inscription over the doorway of Dante's Hell reads:

Through me the way is to the city of woe:
  Through me the way into the eternal pain;
  Through me the way among the lost below.
Righteousness did my maker on high constrain.
  Me did divine authority uprear;
  Me supreme Wisdom and primal Love sustain.
Before I was, no things created were
  Save the eternal, and I eternal abide.
  Relinquish all hope, ye who enter here.

After the rhyme between the first and third lines, the rest of the passage weaves interlocking sets of three rhymes each. In the next to the last line, another rhyme "abide," appears, which sets off another round, and so on throughout the entire canto. Dante's line, common in Italian poetry just as Shakespeare's iambic pentameter is in English, has eleven syllables. He was using, with great technical skill and personal genius, poetic tools that had been honed by the great Italian poets who had labored earlier in the thirteenth century.

The translation used here is Henry Wadsworth Longfellow's. It stays close to the original poetic form without the rhyming system. Nothing, of course, can replace the experience of reading Dante in Italian, which is not overly difficult for anyone who knows some Latin, Spanish, or French. But Longfellow's version possesses the music of a real poet in his own right and gives just about the right flavor of how Dante appears to a modern Italian reader. Dante's Italian is about as modern as, say, Shakespeare's English is for us. But at the same time it contains some archaisms, and unusual expressions need an explanation even for Italians. The reader will need to be patient as we sort out some of the difficulties. Perhaps a certain amount of frustration will be avoided if the reader understands that Dante's poetry ranges from the simply transparent to passages as dense as anything to be found in modern poets such as Valéry or Rilke. The intellectual content, the complexity of the unfolding frame, and the sheer exaltation of the theme require, at times, careful study and no little effort.

But Dante repays study. In the entire history of Christianity, no poet has written a more complete vision of Christian life. Dante's genius assimilated the great century of Christian theology and philosophy that had preceded him, and presents that sometimes arid discourse in terms of quite vivid human drama. Many developments in science, theology, and psychology have occurred since Dante's day. But beyond the obsolete elements, in Dante we are always in touch with an ardent Christian soul, tirelessly seeking to penetrate ever deeper into the mystery of God's Love, and hoping as far as possible to communicate the "bread of angels" to average people in their own language. His was a heroic adventure and a generous labor, and that is why even today, nearly seven hundred years after Dante's death he remains very much alive.

Chapter 1

The Dark Wood

Midway upon the journey of our life
  I found myself within a forest dark,
  For the straightforward pathway had been lost.
Ah me! how hard a thing it is to say
  What was this forest savage, rough, and stern,
  Which in the very thought renews the fear.
So bitter is it, death is little more;
  But of the good to treat, which there I found,
  Speak will I of the other things I saw there.

These lines are among the most famous openings in all literature, but to understand them correctly we need to keep in mind that Dante writes on several levels at once. For example, we can read this passage psychologically as saying that Dante is having a kind of "midlife" crisis. The Middle Ages took numbers seriously. So when they read in Psalm 90 that "the days of our years are threescore years and ten," they presumed that seventy was our normal human life span. Thirty-five represents the height of a person's powers, midway between birth and death, the point at which life begins a return to its origins. When Dante says "Midway" here, he means it literally. He was born in 1265; he turned thirty-five in 1300, the year in which the poem is set.

It is precisely at the height of his human life that he finds himself deeply lost. In the modern world, successful people often feel a hollowness at midlife about the achievements and possessions supposed to make us happy. By 1300, Dante was a well-known poet; he had served honorably in Florence's military campaigns; and in that very year he was elected one of the priors, the highest political office in the city. He had a wife and several children.

To all outward appearances, Dante had achieved the highest success in every field to which he applied himself. Yet he is in crisis. We are not sure what to make of such feelings when they afflict us. Dante and the spiritual tradition he inherited had more sophisticated resources available.

While Dante certainly means more here by his midlife crisis than we do, were he alive today he would not entirely dismiss a psychological analysis. But for him, the personal turmoil would also be an index to something much deeper. Some modern psychologists, the Jungians most prominently, have rightly reconnected such crises to archetypal myths and life-and-death realities. In every human life a time comes when the deep call to understanding and change demands a response. What we need is not merely to reform some bad habits or attitudes; we need to reorient our whole lives and rediscover authentic life, the universal dream of the human race. The alternative is to lose life even while we remain alive. There is no escaping that choice, which is woven into our natures and the world.

In the original Italian, Dante does not say "I found" myself in a dark wood, but something more like "I re-found myself." This is significant. A common pattern in the spiritual life is the passage from original innocence and connection with God, through a period when we seem somehow to have lost him and need to discover what is wrong, and back by means of purgation of faults and restoration of the soul's order to a new illumination. That is one meaning of the journey through the three realms. Strictly speaking, we do not choose this journey; it chooses us. When Dante comes to himself again in the dark forest, he not only does not know how to free himself. He cannot even remember how he got there, "So full was I of slumber at the moment / In which I had abandoned the true way." He was not literally asleep, but part of his spirit—a part difficult to specify at this first moment of spiritual awakening—had not been vigilant. He had imperceptibly been led into a state of fear, confusion, and turmoil.

But in the ways of the spiritual life, paradoxically, that very agony becomes the spur to fullness of life. If we think Dante is exaggerating, he makes sure to say that the mere memory of what he endured is only a little short of death. For many people, only the closing off of all alternatives to a primal choice, whether in the middle of life or at the time of bodily death, will touch the spirit at sufficient depth that, perhaps for the first time, it really chooses. We are so prone to spiritual drift that it is often only through the sharp sense of loss of meaning and direction that God can get our attention. At first, we may only think we need simple measures to pull ourselves together such as therapy or vigorous action. These may help, but Dante suggests that, for this predicament, the real remedy goes much further.

He looks up and sees the sun at the top of a hill. The sun has often been used to represent spiritual illumination. Dante is cheered because he now seems to have found a way out of the dark valley of sin and error, "The pass / That never yet a living person left." He tries to climb toward the light:

> And lo! almost where the ascent began,
>   A panther light and swift exceedingly,
>   Which with a spotted skin was covered o'er!
> And never moved she from before my face,
>   Nay, rather did impede so much my way,
>   That many times I to return had turned.
> The time was the beginning of the morning,
>   And up the sun was mounting with those stars
>   That with him were, what time the Love Divine
> At first in motion set those beauteous things;
>   So were to me occasion of good hope,
>   The variegated skin of that wild beast,
> The hour of time, and the delicious season;
>   But not so much, that did not give me fear
>   A lion's aspect which appeared to me.
> He seemed as if against me he were coming
>   With head uplifted, and with ravenous hunger,
>   So that it seemed the air was afraid of him;
> And a she-wolf, that with all hungerings
>   Seemed to be laden in her meagreness,
>   And many folk has caused to live forlorn!
> She brought upon me so much heaviness,
>   With the affright that from her aspect came,
>   That I the hope relinquished of the height.
> And as he is who willingly acquires,
>   And the time comes that causes him to lose,
>   Who weeps in all his thoughts and is despondent,
> E'en such made me that beast withouten peace,

> Which, coming on against me by degrees
> Thrust me back thither where the sun is silent.

It is spring, the season of new life. Other passages show that, more specifically, it is Easter time, when Christ conquered death. Under these conditions, Dante hoped to escape. But the minute he tries to ascend the mountain he finds several wild beasts in his way: a panther, a lion, and a she-wolf. The three beasts here are probably taken from Jeremiah 5:6 and prefigure the divisions of the *Inferno*—incontinence of appetites, violence, and fraud—that follow below. Confronting them alone in his confusion, Dante loses hope.

Another paradox of the true spiritual way is that it is precisely at this moment of seeming hopelessness that unexpected aid appears:

> While I was rushing downward to the lowland,
> Before mine eyes did one present himself,
> Who seemed from long-continued silence hoarse.
> When I beheld him in the desert vast,
> "Have pity on me," unto him I cried,
> "Whiche'er thou art, or shade or real man!"
> He answered me: "Not man; man once I was,
> And both my parents were of Lombardy,
> And Mantuans by country both of them.
> Sub Julio was I born, though it was late,
> And lived at Rome under the good Augustus,
> During the time of false and lying gods.
> A poet was I, and I sang that just
> Son of Anchises, who came forth from Troy,
> After that Ilion the superb was burned
> But thou, why goest thou back to such annoyance?
> Why climb'st thou not the Mount Delectable
> Which is the source and cause of every joy?"

We might have expected some religious figure—a saint or one of the angels or even Christ himself—to carry out the rescue. In the next canto, we shall see higher powers move him, but the figure here is, curiously, a pagan, the great Roman poet Vergil.

Vergil died shortly before the birth of Christ, and it is instructive that he will be Dante's guide through Hell and Purgatory. The best human reason (Vergil is sometimes considered a symbol of reason in the poem), displays its divine origins in its capacity to direct the human race to its strictly natural perfection in this world. Vergil will be a trustworthy guide for much of Dante's vast spiritual journey—human reason and divine wisdom, properly understood, are not opposed to one another, but are meant to cooperate in producing both worldly and otherworldly happiness. But perhaps added to these abstract formulations and symbols, we have in Vergil simply a figure whom Dante loved:

> "Now, art thou that Virgilius and that fountain
>   Which spreads abroad so wide a river of speech?"
>   I made response to him with bashful forehead.
> "O, of the other poets honour and light,
>   Avail me the long study and great love
>   That have impelled me to explore thy volume!
> Thou art my master, and my author thou,
>   Thou art alone the one from whom I took
>   The beautiful style that has done honour to me.
> Behold the beast, for which I have turned back;
>   Do thou protect me from her, famous Sage."

"Thee it behoves to take another road," Vergil gently explains. Dante's overoptimistic belief that he was free to go directly toward the good was an understandable error. We all like to think we can simply turn to the good without deep changes in ourselves or the world around us. But for the complete journey toward God, Dante must begin by descending into an understanding of the evil in which he has become unconsciously entrapped before he will be free for the ascent.

The she-wolf (fraud), in particular, says Vergil, mates with many other animals and does not allow any to pass. Someday a greyhound will come who will free Italy, and perhaps the world, from her dominance. The prophecy is obscure. But it is clear that Dante's personal liberation and worldly justice are intertwined from the outset. Vergil continues with a description of their itinerary and a promise of their goal:

> Therefore I think and judge it for thy best
>   Thou follow me, and I will be thy guide,
>   And lead thee hence through the eternal place,
> Where thou shalt hear the desperate lamentations,
>   Shalt see the ancient spirits disconsolate,

Who cry out each one for the second death;
And thou shalt see those who contented are
Within the fire, because they hope to come,
Whene'er it may be, to the blessed people;
To whom, then, if thou wishest to ascend,
A soul shall be for that than I more worthy;
With her at my departure I will leave thee;
Because that Emperor, who reigns above,
In that I was rebellious to his law,
Wills that through me none come into his city.
He governs everywhere and there he reigns;
There is his city and his lofty throne;
O happy he whom thereto he elects!"
And I to him: "Poet, I thee entreat,
By that same God whom thou didst never know,
So that I may escape this woe and worse,
Thou wouldst conduct me there where thou hast said,
That I may see the portal of Saint Peter,
And those thou makest so disconsolate."
Then he moved on, and I behind him followed.

So we are now about to enter Hell, where those who suffer from "the second death," the death of the soul's hope for salvation after the first death of the body, will show Dante the depths of depravity and self-willed flight from the light of which we are capable. In many mythological systems and in modern therapies such as psychoanalysis, this descent into the furies of a deeper world is the necessary prelude to ascent.

All this, which occupies only the first canto of one hundred has already moved us far from Dante's initial refinding of himself in the mysterious wood. He has already learned that the slow process by which he lost his bearings is no mere personal drama, but one that literally involves the whole cosmos. His human loves and hates, his worldly successes and failures, and a whole world of good and evil spirits culminating in God himself are intricately woven together in the story of every individual soul, whether we are great or small. All of us will someday find our eternal destiny in one of the eternal realms. It is a daunting truth to recognize that our lives have such significance and even Dante—as sorely driven as he is to escape his spiritual suffering—will hesitate with several typical doubts before finally entrusting himself to the great universe about to open up to him.

Canto 2

> Day was departing, and the embrowned air
>   Released the animals that are on earth
>   From their fatigues; and I the only one
> Made myself ready to sustain the war,
>   Both of the way and likewise of the woe,
>   Which memory that errs not shall retrace.
> O Muses, O high genius, now assist me!
>   O memory, that didst write down what I saw,
>   Here thy nobility shall be manifest!

In keeping with his status as a celebrated poet, Dante invokes the Muses of poetry to help him tell his tale. In other invocations scattered through the *Comedy,* it is clear that Dante does not literally believe in the Muses the way the ancient polytheists did. Rather, he knows that they symbolize a divine inspiration that he requests—and gets in a different way than he expects. The result shows that Dante, as a Christian, sees himself quite differently and works in a very different way than the ancient poets did. Having pointed us toward the fact that here his genius's "nobility shall be manifest," he makes an unexpected turn compared with the self-confident humanism of the classical models:

> And I began: "Poet, who guidest me,
>   Regard my manhood, if it be sufficient.
>   Ere to the arduous pass thou dost confide me.
> Thou sayest, that of Silvius the parent [i.e., Aeneas],
>   While yet corruptible, unto the world
>   Immortal went, and was there bodily.
> But if the adversary of all evil
>   Was courteous, thinking of the high effect
>   That issue would from him, and who, and what,
> To men of intellect unmeet it seems not;
>   For he was of great Rome, and of her empire
>   In the empyreal heaven as father chosen;
> The which and what, wishing to speak the truth,

> Were stablished as the holy place, wherein
> Sits the successor of the greatest Peter.
>
> .   .   .   .
>
> Thither went afterwards the Chosen Vessel [i.e., Paul],
> To bring back comfort thence unto that Faith,
> Which of salvation's way is the beginning.
> But I, why thither come, or who concedes it?
> I not Aeneas am, I am not Paul,
> Nor I, nor others, think me worthy of it.
> Therefore, if I resign myself to come,
> I fear the coming may be ill-advised;
> Thou'rt wise, and knowest better than I speak."

At first sight, this highly stylized account of secular and sacred heroism sounds reasonable and modest. Aeneas helped found one of the two great classical civilizations; and Rome would become the city of the popes. St. Paul, the "chosen vessel" (*vas electionis*) carried out the great missionary voyages. But Dante's reasoning does not impress the reason of Vergil, who sees through Dante's verbal acrobatics:

> "If I have well thy language understood,"
> Replied that shade of the Magnanimous,
> "Thy soul attainted is with cowardice,
> Which many times a man encumbers so,
> It turns him back from honoured enterprise,
> As false sight doth a beast, when he is shy."

These are hard words to a soul in turmoil. But Vergil's comment is intended to cut through the self-deception, hesitancy, false Christian modesty, and rationalizations we use to avoid the high destiny to which we all, by merely being human, are called. We may fear the path to real happiness in this life as much as or more than we fear unhappiness.

If the Christian dispensation means anything, it means that Heaven has taken the initiative toward all who are willing to open their hearts to grace. In Dante's case specifically, the divine life that he had glimpsed in Beatrice while she was alive remains the channel through which, humanly speaking, he will be saved from his sin and torpor. Vergil tells Dante why he may have confidence:

Among those was I who are in suspense,
  And a fair, saintly Lady called to me
  In such wise, I besought her to command me.
Her eyes were shining brighter than the Star;
  And she began to say, gentle and low,
  With voice angelical, in her own language
"O spirit courteous of Mantua,
  Of whom the fame still in the world endures,
  And shall endure, long-lasting as the world;
A friend of mine, and not the friend of fortune,
  Upon the desert slope is so impeded
  Upon his way, that he has turned through terror,
And may, I fear, already be so lost,
  That I too late have risen to his succour,
  From that which I have heard of him in Heaven.
Bestir thee now, and with thy speech ornate,
  And with what needful is for his release,
  Assist him so, that I may be consoled.
Beatrice am I, who do bid thee go;
  I come from there, where I would fain return;
  Love moved me, which compelleth me to speak."

Here we see the early seed, a human love, of that at first distant
and seemingly abstract divine love. When Beatrice says love
moved her and makes her speak, are we to understand this in
human or divine terms? As the *Comedy* unfolds, we gradually see
that the two, rightly understood, are really one. Human love,
especially between a man and a woman, often goes awry, cools,
or breaks off into disorder of one kind or another. In the present
context, however, we see human and divine love nested within
one another.

Vergil asks Beatrice why she does not fear descending into
Hell, and her answer is meant to be instructive for Dante also:

Of those things only should one be afraid
  Which have the power of doing others harm;
  Of the rest, no; because they are not fearful.
God in his mercy such created me
  That misery of yours attains me not,
  Nor any flame assails me of this burning.
A gentle Lady is in Heaven, who grieves
  At this impediment, to which I send thee,

So that stern judgment there above is broken.
In her entreaty she besought Lucia,
    And said, "Thy faithful one now stands in need
    Of thee, and unto thee I recommend him."
Lucia, foe of all that cruel is,
    Hastened away, and came unto the place
    Where I was sitting with the ancient Rachel.
"Beatrice," said she, "the true praise of God,
    Why succourest thou not him, who loved thee so,
    For thee he issued from the vulgar herd?
Dost thou not hear the pity of his plaint?
    Dost thou not see the death that combats him
    Beside that flood, where ocean has no vaunt?"
Never were persons in the world so swift
    To work their weal and to escape their woe,
    As I, after such words as these were uttered,
Came hither downward from my blessed seat,
    Confiding in thy dignified discourse,
    Which honours thee, and those who've listened to it.

. . . What is it, then? Why, why dost thou delay?
    Why is such baseness bedded in thy heart?
    Daring and hardihood why hast thou not,
Seeing that three such Ladies benedight
    Are caring for thee in the court of Heaven,
    And so much good my speech doth promise thee?

The three ladies spoken of here are the Blessed Virgin Mary, the Advocate, whose pity operates so that "stern judgment there above is broken"; St. Lucy; and Beatrice. But ultimately this entire sisterhood of love is a manifestation of divine love. Knowing whence comes Vergil's mission to him, Dante would be both ungrateful and obtuse were he not to recognize the high powers operating for his own good, even if he is not an Aeneas or St. Paul.

And the warmth of that love opens up his spirit:

Even as the flowerets, by nocturnal chill,
    Bowed down and closed, when the sun whitens them,
    Uplift themselves all open on their stems;
Such I became with my exhausted strength,
    And such good courage to my heart there coursed,
    That I began, like an intrepid person:

"O she compassionate, who succoured me,
  And courteous thou, who hast obeyed so soon
  The words of truth which she addressed to thee!
Thou hast my heart so with desire disposed
  To the adventure, with these words of thine,
  That to my first intent I have returned.
Now go, for one sole will is in us both,
  Thou Leader, and thou Lord, and Master thou."
  Thus said I to him; and when he had moved,
I entered on the deep and savage way.

Dante has returned to his original resolve in anticipation of seeing Beatrice. But it is important to keep in mind at this point that he is not acting under mere emotion. He turns to Vergil, that is, to human reason, to guide him through the things that human reason is good for, which he believes are many. Ultimately, love—here something objective and true about both Dante and the universe, not a mere emotion—guides and inspires such reason. And one of the sure signs that Dante is acting realistically is that, though he sets out in confidence in the ultimate goal of his journey, he has not lost sight of the immediate challenge. The last line here might also be translated, "I entered by the high way of the wood (*silvestro*)." Dante's initial effort quickly to flee the evil of the dark wood now turns into the courage to confront and know it as a way of overcoming it.

Canto 3

Through me the way is to the city dolent;
  Through me the way is to eternal dole;
  Through me the way among the people lost.
Justice incited my sublime Creator;
  Created me divine Omnipotence,
  The highest Wisdom and the primal Love.
Before me there were no created things,
  Only eterne, and I eternal last.
  All hope abandon, ye who enter in!

Just as Dante's lines at the opening of his *Comedy* are known to almost everyone, so are these words above the gates of Hell,

always wide open, that lead to perdition. Vergil's guidance is
crucial:

> Here all suspicion needs must be abandoned,
> All cowardice must needs be here extinct.
> We to the place have come, where I have told thee
> Thou shalt behold the people dolorous
> Who have foregone the good of intellect.

Courage, we are reminded again, must be our constant compan-
ion in facing what must be faced. But understanding too must be
constantly won. There is probably no more difficult doctrine to
modern Christians than the notion of Hell, or eternal punishment
for sin. Almost no human failing seems to warrant eternal penal-
ties. But Dante, the poet of love, takes the view that "the Primal
Love" itself was moved to create Hell, along with the Justice,
Omnipotence, and Wisdom that are in God. In fact, the power,
wisdom, and love mentioned here are meant to suggest that the
Father, Son, and Holy Spirit—the Holy Trinity—made Hell.

What are we to make of this? Dante, like much of the Christian
tradition before and after him, believes in the eternal significance
of what we do on Earth. In this view, it was an act of divine love
that gave us freedom to love and choose the right things as per-
sons made in the image and likeness of the Creator. Despite that
fact, Hell too has a divine origin and exists to accommodate
wrong loves. Vergil also describes the people here as those who
"have lost the good of the intellect." This may appear a cold
expression, as if simply because of some wrong reasoning people
are being condemned to eternal torture.

But Vergil and Dante have something quite different in mind.
The great love that moves through all the universe is not to be
thought of as separate from truth and understanding. In fact, in
God all these principles are united together. We may recall here
that Christ described himself as "the Way, the Truth, and the
Life." Salvation must mean that not only body and spirit but the
human mind come into the presence of God, that the whole
human person reaches beatitude. And if one or more of these
three departs from God definitively, it cannot exist with God
except in Hell. A hard saying, and Dante notes as much. But cou-
pled with this teaching about the need for cooperation between

will and understanding to achieve salvation—which is really a statement about the dignity of human nature—we shall see later that all sorts of human and divine help becomes available, if we start to open our hearts and minds to it.

Indeed, Vergil, turns with tenderness and gladness to Dante because Reason knows that seeing and rejecting the mysteries of unreason will lead to beatitude:

> And after he had laid his hand on mine
> With joyful mien, whence I was comforted,
> He led me in among the secret things.

As Dante enters through the wide gate, the first group he encounters consists of a kind of person we may never have thought seriously about. They are people who refused to enter the whole spiritual drama that Dante rediscovered in the Dark Wood. (In keeping with a medieval legend, Dante also refers to angels who neither rebelled with Lucifer nor stayed with God.) All of us spend a great deal of time every day at occupations and diversions that do not have much to do with cosmic issues directly. A lot of the time that is as it should be. We should go about the daily tasks focused on doing them well, provided that at those times when we are called upon to decide the larger purposes and directions of our lives, we do not, out of indifference or sloth, simply refuse anything more ambitious. As Vergil understands those who are here:

> This miserable mode
> Maintain the melancholy souls of those
> Who lived without infamy or praise.
> Commingled are they with that caitiff choir
> Of Angels, who have not rebellious been,
> Nor faithful were to God, but were for self.
> The heavens expelled them, not to be less fair;
> Nor them the nethermore abyss receives,
> For glory none the damned would have from them.

To be "for self," a thing many people advocate today, has a kernel of truth since we must love our neighbor as ourselves. But the two must be lived together; otherwise, as appears here, the focus on self means we shut ourselves into a state open to neither evil nor good.

Dante asks for some clarification at this point of how the whole process works.

> He answered: "I will tell thee very briefly.
> These have no longer any hope of death;
>   And this blind life of theirs is so debased,
>   They envious are of every other fate.
> No fame of them the world permits to be;
>   Misericord and Justice both disdain them.
>   Let us not speak of them, but look, and pass."
> And I, who looked again, beheld a banner,
>   Which, whirling round, ran on so rapidly,
>   That of all pause it seemed to me indignant;
> And after it there came so long a train
>   Of people, that I ne'er would have believed
>   That ever Death so many had undone.
>
> .   .   .   .
>
> Forthwith I comprehended, and was certain,
>   That this the sect was of the caitiff wretches
> Hateful to God and to his enemies.
>   These miscreants, who never were alive,
>   Were naked, and were stung exceedingly
> By gadflies and by hornets that were there.
>   These did their faces irrigate with blood,
>   Which, with their tears commingled, at their feet
> By the disgusting worms was gathered up.

What might seem mere lukewarmness over difficult questions of theology here shows a fearful dimension. These are people "who were never alive" in the full human sense, though they lived physically on earth. They are beyond the reach of both mercy and justice, hateful to God and the devil alike. Their punishment is to be stung by gadflies and hornets, the kinds of spurs that in life should have led them to basic decisions, but that now, observing the kind of just recompense that Dante will show everywhere in the otherworld, are applied to them forever, a useless good, the blood itself resulting in no redemptive movement, but merely being consumed. We shall see many punishments in Hell for sins that are far more familiar, but it is only here that Dante expresses surprise that "Death had undone so many." The Middle Ages are often considered an age of faith. Dante suggests here that even then—and perhaps in all times—many people never even allow themselves into the play of Primal Love.

Dante and Vergil now come to the banks of the river Acheron, which the ancient pagans thought separated this world from the next. They find Charon, the ferryman, engaged in his perpetual task of carrying the souls down to Hades. But though Charon takes in thousands and millions of souls, he knows which are intended for his realm, which for the others. Dante is still alive, and Charon wants to refuse him passage until Vergil invokes the divine authority for this journey:

> "Vex thee not, Charon;
>   It is so willed there where is power to do
>   That which is willed; and farther question not."
> Thereat were quieted the fleecy cheeks
>   Of him the ferryman of the livid fen,
>   Who round about his eyes had wheels of flame.
> But all those souls who weary were and naked
>   Their colour changed and gnashed their teeth together,
>   As soon as they had heard those cruel words.
> God they blasphemed and their progenitors,
>   The human race, the place, the time, the seed
>   Of their engendering and of their birth!
> Thereafter all together they drew back,
>   Bitterly weeping, to the accursed shore,
>   Which waiteth every man who fears not God.

Dante says that vast numbers rush to assemble at the shore even before Charon can return from taking the souls he has across. At the sight of these teeming souls, Dante will faint. But before that happens, Vergil—good guide that he is—reminds him that those who have condemned themselves to Hell by the direction of their wills have their fear turned into desire. Indeed, it may be that here, where our choices reveal themselves for what they truly are, we find that all along we have been pursuing Hell. They rush toward perdition. And the canto ends with Dante's swooning after a kind of red lightning flash into deeper darkness:

> The land of tears gave forth a blast of wind,
>   And fulminated a vermilion light,
>   Which overmastered in me every sense,
> And as a man whom sleep hath seized I fell.

CROSS-SECTION OF THE EARTH

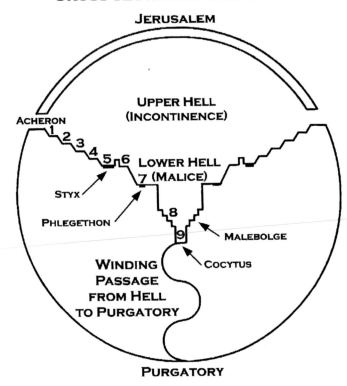

UPPER HELL
1. LIMBO
2. LUST
3. GLUTTONY
4. AVARICE AND PRODIGALITY
5. ANGER

LOWER HELL
6. HERESY
7. VIOLENCE
   (AGAINST: OTHERS, SELF, GOD, AND NATURE)
8. FRAUD
9. TREACHERY

Canto 4

The lightning and thunder that overcome the pilgrim as he enters
into Hell warn us that the challenges ahead will tax human
power. For we are about to descend into states of the soul that are
not mixed, as in everyday life, with shades of light and dark and
comforting social distractions. Many of the figures to be met with
along this journey will be well-known historical personalities:
Dante will try to render a judgment on the balance of their lives
and the final direction of their loves. Other souls in the afterlife
will be people Dante knew personally, some of prominence,
others virtually unknown. It has often been said of these people
that Dante "punishes his enemies" and rewards his friends from
Earth. But many figures that Dante admires wind up in Hell;
others—determined sinners or his political enemies—sometimes
repent and gain Heaven. Whatever misjudgments Dante may
have made about specific people, everything he says has a steady
moral and theological ground.

One indication of this appears in canto 4. After the dramatic
swoon and the lightning and thunder, we might have expected
Dante to regain consciousness amid terrible punishments. But
both Dante and Vergil, when they write about the descent into
Hell, speak of its gradual and easy—almost imperceptible—
unfolding. Dante said he was "full of sleep" when he entered the
Dark Wood; now, as he enters Hell proper, he returns to his
senses and sees Vergil with a pained expression on his face.
Dante attributes this to fear; but Vergil explains that it is rather
pity for the anguish of the people they are about to meet.

For the First Circle of Hell is the place of virtuous pagans, the
place where Vergil himself has been assigned for all eternity.
Dante, who always shows great respect for human reason prop-
erly used, does not envision these good pagans as suffering tor-
ments, but because of their failure to intuit the fullness of the law
written in their hearts, they live aspiring to a life that paganism
leaves unfulfilled. The two poets come to a region of melancholy
calm:

> There, as it seemed to me from listening,
>   Were lamentations none, but only sighs,

That tremble made the everlasting air.
And this arose from sorrow without torment,
    Which the crowds had, that many were and great
    Of infants and of women and of men.
To me the Master good: "Thou dost not ask
    What spirits these, which thou beholdest, are?
    Now will I have thee know, ere thou go farther,
That they sinned not; and if they merit had,
    'Tis not enough, because they had not baptism
    Which is the portal of the Faith thou holdest;
And if they were before Christianity,
    In the right manner they adored not God;
    And among such as these am I myself
For such defects, and not for other guilt,
    Lost are we and are only so far punished,
    That without hope we live on in desire."

For modern readers, this is a difficult state to grasp. We tend to believe that if people are without sin or other "defects" they are, in God's justice, good candidates for Heaven. Yet, as with the earlier troop of people and angels who never chose God or Satan, these virtuous pagans represent a state of the soul worth understanding. There is no question that Dante means us to find an inherent dignity in those who have brought various human realms to their natural perfections. But in the mysterious dialogue between God and the soul, this group went no farther than human perfections. Some pagans were saved without baptism and in anticipation of Christ's coming. Here, however, we are given certain pagans as they might have understood themselves, as moral, hungry for something that transcended their own world, but ultimately frustrated by the belief that no such transcendence existed. The modern world may contain many such people who, thinking perfect happiness in an afterlife cannot be believed, "without hope . . . live on in desire." Still, these figures are worthy of human honor, a word that will be repeated frequently in the lines that follow.

Adam, Abel, Noah, Abraham, Moses, Rachel, David, and others were brought out when Christ, not long after Vergil's own death, descended into Hell. Those who remain, inhabit a kind of city of light that reflects the proper honor due to them, beginning with the great ancient poets, of whom Vergil is preeminent:

> Not very far as yet our way had gone
>> This side the summit, when I saw a fire
>> That overcame a hemisphere of darkness.
> We were a little distant from it still,
>> But not so far that I in part discerned not
>> That honourable people held that place.
> "O thou who honourest every art and science,
>> Who may these be, which such great honour have,
>> That from the fashion of the rest it parts them?"
> And he to me: "The honourable name,
>> That sounds of them above there in thy life,
>> Wins grace in Heaven, that so advances them."
> In the mean time a voice was heard by me:
>> "All honour be to the pre-eminent Poet;
>> His shade returns again, that was departed."
> After the voice had ceased and quiet was,
>> Four mighty shades I saw approaching us;
>> Semblance had they nor sorrowful nor glad.

This state that is neither sorrowful nor glad is precisely the eternal status of these souls because they are neither condemned for sins they did not commit nor credited with a faith they did not have. The four shades are four great poets—Homer, Horace, Lucan, and Ovid—who walk together with Vergil and Dante. Dante says, without false modesty here,

> And more of honour still, much more, they did me,
>> In that they made me one of their own band
>> So that the sixth was I, 'mid so much wit.

They approach a castle which is the proper abode of these souls in Limbo:

> We came unto a noble castle's foot,
>> Seven times encompassed with lofty walls,
>> Defended round by a fair rivulet;
> This we passed over even as firm ground;
>> Through portals seven I entered with these sages
>> We came into a meadow of fresh verdure.

> People were there with solemn eyes and slow,
>> Of great authority in their countenance;
>> They spake but seldom, and with gentle voices.

Many commentators have tried to explain the repetition of sevens in this passage. The seven walls, shutting out the evils of the rest of Hell are often taken to mean philosophical virtues: Prudence, Justice, Temperance, Fortitude, Wisdom, Knowledge, and Understanding. The seven gates may correspond to the medieval liberal arts: Grammar, Logic, Rhetoric, Music, Arithmetic, Geometry, and Astronomy. In any case, the castle is a fortress against evil proper, an indication of the achievements and limitations of even the best human life when it remains strictly on the natural plane.

Within the walls of the castle, Dante sees many noble figures from ancient Roman history. Aristotle occupies a special place among these distinguished men and women as "the master of those who know." His philosophy had been rediscovered in the universities not long before Dante was born. And it had been incorporated into Christian thought by many scholastic thinkers, most notably by St. Thomas Aquinas. As we shall see, that somewhat christianized Aristotle forms the backbone of the moral and spiritual judgments Dante makes about Hell and Purgatory, the realms that, in his view, can be partly understood without specifically Christian interpretation. Evil, at least until we get down to the radical betrayal of God as represented by Satan at the bottom of the universe, can largely be understood in human terms. So can the discipline of Purgatory. Understanding these things is not necessarily the same as overcoming them, and there are hints throughout the poem that grace is operative at the sticking points. But it is worth keeping in mind that Dante here honors the best available human thought in his day as being a kind of preparation and guide to higher things for those souls who are properly disposed for them.

Dante breaks off his catalogue. The band of six poets departs and we move into a very different part of the underworld, "where nothing shines."

Canto 5

We are entering Hell proper now. Behind us lie the confusions of this life, the hesitations, the inertia of those who never got started in the spiritual life, and the suspension in Limbo of those human goods that do not partake of either salvation or damnation. In short, we are about to embark upon the realm of real sin and evil. But how does Dante understand these notions, which have been palpable to the human race since the beginning of recorded history and yet have retained a certain mystery? How is it that we do things that are good neither for ourselves nor for others? Dante's answer is clear: we do everything, even evil, because of one or another love.

Why and how the initial sin began of preferring a different order of love than God intended remains a mystery, but its effects are clear. The first real sin that leads to damnation is precisely a disordered love between man and woman. Some people, hearing the frequent warnings by Christian clergy about the evils of fornication and adultery, have come to assume that, in the Christian scheme of things, this is the most serious of sins. Dante and the whole medieval tradition thought otherwise. As we discover here, the sins of the flesh were the least serious sins for which souls might be damned, precisely because, though disordered, the love between man and woman is an image of the love between God and the soul, Christ and the church. Though it is a counterfeit form, it still retains some of that glory.

Yet it also merits damnation, and that should never be lost from sight. Dante begins his account of Lust, our abandoning ourselves to mere emotion, with the observation that, however much it may feel like an expansion to the parties concerned, it begins to lead us into a narrower world. At its entrance stands Minos, the pagan judge of the underworld, assigning the souls who enter here to the places that their actions merited:

> Thus I descended out of the first circle
>   Down to the second, that less space begirds,
>   And so much greater dole, that goads to wailing.
> There standeth Minos horribly, and snarls;
>   Examines the transgressions at the entrance;
>   Judges, and sends according as he girds him.

I say, that when the spirit evil-born
  Cometh before him, wholly it confesses;
  And this discriminator of transgressions
Seeth what place in Hell is meet for it;
  Girds himself with his tail as many times
  As grades he wishes it should be thrust down.
Always before him many of them stand;
  They go by turns each one unto the judgment;
  They speak, and hear, and then are downward hurled.

Minos notices that Dante is a still living soul and warns him to be careful whom he trusts in entering this netherworld:

"O thou, that to this dolorous hostelry
  Comest," said Minos to me, when he saw me,
  Leaving the practice of so great an office,
"Look how thou enterest, and in whom thou trustest;
  Let not the portal's amplitude deceive thee."
  And unto him my Guide: "Why criest thou too?
Do not impede his journey fate-ordained;
  It is so willed there where is power to go
  That which is willed; and ask no further question."

Why this warning? Christ himself warned, "Enter through the narrow gate; for the gate is wide and the road is easy that leads to destruction" (Matthew 7:13). All sin in our fallen condition appears easy, free, and attractive. But as all the love laments of the ages agree, false love between a man and a woman is particularly deceptive because Lust so closely mimics Love.

Dante finds among the carnal sinners not peace and joy but the eternal agitation of unbounded desire:

I came into a place mute of all light,
  Which bellows as the sea does in a tempest,
  If by opposing winds 't is combated.
The infernal hurricane that never rests
  Hurtles the spirits onward in its rapine;
  Whirling them round, and smiting, it molests them.
When they arrive before the precipice,
  There are the shrieks, the plaints, and the laments,
  There they blaspheme the puissance divine.
I understood that unto such a torment
  The carnal malefactors were condemned,

> Who reason subjugate to appetite.
> And as the wings of starlings bear them on
>   In the cold season in large band and full,
>   So doth that blast the spirits maledict;
> It hither, thither, downward, upward, drives them;
>   No hope doth comfort them for evermore,
>   Not of repose, but even of lesser pain.

One couple in particular catches Dante's eye, and he courteously seeks to talk with them when the heaving air permits it. The tone of this passage reflects the atmosphere of courtly love prominent in late medieval culture:

> As turtle-doves, called onward by desire,
>   With open and steady wings to the sweet nest
>   Fly through the air by their volition borne,
> So came they from the band where Dido is,
>   Approaching us athwart the air malign,
>   So strong was the affectionate appeal.
> "O living creature gracious and benignant,
>   Who visiting goest through the purple air
>   Us, who have stained the world incarnadine,
> If were the King of the Universe our friend,
>   We would pray unto him to give thee peace,
>   Since thou hast pity on our woe perverse."

The very civility of the exchange conceals the self-deception and profound error of these two souls. God himself is not "our friend" because he did not condone our adultery. They regard their punishment and not their acts as "perverse." The distinctive trait of this disordered love is to place itself above Love itself.

These two are the famous Paolo and Francesca, who were killed by the latter's jealous husband. Dante chose a difficult case that is often thought to justify infidelity; his judgment is that it does not. Francesca was given in a politically arranged marriage to Giovanni Malatesta of Rimini. Giovanni was a brave warrior, but lame and possibly deformed in other ways. Legends say that his brother, Paolo, stood in for him during the courtship or marriage, and that Francesca may have been deceived about whom she was consenting to marry. In any event, these two, each married to another, began an affair, and were subsequently murdered by Giovanni.

Dante allows Francesca to give a theology of courtly love, with three different statements about love that form a trinitarian rationalization:

> Love, that on gentle heart doth swiftly seize,
>> Seized this man for the person beautiful
>> That was ta'en from me, and still the mode offends me.
> Love, that exempts no one beloved from loving,
>> Seized me with pleasure of this man so strongly,
>> That, as thou seest, it doth not yet desert me;
> Love has conducted us unto one death;
>> Caina waiteth him who quenched our life!

Dante conveys the full force of the attempt at justification here. The "gentle" heart, which is to say a person of refined sensibilities, is quick to respond to love. Love produces love in return. Love, in a perversion of the true version of the saying, is even in Hell stronger than death. All of this is quite plausible and moving, if, like the damned souls themselves, we forget their responsibilities to God and other people.

Dante even recognizes how wonderful their feelings must have been:

> "Alas!
> How many pleasant thoughts, how much desire,
> Conducted these unto the dolorous pass!"
> Then unto them I turned me, and I spake,
>> And I began: "Thine agonies, Francesca,
>> Sad and compassionate to weeping make me.
> But tell me, at the time of those sweet sighs,
>> By what and in what manner Love conceded,
>> That you should know your dubious desires?"
> And she to me: "There is no greater sorrow
>> Than to be mindful of the happy time
>> In misery, and that thy Teacher knows.
> But, if to recognise the earliest root
>> Of love in us thou hast so great desire,
>> I will do even as he who weeps and speaks."

She tells how it was precisely stories about illicit loves—the medieval equivalent of the books, television programs, and films that portray what appear to be justifiable infidelities—turned the trick:

> One day we reading were for our delight
>> Of Launcelot, how Love did him enthral.
>> Alone we were and without any fear.
> Full many a time our eyes together drew
>> That reading, and drove the colour from our faces;
>> But one point only was it that o'ercame us.
> When as we read of the much-longed-for smile
>> Being by such a noble lover kissed,
>> This one, who ne'er from me shall be divided,
> Kissed me upon the mouth all palpitating.
>> Galeotto was the book and he who wrote it.
>> That day no farther did we read therein."

Galeotto was a famous pander in medieval literature, and the whole is a common occurrence, one to which Dante himself may have succumbed, since he tells us elsewhere that he will have to expiate many sins of the flesh in Purgatory. In fact, as we shall see when we reach the summit of the mountain of purgation, carnal sins are the last to be purged before souls are admitted back into the earthly Paradise. Love for another, even disordered, remains close to love of God. But Dante's conclusion at this point, despite all the sighs, yearnings, and delicacy is that a subtle but decisive self-indulgence on these matters is the gateway to perdition. He concludes:

> And all the while one spirit uttered this,
>> The other one did weep so, that, for pity,
>> I swooned away as if I had been dying,
> And fell, even as a dead body falls.

That "dead body" is the weight of human flesh without the light of the spirit. Feelings of lightness and elevation notwithstanding, turning to a good different from the good God placed in the order of the universe will now lead into heavier and far less attractive forms of sin.

Canto 6

In the following canto, we come upon the gluttons. The very notion that our eating and drinking may be sinful has largely disappeared, even from Christian circles. In modern societies, we may think that overeating or its contrary, anorexia, reflects psychological deformations. Insofar as these psychological discoveries help us better to understand the ways of the soul, they are helpful. Many people eat to fill up an emptiness or an absence of other goods. In the contrary direction, some people, especially young girls and women in our society, can forgo food to the point of illness in order to live up to exaggerated notions of thinness and glamour.

Had he known these psychological theories, Dante probably would not have been surprised. What he reminds us, however, is that these explanations are not ultimate justifications or excuses. It was a commonplace of medieval moral theology that some of those who did not know or turned away from the source of ultimate satisfaction, namely, God, would necessarily overindulge in other, otherwise perfectly licit, goods to try to fill up the emptiness in their lives. Similarly, even the excessive refusal of food cannot be merely explained away as a striving to live up to social expectations. We have also to explain why the soul accepts that disordered end and pursues it by refusing one of God's intended goods of the body. As with every type of sin, there is obviously a great difference between occasional minor excesses and defects and a deep-seated orientation toward a bad end. Medical science may help people in the throes of obesity and anorexia, but except in unusual cases, we might find that recovering the spiritual dimension of these disordered loves would also help liberate people from false gods.

Dante does not only leave this question of gluttony at a bodily level, however. For him, the excessive desire to possess bodily goods is the root of many political disorders as well. He may well have had in mind here how Esau sold his birthright as inheritor of God's promise to Abraham to Jacob because returning from hunting he was very hungry. In the opening canto, we saw that the ravening she-wolf could only be chased away by a greyhound who would not feed upon Earth. As we shall see in this canto, there are concrete ways in which our seemingly private appetites have large public consequences.

When Dante awakens from his fainting spell after hearing Paolo and Francesca's story, he says:

New torments I behold, and new tormented
    Around me, whichsoever way I move,
    And whichsoever way I turn, and gaze.
In the third circle am I of the rain
    Eternal, maledict, and cold, and heavy;
    Its law and quality are never new.
Huge hail, and water sombre-hued, and snow,
    Athwart the tenebrous air pour down amain;
    Noisome the earth is, that receiveth this.

The gluttonous pursuit of the fruits of the Earth has turned what might have given nourishment and growth into a sodden mass.

He encounters one figure whom he knew in his place of birth, a certain Ciacco. There is no record of who this Ciacco might have been. All that we know, we know from this passage: that he must have been an acquaintance of Dante and, perhaps, as Dante was, involved in the politics of Florence. The hunger that gobbles up Earth here leads to the first of Dante's political comments:

I answered him: "Ciacco, thy wretchedness
    Weighs on me so that it to weep invites me;
    But tell me, if thou knowest, to what shall come
The citizens of the divided city;
    If any there be just; and the occasion
    Tell me why so much discord has assailed it."

The souls in the other world can see the future, and Ciacco goes on to say how the various factions in Florence will by turns conquer and submit to one another. As for just men, there are as few there as in the story in the book of Genesis where Abraham asks God to spare Sodom for the sake of a few who are just.

Ciacco, blinded by allowing animal desires to possess his soul, will not awake from the mire until Christ shall come, each soul shall be reunited with its body, and final judgment will be pronounced. This statement gets Dante to thinking, and he asks a question:

Wherefore I said: "Master, these torments here,
    Will they increase after the mighty sentence,
    Or lesser be, or will they be as burning?"
And he to me: "Return unto thy science,
    Which wills, that as the thing more perfect is,
    The more it feels of pleasure and of pain.

> Albeit that this people maledict
> > To true perfection never can attain,
> > Hereafter more than now they look to be."

The point of this reply is that we human beings are by nature most perfect when, as the ancient and medieval philosophers believed, our souls are united with proper bodies. That composite of body and soul is "more perfect" than the soul alone, and therefore when the souls of the gluttonous are reunited with their bodies, they will feel great torments because, though barred from true perfection, their bodies and spirits will be functioning at the greatest degree of sensibility of which they are capable in this state.

Canto 7

We have been moving deeper and deeper into the rejection of God that is Hell. The lustful and the gluttons occupy the first two circles in this part of Hell. Now we enter a circle that presents far clearer edges and punishments: the circle of the greedy and the prodigal. Getting or spending money presents dangers quite vivid to us. But we tend to see them as displacing other important things in this world such as spouses, children, and enjoyment of nature. Dante would not deny this. In fact, the punishment for this sin is a perpetual clash with others. But in his cosmic scheme of all things, disordered love of money and things is an idolatry that turns us away from the Absolute Love, God. Once again, therefore, he begins the canto with a bizarre figure from pagan mythology to suggest graphically that this sin literally puts us under the torments of a non-Christian demon:

> "Pape Satan, Pape Satan, Aleppe!"
> > Thus Plutus with his clucking voice began;
> > And that benignant Sage, who all things knew,
> Said, to encourage me: "Let not thy fear
> > Harm thee; for any power that he may have
> > Shall not prevent thy going down this crag."
> Then he turned round unto that bloated lip,
> > And said: "Be silent, thou accursed wolf;
> > Consume within thyself with thine own rage.

> Not causeless is this journey to the abyss;
>> Thus is it willed on high, where Michael wrought
>> Vengeance upon the proud adultery."

Commentators have tried to explain the first line of this passage with little success. Perhaps the reason is that as we begin to descend further into the realms of unreason, there is no fully intelligible reason for sin, except a strange perversity of will. The last word in this section is one of the few places where Longfellow's translation is simply wrong. Michael did not avenge nor does Dante speak of "adultery," which suggests sexual misconduct. What Dante wrote here is "proud rebellion," the revolt, that is to say, of angels who then became devils. This sin, unlike the earlier carnal weaknesses, is much more substantially a revolt against God:

> Here saw I people, more than elsewhere, many,
>> On one side and the other, with great howls,
>> Rolling weights forward by main force of chest.
> They clashed together, and then at that point
>> Each one turned backward, rolling retrograde,
>> Crying, "Why keepest?" and, "Why squanderest thou?"
> Thus they returned along the lurid circle
>> On either hand unto the opposite point,
>> Shouting their shameful metre evermore.
> Then each, when he arrived there, wheeled about
>> Through his half-circle to another joust.

Anyone familiar with classical mythology will recall, reading this, the figure of Sisyphus, condemned forever to roll a rock up a hill only to have it roll back down again. Dante shifts that pagan torment into a perpetual dancing in a circle where the hoarders and wasters of money roll enormous rocks into clashes with one another. That this failing is common appears from the fact that Dante claims he sees more people here than in the earlier circles; in addition, he sees clerics, people in religious life, who nonetheless are greedy for worldly goods.

Dante would like to see if he knew any of these sinners in life, but Vergil says it is impossible to recognize them now:

> Vain thought thou entertainest;
> The undiscerning life which made them sordid

Now makes them unto all discernment dim.
Forever shall they come to these two buttings;
    These from the sepulchre shall rise again
    With the fist closed, and these with tresses shorn.
Ill giving and ill keeping the fair world
    Have ta'en from them, and placed them in this scuffle;
    Whate'er it be, no words adorn I for it.
Now canst thou, Son, behold the transient farce
    Of goods that are committed unto Fortune,
    For which the human race each other buffet;
For all the gold that is beneath the moon,
    Or ever has been, of these weary souls
    Could never make a single one repose.

We are used to thinking of Fortune as fickle, as a force that ran-
domly upsets our plans and prevents, at times, honest efforts
from reaping a just reward. Vergil wants Dante to understand
that the instability of this life, far from being an evil, is actually
an instrument of Divine Providence:

He whose omniscience everything transcends
    The heavens created, and gave who should guide them,
    That every part to every part may shine,
Distributing the light in equal measure;
    He in like manner to the mundane splendours
    Ordained a general ministress and guide,
That she might change at times the empty treasures
    From race to race, from one blood to another,
    Beyond resistance of all human wisdom.
Therefore one people triumphs, and another
    Languishes, in pursuance of her judgment,
    Which hidden is, as in the grass a serpent.
Your knowledge has no counterstand against her;
    She makes provision, judges, and pursues
    Her governance, as theirs the other gods.
. . . .
Her permutations have not any truce;
    Necessity makes her precipitate,
    So often cometh who his turn obtains.
And this is she who is so crucified
    Even by those who ought to give her praise,
    Giving her blame amiss, and bad repute.

Vergil does not feel obliged to explain any further, but counsels that they continue on since they still have a long path to traverse. They follow a mysterious, dark stream down a gully and come to the next circle, where they find a marsh in which the souls strike and tear each other with their teeth:

> Said the good Master: "Son, thou now beholdest
> The souls of those whom anger overcame;
> And likewise I would have thee know for certain
> Beneath the water people are who sigh
> And make this water bubble at the surface,
> As the eye tells thee wheresoe'er it turns.
> Fixed in the mire they say, 'We sullen were
> In the sweet air, which by the sun is gladdened,
> Bearing within ourselves the sluggish reek;
> Now we are sullen in this sable mire.'
> This hymn do they keep gurgling in their throats,
> For with unbroken words they cannot say it."

As with the opposite but related sins of overhoarding and over-spending, Dante here comes upon those who were wrathful toward others, bespattered with mud. The sullen, those who did not enjoy the pleasures to be found in God's creation, are sunken in the mire and unable even to speak their woe. For a modern person, the sullen may resemble nothing so much as people who are deeply depressed, take no joy in life, and cannot even talk. Some psychologists attribute this to a kind of introverted anger at life situations. But once again, Dante forces us to open out our psychological diagnosis to situate it in the larger scheme of God's universe. Medical treatment and therapy provide useful insight into depression, but ultimately the depressed person must find a way to choose something besides despair.

Dante and Vergil come upon an ominous sign that will mark the transition from the several forms of incontinence to far more wicked evils:

> Thus we went circling round the filthy fen
> A great arc 'twixt the dry bank and the swamp,
> With eyes turned unto those who gorge the mire;
> Unto the foot of a tower we came at last.

Canto 8

The tower is one of many in the City of Dis, which appears to have minarets such as the Muslim heretics, in Dante's view, build. The poets enter into the boat of another infernal ferryman, who will take them to the gates of the city. But they are refused entry by the devils. Vergil himself cannot overcome them, but says someone who can will soon arrive.

Canto 9

While the poets wait for this mysterious person, they see several monsters on the parapets of the city walls. The demons threaten to bring out Medusa, the mythical monster with hair made of snakes who turned anyone who looked at her into stone. Reason, Vergil, has to make sure that Dante does not look directly on a certain kind of evil because, it seems, it would infect his own will in a way that would render him damnable. This strategy works and the expected help arrives.

> More than a thousand ruined souls I saw,
> > Thus fleeing from before one who on foot
> > Was passing o'er the Styx with soles unwet
> From off his face he fanned that unctuous air,
> > Waving his left hand oft in front of him,
> > And only with that anguish seemed he weary.
> Well I perceived one sent from Heaven was he,
> > And to the Master turned; and he made sign
> > That I should quiet stand, and bow before him.
> Ah how disdainful he appeared to me!
> > He reached the gate, and with a little rod
> > He opened it, for there was no resistance.
>
> . . . .
>
> Then he returned along the miry road,
> > And spake no word to us, but had the look
> > Of one whom other care constrains.

This scene is complex with many possible meanings, but for present purposes it is clear that where reason reaches a sticking point in negotiating with evil, divine power can become available to make the path toward truth wide open.

Canto 10

Now that we have entered Hell proper in the City of Dis, we move from the spirits of those who have gone beyond incontinence and self-indulgence to spirits who have engaged in malice toward themselves, toward others, and toward God. One of the curious things we shall observe is how Dante sees these various forms of malice nested within one another so that hatred of one of God's creatures, whether ourselves or our neighbor, ultimately reflects a hatred of the Creator. This becomes manifest immediately in cantos 9 and 10, where Dante sees heretics lying in red-hot tombs that, for the moment, remain uncovered. We might be inclined to think that the heretics belong further down in Hell as directly denying God or some truth about him, but for Dante a moral, spiritual, and psychological threshold must first be crossed to indulge in true hatred. And Vergil warns him ominously, "And much/more than thou thinkest laden are the tombs." Freely chosen alienation from God is greater than Dante, a medieval man living at a time when the possibility of damnation was preached far more often than it is today, would suppose.

As we have seen in our general sketch of Dante's life, one of the common expressions of hatred in his day was through factional politics. The parties of the pope and the emperor were at constant war in Florence and by all accounts the Ghibellines, who followed the emperor's banner, were tainted with "Epicureanism." Medieval philosophers did not have a great knowledge of the real Epicurus (342–270 B.C.) or his doctrines, but they knew that he did not believe that the soul survived after death and consequently made physical pleasure and absence of pain the highest good. As Dante will mention, the emperor Frederick II was widely rumored to have been an Epicurean. Many figures who made political violence a means of satisfying their wills and obtaining their own aims must have abandoned any other standard than personal pleasure and any worry about future judgment before they could have acted as they did.

For Dante there is no doubt that this stance is evil and leads to all the other big sins. As he says in book 2 of his *Banquet:* "I say that of all the stupidities that is the most foolish, the basest, and the most pernicious, which believes that after this life there is no other; for if we turn over all the writings both of the philosophers and the other wise authors, all agree that within us there is a certain part that endures." One reason this view is so pernicious is that it makes it impossible for there to be an ultimate accounting for all that we have been and done; another reason it leads us astray is that it tells us that, even in this world, there are no higher authorities than the wants of our small, individual human wills.

Dante chooses two figures to represent this heresy. The first, Farinata degli Uberti, was a legendary leader of the emperor's Ghibellines in Florence. As we shall see in a variety of details, Dante admires the worldly force of Farinata but thinks ultimately that his pride and heresy were his undoing. Yet a certain dignity still adheres to Farinata, who hears Dante passing and addresses him nobly:

> "O Tuscan, thou who through the city of fire
>> Goest alive, thus speaking modestly,
>> Be pleased to stay thy footsteps in this place.
> Thy mode of speaking makes thee manifest
>> A native of that noble fatherland,
>> To which perhaps I too molestful was."
>
> . . . .
>
> I had already fixed mine eyes on his,
>> And he uprose erect with breast and front
>> E'en as if Hell he had in great despite.

The disdain that Farinata has for Hell even as he is tormented shows a certain nobility of spirit, but the very same pride in his own dignity is the very fault that brought him to this terrible end. A few lines later, Farinata even admits that the political failures of his party "more tormenteth me, than doth this bed."

By contrast, the other main figure in the canto is a Guelf and a more emotional being. Cavalcante dei Cavalcanti was the father of Dante's best friend, the poet Guido Cavalcanti. Both father and son seem to have denied the immortality of the soul and thus, despite friendship and membership in the same political factions, Dante consigns them to this circle of heretics. One dimension of their heresy seems to have been an overemphasis on individual genius, as we see when Cavalcante's shade arises in a tomb next to Farinata's:

Weeping, he said to me: "If through this blind
   Prison thou goest by loftiness of genius,
   Where is my son? and why is he not with thee?"
And I to him: "I come not of myself;
   He who is waiting yonder leads me here,
   Whom in disdain perhaps your Guido had."

The interweaving in this canto of personal destiny, political events, and spiritual insight is typical of Dante's firm belief in the unity of the world created by God. Unlike the Epicureans, he thinks that not only do his past and future ups and downs have personal meaning; they have worldly and even heavenly significance. Genius is, therefore, not merely a power we possess but a gift. The ultimate fate of souls who do not see these truths is not merely condemnation to Hell but, when the world comes to an end, a closing off of knowledge and closing of selves into the eternal tombs of torment that are the fitting recompense for their heresy—which in the end is a refusal of love.

Cantos 11–13

From this point on, we will take a much more rapid descent into the Inferno, stopping at a few key points, especially as we reach the very bottom of Hell and Dante's vision of Lucifer himself. In many ways, as we reach a certain depth of depravity, the lessons become merely notional, outside of our experience and imagination. We appreciate the images Dante presents of what such grave sinners have turned themselves into. But the very depravity and narrowness of soul among the worst sinners almost always remains distant from most of us.

Dante himself provides a brief summary at this point in the poem of much of what exists below. Vergil tells Dante that they must pause until they become accustomed to the stench. This in itself marks a change. Until now they have, more or less, been able to bear the condition of the evildoers. All of them, with the exception of the heretics, were what the medievals called incontinent, incapable of controlling their appetites. While these are serious sins for the people who have finished in Hell, they do not have by nature the grave malice within them that we are about to encounter. Even the heretics have, by comparison, a certain nobility in their stiff error. Since they do not wish to waste time, Dante asks Vergil to tell him what is to come. Vergil begins to divide up the lower circles according to a common philosophical scheme harking back to Aristotle. We do malice either by violence or fraud. Violence is something we share with wild beasts, but fraud requires human reason and therefore is a graver sin against our nature. These two, force and fraud, are further divided within themselves. We may indulge in violence, "To God, to ourselves, and to our neighbour. . . ." Murder and other injuries thus occupy the first circle of the violent; suicides the second; blasphemers, sodomites, and usurers the third.

Below the violent, the fraudulent are divided into two large groups: those who betrayed someone connected to them by special demands of affection or obedience and those who simply practiced fraud on strangers. Since the first adds another sin, treachery, on top of fraud, it is punished farther down. The others include people who practice:

Hypocrisy, flattery, and who deals in magic,
Falsification, theft, and simony,
Panders, and barrators, and the like filth.

In later cantos, we will see concretely what Dante means.

Canto 12

The violent against neighbors are punished by mythological figures, the Centaurs, who are half man and half beast. This may be meant to suggest that people who indulge in unjust violence against their neighbor make themselves something other than wholly human. Specifically, the Centaurs keep the condemned souls immersed in a boiling, circular river of blood. The worst offenders, such as bloody tyrants, are wholly submerged; lesser offenders are immersed to a degree commensurate with their offenses. Dante and Vergil observe this just punishment and cross the river at its shallowest point to go down to the next circle.

Here suicides, those who have perpetrated unjust violence against themselves, are punished by having their souls pent up in tangled and gnarled trees. Perhaps the eeriest feature of the suicides is the voice they now have. With their souls in these deformed trees, their speech is only let out if someone breaks off a branch. Then, voice and blood issue from the break in a spooky hissing sound.

> After it had become embrowned with blood,
>   It recommenced its cry: "Why dost thou rend me?
>   Hast thou no spirit of pity whatsoever?
> Men once we were, and now are changed to trees;
>   Indeed, thy hand should be more pitiful,
>   Even if the souls of serpents we had been."
> As out of a green brand, that is on fire
>   At one of the ends, and from the other drips
>   And hisses with the wind that is escaping;
> So from that splinter issued forth together
>   Both words and blood; whereat I let the tip
>   Fall, and stood like a man who is afraid.

The punishment again fits the crime. Leaving aside for the moment our modern medical theories about the mechanisms by which some people are driven, beyond their own fault, to suicide, Dante rightly says that those who deliberately choose death to avoid shame or some other minor inconvenience, have thrown away the bodily life God intended for them. One, the emperor's counselor Pier delle Vigne, did so solely because envious detractors had accused him of plotting against his lord. In Dante, there is no Samurai-like belief that it is better to kill onself than suffer dishonor. To give up the animal and human enjoyment of life for relatively lesser goods means making oneself into a bare living being, like a tree, possessing life but without the added faculties of animals and men. Even at the last judgment, these sinners will not enjoy the reincarnation of the body, for it is not just, says Dante, for them to have in eternity what they threw away in the temporal world.

Canto 14

Vergil and Dante pass on to a deeper form of violence, the part of Hell for those who have been violent against God, man, and nature through blasphemy, usury, and homosexuality. Though this grouping may seem odd to us, it proceeds from the medieval notion that all these flaws stem from a movement against the natural order that results in sterility or, in the case of usury, unnatural fecundity. All the spirits in this region inhabit a desert waste that Dante is careful to say repels every plant from its bed. Flakes of fire, like large snowflakes, fall upon the three types of spirits, perhaps a reminiscence of the fire that God sent on Sodom. The three groups are condemned to three different postures on the fiery sand:

> Supine upon the ground some folk were lying;
>   And some were sitting all drawn up together,
>   And others went about continually.
> Those who were going round were far the more,
>   And those were less who lay down to their torment,
>   But had their tongues more loosed to lamentation.

Those lying immobile are the blasphemers, among whom the classical figure of Capaneus so disdains God that he lies immobile even under the torment and exclaims:

>   "Such as I was living, am I, dead
> If Jove should weary out his smith, from whom
>   He seized in anger the sharp thunderbolt,
>   Wherewith upon the last day I was smitten . . .
> He would not have thereby a joyous vengeance."

Again we are told that whatever we were in life so we continue in eternity, and in this instance the resistance to the origin of the universe itself has a horrible retribution. Dante says that Vergil—here surely the voice of natural Reason speaking of our natural obligation to acknowledge the Creator—shouts louder than ever:

> "O Capaneus, in that is not extinguished
> Thine arrogance, thou punished art the more;
>   Not any torment, saving thine own rage,
>   Would be unto thy fury pain complete."

Unlike the heretics, Capaneus believes God exists but flouts him anyway. Dante touches a point about stubbornness; it often resists even when it knows the truth.

The only way the poets can cross the burning sand and the

rain of fire is across a bridge bordered by streams descending from Phlegethon, the river of blood in the circle above. Dante asks where this river comes from, and Vergil hints that all the evils of the world since the fall and the decline of nations are gathered together and flow down to be collected in Hell until they come to the very bottom of the universe to be frozen forever in the lake of Cocytus.

Canto 15

The poets begin to cross the scorching desert on the bridge, which protects them from the falling flakes of fire. As they do, they encounter some of the running spirits, the largest group in this circle. Nowhere is it mentioned, but we know from Vergil's earlier explanation that these are the sodomites—in our terms, homosexuals. While Dante puts these sinners in the circle where he thinks they properly belong, it is hard not to detect a certain sadness, as in the case of the disordered love of Paolo and Francesca, that the figures he encounters have come to this pass. In one of the most touching scenes in the whole of the *Inferno*, Dante meets Brunetto Latini, a notary and a gifted public figure during the poet's youth. It was once thought that Dante must have been Brunetto's student because of the respectful language bordering almost on a father–son relationship. But it now appears that the exchange here more accurately reflects that Dante learned much from the older man about how to conduct oneself with honor in public affairs. After the initial shock in which Dante exclaims, "Are you here, Ser Brunetto?" Brunetto himself is surprised to see a still living Dante:

> "What fortune or what fate
> Before the last day leadeth thee down here?
> And who is this that showeth thee the way?"
> "Up there above us in the life serene,"
> I answered him, "I lost me in a valley,
> Or ever yet my age had been completed.
> But yestermorn I turned my back upon it;
> This one appeared to me, returning thither,
> And homeward leadeth me along this road."
> And he to me: "If thou thy star do follow,

> Thou canst not fail thee of a glorious port,
> If well I judged in the life beautiful.
> And if I had not died so prematurely,
>   Seeing Heaven thus benignant unto thee,
>   I would have given thee comfort in the work."

Brunetto denounces the corrupt and violent elements that have come into Florence and warns Dante about the ill fortune that will soon overtake him. Dante replies not to worry:

> "If my entreaty wholly were fulfilled,"
>   Replied I to him, "not yet would you be
>   In banishment from human nature placed;
> For in my mind is fixed, and touches now
>   My heart the dear and good paternal image
>   Of you, when in the world from hour to hour
> You taught me how a man becomes eternal."

This is one of the few places in the poem where the translation needs correction. Dante actually says, "you taught me how a man 'eternals himself'"; by this novel expression Dante presumably wishes to suggest that the kind of virtue needed for this end requires special cultivation, almost unheard-of in normal life. The kind of making oneself eternal that Dante has in mind is not the reaching out spiritually to the eternal realms but the doing of noble earthly deeds worthy of being remembered for as long as the human race endures.

Indeed, such is the nobility Brunetto inspires in Dante that he compares the figure of Brunetto as he runs off at their parting to the winner of a footrace usually held on the first Sunday in Lent in the northern Italian city of Verona:

> Then he turned round, and seemed to be of those
>   Who at Verona run for the Green Mantle
>   Across the plain; and seemed to be among them
> The one who wins, and not the one who loses.

What are we to make of the spiritual import of all of this? As in the past, the rule is "what I was living, so am I dead." Dante does not feel much need to argue about this sin, which was universally condemned by the moral tradition. Instead he hints at a kind of delicacy among those in this circle, not only Brunetto but teachers and others, whose perceptiveness adds to the refinement of the race yet is vitiated by their turn into homosexual relations.

Canto 17

Dante sees a monster rise that we might have expected to appear in a book of medieval chivalry where knights battle dragons. But this is no merely mythical beast. This monster breaks all natural and manmade restraints in its flight:

"Behold the monster with the pointed tail,
  Who cleaves the hills, and breaketh walls and weapons,
  Behold him who infecteth all the world."
Thus unto me my Guide began to say,
  And beckoned him that he should come to shore,
  Near to the confine of the trodden marble;
And that uncleanly image of deceit
  Came up and thrust ashore its head and bust,
  But on the border did not drag its tail.
The face was as the face of a just man,
  Its semblance outwardly was so benign,
  And of a serpent all the trunk beside.
Two paws it had, hairy unto the armpits;
  The back, and breast, and both the sides it had
  Depicted o'er with nooses and with shields.
With colours more, groundwork or broidery
  Never in cloth did Tartars make nor Turks,
  Nor were such tissues by Arachne laid. . .
His tail was wholly quivering in the void,
  Contorting upwards the envenomed fork,
  That in the guise of scorpion armed its point.

This bizarre beast with the face of a good man, the body of a serpent, and the sting of a scorpion is Geryon. Dante has concocted him from both classical mythology and chapter 9 of the book of Revelation, where a horde of locusts is said to have human faces but a scorpion's sting. The oddness of this appearance of humanity coupled with bestial harm is meant to warn us about the kind of fraud we encounter in the world and in ourselves. Its face is familiar and comfortable. But the more we get to know it the more inhuman it is.

Dante and Vergil stand at the edge of a kind of large well, into which they must now descend deeper. The two wayfarers must move aside to allow Geryon room to get turned around. As they do so, Dante notices some usurers sitting on the burning sand and goes off to talk with them briefly, a hint that perhaps usury borders on fraud. When he turns back to Vergil, we see the allegory beneath the literal story. As Reason, Vergil is Dante's sole support as the two of them are about to begin a dizzying descent on the back of Geryon into the circles of fraud:

I found my Guide, who had already mounted
   Upon the back of that wild animal,
   And said to me: "Now be both strong and bold.
Now we descend by stairways such as these;
   Mount thou in front, for I will be midway,
   So that the tail may have no power to harm thee."
Such as he is who has so near the ague
   Of quartan that his nails are blue already,
   And trembles all, but looking at the shade;
Even such became I at those proffered words;
   But shame in me his menaces produced,
   Which maketh servant strong before good master.
I seated me upon those monstrous shoulders;
   I wished to say, and yet the voice came not
   As I believed, "Take heed that thou embrace me."
But he, who other times had rescued me
   In other peril, soon as I had mounted,
   Within his arms encircled and sustained me,
And said: "Now, Geryon, bestir thyself;
   The circles large, and the descent be little;
   Think of the novel burden which thou hast."

Like all of us, Dante must be held fast by truth as he enters a spiritual realm that has established itself on the principle of falsehood. Anyone who has ever had the experience of being deliberately deceived with an intention to harm knows this sense of falling without, apparently, anything to grasp on to. But more than a psychological reaction, Dante sees in this sense a true expression of the spiritual reality that opens up when one human being draws another in with insubstantial lies:

Onward he goeth, swimming slowly, slowly;
  Wheels and descends, but I perceive it only
  By wind upon my face and from below.
I heard already on the right the whirlpool
  Making a horrible crashing under us;
  Whence I thrust out my head with eyes cast downward.
Then was I still more fearful of the abyss;
  Because I fires beheld, and heard laments,
  Whereat I, trembling, all the closer cling.
I saw then, for before I had not seen it,
  The turning and descending, by great horrors
  That were approaching upon divers sides.

The strange floating feeling here coupled with the spiral descent and highlighted by the crashing waters as we rush headlong into deeper sin create a kind of vertigo. Dante has earlier seen fearful punishments for serious sins, but these have always been held at arm's length, as it were, by the fact that he was merely seeing a manifestation of judgment and just punishment. But as we draw deeper into evil our very senses and sense of judgment begin to become disoriented by the loss of all the certainties that we formerly had. As we now go through the ten circles of fraud, Dante and Vergil, the symbol of Reason, will themselves sometimes be deceived by spirits who have made deception their life, perhaps suggesting hidden and intractable effects in our own personalities.

Canto 18–19

We are now in Malebolge ("evil pouch"), which contains the sinners who have committed fraud, a direct violation of the truthfulness and right action with which the human being is particularly gifted by God. As the betrayal of the gift is greater, so, justly, is the punishment. The place is all stone and iron to reinforce the notion of a prison house. Here there are ten concentric circles containing sinners who have perpetrated different forms of fraud and are punished diversely. And we are warned early on that there is in the midst of even these levels of human depravity a large well that goes down to a level still lower. The figure on page 80 gives a view from above the realm Dante describes. We shall only stop at a few points here.

THE MALEBOLGE:
THE EIGHTH
CIRCLE
OF HELL

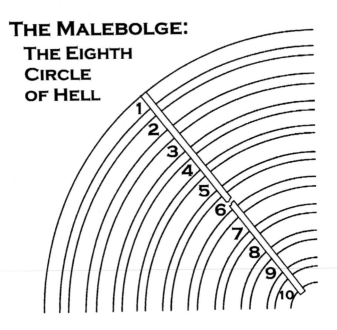

1. PANDERS AND SEDUCERS
2. FLATTERERS
3. SIMONISTS
4. SOOTHSAYERS
5. BARRATORS

6. HYPOCRITES
7. THIEVES
8. EVIL COUNSELORS
9. CREATORS OF STRIFE
10. FALSIFIERS

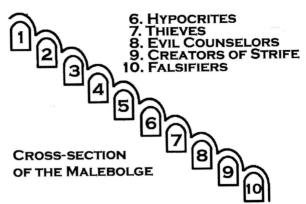

CROSS-SECTION
OF THE MALEBOLGE

Canto 20

In one circle, Dante comes upon a sorrowful image of what
human nature can do to itself, and the distortion causes him to
weep:

> And people saw I through the circular valley,
>   Silent and weeping, coming at the pace
>   Which in this world the Litanies assume.
> As lower down my sight descended on them,
>   Wondrously each one seemed to be distorted
>   From chin to the beginning of the chest;
> For tow'rds the reins the countenance was turned,
>   And backward it behoved them to advance,
>   As to look forward had been taken from them.
> Perchance indeed by violence of palsy
>   Some one has been thus wholly turned awry;
>   But I ne'er saw it, nor believe it can be.
> As God may let thee, Reader, gather fruit
>   From this thy reading, think now for thyself
>   How I could ever keep my face unmoistened,
> When our own image near me I beheld
>   Distorted so, the weeping of the eyes
>   Along the fissure bathed the hinder parts.

These souls are those of the diviners, or fortune-tellers, who
longed to look far ahead and now look forever backwards.
Certainly, Dante believed some people might be inspired by God
to issue prophetic warnings. But what he is describing here are
the many ways in which fortune-tellers, magicians, and others
play upon the weakness of people who do not trust sufficiently
in God. They want an advance warning or a magical means to
ward off what is to come. Vergil, ever the voice of Reason,
rebukes Dante:

> Truly I wept, leaning upon a peak
>   Of the hard crag, so that my Escort said
>   To me: "Art thou, too, of the other fools?
> Here pity lives when it is wholly dead;
>   Who is a greater reprobate than he
>   Who feels compassion at the doom divine?"

The rebuke has a double purpose. The last line in Dante's Italian reads more literally "who sorrows at the divine judgment." The rebuke, then, criticizes both those who refused to trust the divine will in this life and a misplaced compassion toward them when they are forced to endure the divine will in death.

Canto 21

Dante next meets the barrators, who sold the public good for money and other benefits. The description of these sinners extends over the better part of three cantos, perhaps reflecting Dante's own experience with corrupt politicians. He begins with a graphic description of the state of these sinners, which reflects the frightening world that they created:

> As in the Arsenal of the Venetians
>> Boils in the winter the tenacious pitch
>> To smear their unsound vessels o'er again,
> For sail they cannot; and instead thereof
>> One makes his vessel new, and one recaulks
>> The ribs of that which many a voyage has made;
> One hammers at the prow, one at the stern,
>> This one makes oars, and that one cordage twists,
>> Another mends the mainsail and the mizzen;
> Thus, not by fire, but by the art divine,
>> Was boiling down below there a dense pitch
>> Which upon every side the bank belimed.

Like corrupt politics, this part of hell bustles, but blackly. A pool of pitch bubbles in the moatlike circle and almost hypnotizes Dante:

> I saw it, but I did not see within it
>> Aught but the bubbles that the boiling raised,
>> And all swell up and resubside compressed.
> The while below there fixedly I gazed,
>> My Leader, crying out: "Beware, beware!"
>> Drew me unto himself from where I stood.
> Then I turned round, as one who is impatient
>> To see what it behoves him to escape,
>> And whom a sudden terror doth unman.
> Who, while he looks, delays not his departure;

And I beheld behind us a black devil,
Running along upon the crag, approach.
Ah, how ferocious was he in his aspect!
And how he seemed to me in action ruthless,
With open wings and light upon his feet.
His shoulders, which sharp-pointed were and high,
A sinner did encumber with both haunches,
And he held clutched the sinews of the feet.

Like the souls of the sinners in this circle, the devils too are becoming more fearful. The demon who rushes along here, like a butcher with a slain animal on his shoulders, is eager to drag souls down to torment and barely waits a moment after throwing this soul into the pitch before returning to Earth for another. The other demons make sure the soul stays covered with the hot sticky fluid so that he will suffer more:

They seized him then with more than a hundred rakes;
They said: "It here behoves thee to dance covered,
That, if thou canst, thou secretly mayest pilfer."
Not otherwise the cooks their scullions make
Immerse into the middle of the caldron
The meat with hooks, so that it may not float.

With vicious spirits like this about, Vergil decides to leave Dante behind a rock and talk with the devils:

With the same fury, and the same uproar,
As dogs leap out upon a mendicant,
Who on a sudden begs, where'er he stops,
They issued from beneath the little bridge,
And turned against him all their grappling-irons;
But he cried out: "Be none of you malignant!
Before those hooks of yours lay hold of me,
Let one of you step forward, who may hear me,
And then take counsel as to grappling me."
They all cried out: "Let Malacoda go;"
Whereat one started, and the rest stood still,
And he came to him, saying: "What avails it?"
"Thinkest thou, Malacoda, to behold me
Advanced into this place," my Master said,
"Safe hitherto from all your skill of fence,
Without the will divine, and fate auspicious?

> Let me go on, for it in Heaven is willed
>   That I another show this savage road."

The devils reluctantly stop threatening Vergil, who calls Dante out. In circumstances like these, where treachery is followed by violence, only Reason can be a sure guide and Dante shows it by his actions:

> Close did I press myself with all my person
>   Beside my Leader, and turned not mine eyes
>   From off their countenance, which was not good.
> They lowered their rakes, and "Wilt thou have me hit him,"
>   They said to one another, "on the rump?"
>   And answered: "Yes; see that thou nick him with it."
> But the same demon who was holding parley
>   With my Conductor turned him very quickly,
>   And said: "Be quiet, be quiet, Scarmiglione;"
> Then said to us: "You can no farther go
>   Forward upon this crag, because is lying
>   All shattered, at the bottom, the sixth arch.
> And if it still doth please you to go onward,
>   Pursue your way along upon this rock;
>   Near is another crag that yields a path.
> Yesterday, five hours later than this hour,
>   One thousand and two hundred sixty-six
>   Years were complete, that here the way was broken."

This refers to the harrowing of Hell by Christ. Since legend held that Christ died at the age of thirty-three, that number plus 1,266 years, plus another year just completed at Easter, equals exactly 1300. All of this is superficially reassuring to Dante and Vergil, who have been warned about the difficulty of the way ahead and had the reason explained by a true reference. The semblance of order and proper rule continues as the lead devil orders the others to accompany the poets. In a parody of military discipline, they form up and salute:

> I send in that direction some of mine
>   To see if any one doth air himself;
>   Go ye with them; for they will not be vicious.
> Step forward, Alichino and Calcabrina,"
>   Began he to cry out, "and thou, Cagnazzo;
>   And Barbariccia, do thou guide the ten.

> Come forward, Libicocco and Draghignazzo,
>   And tusked Ciriatto and Graffiacane,
>   And Farfarello and mad Rubicante;
> Search ye all round about the boiling pitch;
>   Let these be safe as far as the next crag,
>   That all unbroken passes o'er the dens."

The names of these demons are daunting enough, and Dante does not trust this apparent order:

> "O me! what is it, Master, that I see?
>   Pray let us go," I said, "without an escort,
>   If thou knowest how, since for myself I ask none.
> If thou art as observant as thy wont is,
>   Dost thou not see that they do gnash their teeth,
>   And with their brows are threatening woe to us?"
> And he to me: "I will not have thee fear;
>   Let them gnash on, according to their fancy,
>   Because they do it for those boiling wretches."
> Along the left-hand dike they wheeled about;
>   But first had each one thrust his tongue between
>   His teeth towards their leader for a signal;
> And he had made a trumpet of his rump.

With this bizarre salute they are off. But, as one who has suffered under false appearance of authority on Earth, Dante has rightly sensed something awry that even Vergil does not see.

Canto 22

After some scuffling, Dante and Vergil wisely choose to leave this untrustworthy escort and go on by themselves. But they have one more surprise in store from these devils. They hasten to get to the next circle, and see the devils pursuing them. Since they were told the bridge over this circle was broken, Vergil decides to slide down the embankment to the next circle holding Dante.

> Hardly the bed of the ravine below
>   His feet had reached, ere they had reached the hill
>   Right over us; but he was not afraid;
> For the high Providence, which had ordained
>   To place them ministers of the fifth moat,
>   The power of thence departing took from all.

In the allegorical dimension of the poem, this scene may be intended to suggest that Reason may be able to contrive some escapes from the more obvious threats of fraud. But Reason has only a limited use when confronted with the wiles of beings who have abandoned truth.

In the new circle to which the poets come, they encounter the hypocrites being punished in the fashion that their sin requires:

> A painted people there below we found,
>   Who went about with footsteps very slow,
>   Weeping and in their semblance tired and vanquished.
> They had on mantles with the hoods low down
>   Before their eyes, and fashioned of the cut
>   That in Cologne they for the monks are made.
> Without, they gilded are so that it dazzles;
>   But inwardly all leaden and so heavy
>   That Frederick used to put them on of straw.

The last line is an obscure reference to the emperor Frederick II, who used to put a lead mantle over traitors and then have it melted with them inside over a fire. Souls here are entombed in heavy lead mantles. The shining exteriors, painted, as were the whited sepulchers in the Gospel, give the impression of brightness and happiness but conceal heavy torments within.

In addition to marveling at this novel punishment, Vergil, as the voice of Reason, marvels and grows angry to find that the devils in the previous canto had been deceiving him about the lack of a bridge over the pitch. Presumably, they would have tried to do the two poets mischief before long. Dante is probably expressing here the limits of our reason, which takes many things at face value, but is less than wholly reliable when confronted with profound evils. The Father of lies has too many tricks. A certain weariness with the unrelieved and unredeemable nature of these sinners inevitably begins to set in for the poets and for the reader as well. Neither they nor we are likely to be in danger of such sins, and their very darkness is not very illuminating. But there is still much more evil in human nature, and for the purposes of exhausting its hold and as a prelude to a better spiritual life, Dante must complete his voyage to the bottom of the universe.

Canto 24

Peering through the smoky air, Dante sees the spirits of the
thieves who, by not respecting other's property, have erased the
necessary distinction between the boundaries of one person's life
and another's. Their punishments stem from the nature of their
offense. In a strange, otherworldly version of apprehension and
arrest, we see these souls:

> They had their hands with serpents bound behind them;
>> These riveted upon their reins the tail
>> And head, and were in front of them entwined.

But that is not all. The serpents attack these once-human figures:

> And lo! at one who was upon our side
>> There darted forth a serpent, which transfixed him
>> There where the neck is knotted to the shoulders.
> Nor "O" so quickly e'er, nor "I" was written,
>> As he took fire, and burned; and ashes wholly
>> Behoved it that in falling he became.
> And when he on the ground was thus destroyed,
>> The ashes drew together, and of themselves
>> Into himself they instantly returned.

A Centaur shows up with a dragon to punish one soul further:

> He fled away, and spake no further word;
>> And I beheld a Centaur full of rage
>> Come crying out: "Where is, where is the scoffer?"
> I do not think Maremma has so many
>> Serpents as he had all along his back,
>> As far as where our countenance begins.
> Upon the shoulders, just behind the nape,
>> With wings wide open was a dragon lying,
>> And he sets fire to all that he encounters.

The scene shifts rapidly, and Dante begs the reader not to dis-
count the sequel. Serpents fasten on human forms and meld into
grotesque shapes with them; others exchange human for serpent
form. In a world of unbounded thievery, no one's form is pre-
served, but is horribly exchanged with others in a perpetual
shape shifting of evil. This goes on among various thieves, sev-
eral of whom are Florentines.

Canto 26

So Dante sarcastically congratulates Florence for all the representatives she has at these great depths:

> Rejoice, O Florence, since thou art so great,
>> That over sea and land thou beatest thy wings,
>> And throughout Hell thy name is spread abroad!
> Among the thieves five citizens of thine
>> Like these I found, whence shame comes unto me,
>> And thou thereby to no great honour risest.

The poets move on to the eighth circle, and Dante says curiously:

> When I direct my mind to what I saw,
> And more my genius curb than I am wont,
> That it may run not unless virtue guide it;
>> So that if some good star, or better thing,
>> Have given me good, I may myself not grudge it.

Why does he feel the need to control his talents here? He says he saw multitudinous fires in the ditch below, as many as fireflies in the country during the springtime, and each turns out to be a flame in which a soul is concealed. These flames contain the spirit of evil counselors, and we have here the explanation for Dante's warning: intelligence is good, but not when God-given gifts run amok against God's purposes.

Dante asks Vergil to speak to one flame in particular, a large one that holds the spirit of the great Ulysses. The text of Homer's *Odyssey* was still unknown in Dante's day; but Dante must have had some knowledge of Ulysses' wide wanderings from other classical sources. Dante constructs a story about Ulysses, perhaps under the mistaken impression that Ulysses liked wandering, that serves as a cautionary tale. The flame begins to hiss and speak, like a fire blown by the wind:

> Nor fondness for my son, nor reverence
>> For my old father, nor the due affection
>> Which joyous should have made Penelope,
> Could overcome within me the desire
>> I had to be experienced of the world,
>> And of the vice and virtue of mankind;

But I put forth on the high open sea
  With one sole ship, and that small company
  By which I never had deserted been.
Both of the shores I saw as far as Spain,
  Far as Morocco, and the isle of Sardes,
  And the others which that sea bathes round about.
I and my company were old and slow
  When at that narrow passage we arrived
  Where Hercules his landmarks set as signals,
That man no farther onward should adventure.
  On the right hand behind me left I Seville,
  And on the other already had left Ceuta.
"O brothers, who amid a hundred thousand
  Perils," I said, "have come unto the West,
  To this so inconsiderable vigil
Which is remaining of your senses still
  Be ye unwilling to deny the knowledge,
  Following the sun, of the unpeopled world.
Consider ye the seed from which ye sprang;
  Ye were not made to live like unto brutes,
  But for pursuit of virtue and of knowledge."

Several elements are at play in this passage. The flickering flame
reflects an inconstant spirit that casts a shadow over what might
otherwise seem heroic. Ulysses gave himself up to a reckless
curiosity without regard for his family. He went beyond the
Pillars of Hercules at the western edge of the Mediterranean to
his doom. What's more, he counseled his men to follow him in
pursuit of virtue and knowledge, a truly noble end, but pursued
through evil means:

Five times rekindled and as many quenched
  Had been the splendour underneath the moon,
  Since we had entered into the deep pass,
When there appeared to us a mountain, dim
  From distance, and it seemed to me so high
  As I had never any one beheld.
Joyful were we, and soon it turned to weeping;
  For out of the new land a whirlwind rose,
  And smote upon the fore part of the ship.
Three times it made her whirl with all the waters,
  At the fourth time it made the stern uplift,

> And the prow downward go, as pleased Another,
> Until the sea above us closed again.

In other words, five months after they sailed west into the
Atlantic they all drowned. The mysterious mountain they dis-
covered was the mountain of Purgatory. Had they approached it
the right way, as Dante and Vergil will in the next *cantica*, rather
than through idle curiosity, it might indeed have led them to
knowledge and virtue.

To us who have knowledge of the successes of explorers who,
less than two centuries after Dante, would discover the Ameri-
cas, this may appear a strange argument. But the truth may be
that it is we who are relatively blind to the kind of idle curiosity
we engage in all the time without attending to the true needs and
potential discoveries of the soul. The world always presents dis-
tracting adventures that, however interesting in themselves, may
not do us any spiritual good and may lead to great harm. In an
age when all forms of exploration are considered unqualifiably
good, this canto makes a strong case for wise counsel in our
exploring.

Canto 27

Another sort of evil counselor comes forward, the treacherous
political adviser Guido da Montefeltro. Like Ulysses, he is one of
the most unforgettable characters in the *Inferno*. Guido speaks
gently from his flame and inquires after his beloved region, the
Romagna. Dante tells him no war is currently raging there. Then
Dante asks a favor in return, Guido's name and story. In a pas-
sage that T. S. Eliot made even more famous by placing it as an
epigraph to his poem "The Love Song of J. Alfred Prufrock,"
Guido responds:

> If I believed that my reply were made
>   To one who to the world would e'er return,
>   This flame without more flickering would stand still;
> But inasmuch as never from this depth
>   Did any one return, if I hear true,
>   Without the fear of infamy I answer . . .

Guido was a man of arms who had given up war and political machinations for repentance and a cloister with the Franciscans. Or, as he puts it, echoing the previous episode of Ulysses' wild adventures on the sea:

> The machinations and the covert ways
>   I knew them all, and practised so their craft,
>   That to the ends of earth the sound went forth.
> When now unto that portion of mine age
>   I saw myself arrived, when each one ought
>   To lower the sails, and coil away the ropes,
> That which before had pleased me then displeased me;
>   And penitent and confessing I surrendered,
>   Ah woe is me! and it would have bestead me. . .

But in his monastic retirement, Pope Boniface VIII, Dante's adversary, whom Guido calls the "Prince of the modern pharisees," came and asked him to perform one last trick. Boniface wants to overrun the city known today as Palestrina. When Guido objects that he has given up such evil, Boniface falsely tells him that, as pope, he holds the keys of the kingdom and can forgive him in advance. Reassured, Guido counsels Boniface to declare a false amnesty for his political enemies, but to destroy them as soon as their guard is down.

This part of the story is interesting for what it tells us of political maneuvering in Dante's day. But the sequel, what happened to Guido right after his death, has relevance to everyone who thinks mere formal absolution, even by a pope, without true penitence, can relieve us of sin. Since Guido returned to the monastery after his evil counsel, he was at least nominally a follower of Francis of Assisi at death:

> Francis came afterward, when I was dead,
>   For me; but one of the black Cherubim
>   Said to him: "Take him not; do me no wrong;
> He must come down among my servitors,
>   Because he gave the fraudulent advice
>   From which time forth I have been at his hair;
> For who repents not cannot be absolved,
>   Nor can one both repent and will at once,
>   Because of the contradiction which consents not.
> O miserable me! how I did shudder

> When he seized on me, saying: 'Peradventure
> Thou didst not think that I was a logician!'"

We are not normally accustomed to think of the devil as a logician. But the law of contradiction is such that we cannot both sin and claim absolution without the actual act of repentance. Guido has the honor of being the only soul in the whole of the *Inferno* who has wound up there because he was outwitted by the devil's own logic. Evil counselors, by nature, use the intellect for purposes that the intellect was not made to pursue. And their fault is not crafty enough to become its own excuse.

Canto 28

In the next circle, we meet up with those who not only counseled evil but actually sowed discord. First among these is Mahomet, whom the medievals thought had sown dissension in the church by setting up a kind of internal schism. The punishment for Mahomet and his son-in-law, Ali, who introduced a further split within Mohammedanism itself, is, as usual, fitting:

> A cask by losing centre-piece or cant
>   Was never shattered so, as I saw one
>   Rent from the chin to where one breaketh wind.
> Between his legs were hanging down his entrails;
>   His heart was visible, and the dismal sack
>   That maketh excrement of what is eaten.
> While I was all absorbed in seeing him,
>   He looked at me, and opened with his hands
>   His bosom, saying: "See now how I rend me;
> How mutilated, see, is Mahomet;
>   In front of me doth Ali weeping go,
>   Cleft in the face from forelock unto chin;
> And all the others whom thou here beholdest,
>   Disseminators of scandal and of schism
>   While living were, and therefore are cleft thus."

To add to the torment, these wounds heal as the spirits go around the circle and are administered to them again, for all eternity, by a devil with a sword. The poets meet with various classical and contemporary figures famous for sowing discord, but one in particular interests Dante, a certain Mosca, who was the source of a famous saying in Tuscany:

> And one, who both his hands dissevered had,
>   The stumps uplifting through the murky air,
>   So that the blood made horrible his face,
> Cried out: "Thou shalt remember Mosca also,
>   Who said, alas! 'A thing done has an end!'
>   Which was an ill seed for the Tuscan people."
> "And death unto thy race," thereto I added;
>   Whence he, accumulating woe on woe,
>   Departed, like a person sad and crazed.

Dante's curse may seem cruel here, but in the early part of the thirteenth century this Mosca de' Lamberti had counseled the murder of Buondelmonte de' Buondelmonti, one of the Florentine leaders with the words, "*Cosa fatta capo ha.*" But this was bad advice, because the murder was not the end but the beginning of many troubles. Carried out almost like a Mafia execution on the Ponte Vecchio on Easter morning of 1215, it led to even more violent factions and the civic strife that produced so much bloodshed.

Canto 31

The poets have left the ten circles of Malebolge, and in the gloom they hear a deafening trumpet sound:

> So loud it would have made each thunder faint,
>   Which, counter to it following its way,
>   Mine eyes directed wholly to one place.
> After the dolorous discomfiture
>   When Charlemagne the holy emprise lost,
>   So terribly Orlando sounded not.

This is a reference to the famous story of Roland, who sounded a warning to the retreating Charlemagne at Roncesvalles, that the Muslims were attacking. Roland blew so loudly that he died from the effort. But even that was as nothing compared to what Dante hears. Dante also thinks he sees a city with towers up ahead, but Vergil says as they approach and can see more clearly that, in fact, they are giants standing in a pit and are only visible from the waist up. These giants are a combination of the giants in Scripture and the classical giants destroyed by Zeus. Dante feels fear and remarks that such bulk combined with the powers of the intellect—like human powers so used—become unnatural behemoths as well:

> Certainly Nature, when she left the making
>   Of animals like these, did well indeed,
>   By taking such executors from Mars;
> And if of elephants and whales she doth not
>   Repent her, whosoever looketh subtly
>   More just and more discreet will hold her for it;
> For where the argument of intellect
>   Is added unto evil will and power,
>   No rampart can the people make against it.

There are four giants here and Antaeus, one of the four who is at Vergil's command, picks up the pair and deposits them gently on the last level of evil.

Canto 32

> If I had rhymes both rough and stridulous,
>   As were appropriate to the dismal hole
>   Down upon which thrust all the other rocks,
> I would press out the juice of my conception
>   More fully; but because I have them not,
>   Not without fear I bring myself to speak;
> For 'tis no enterprise to take in jest,
>   To sketch the bottom of all the universe.

The bottom of the universe! A phrase that in the spiritual world of Dante has profound echoes. It is not possible for any being to go lower than what we are about to see. We have come to Cocytus, a frozen waste wherein souls have become so wicked that they are stuck forever in a bleakness of their own making. Dante finds souls frozen in this lake with their teeth chattering violently and held in a tortured posture:

> Each one his countenance held downward bent:
>   From mouth the cold, from eyes the doleful heart

Among them witness of itself procures.
When round about me somewhat I had looked

. . . .

Then I beheld a thousand faces, made
    Purple with cold; whence o'er me comes a shudder,
    And evermore will come, at frozen ponds.
And while we were advancing tow'rds the middle,
    Where everything of weight unites together,
    And I was shivering in the eternal shade,
Whether 'twere will, or destiny, or chance,
    I know not; but in walking 'mong the heads
    I struck my foot hard in the face of one.
Weeping he growled: "Why dost thou trample me?
    Unless thou comest to increase the vengeance
    Of Montaperti, why dost thou molest me?"

Dante seems to recognize this spirit and, moved by ire at his
wickedness, threatens to add to his torment:

Then by the scalp behind I seized upon him,
    And said: "It must needs be thou name thyself,
    Or not a hair remain upon thee here."
Whence he to me: "Though thou strip off my hair,
    I will not tell thee who I am, nor show thee,
    If on my head a thousand times thou fall."
I had his hair in hand already twisted,
    And more than one shock of it had pulled out,
    He barking, with his eyes held firmly down,
When cried another: "What doth ail thee, Bocca?
    Is't not enough to clatter with thy jaws,
    But thou must bark? what devil touches thee?"

Through the treachery of another soul, treachery being the sin
punished in this deep part of Hell, Dante has learned that Bocca
degli Abbati, who traitorously turned on the Florentine Guelphs
during a battle at Montaperti, is in his hands. And he intends to
tell of this soul's shame in Hell when he returns to Earth. But he
does not tarry:

Already we had gone away from him,
    When I beheld two frozen in one hole,
    So that one head a hood was to the other;
And even as bread through hunger is devoured,

> The uppermost on the other set his teeth,
> There where the brain is to the nape united.

These two souls, frozen in the ice up to the neck and close to one
another are among the most famous in all of Dante's *Inferno*. One
is Ugolino della Gherardesca, himself a traitor, betrayed by the
Archbishop of Pisa, Ruggieri degli Ubaldini, whose head he
gnaws on.

Canto 33

> His mouth uplifted from his grim repast,
>> That sinner, wiping it upon the hair
>> Of the same head that he behind had wasted
> Then he began: "Thou wilt that I renew
>> The desperate grief, which wrings my heart already
>> To think of only, ere I speak of it;
> But if my words be seed that may bear fruit
>> Of infamy to the traitor whom I gnaw,
>> Speaking and weeping shalt thou see together. . . ."

Ugolino tells of having been shut up—tragically with his own
young sons—in a prison tower in Pisa, now known as the Tower
of Hunger because of what happened there. He dreamed of the
archbishop as a savage hunter of wild wolves while imprisoned
there. When he awakes, things take a piteous turn:

> Moaning amid their sleep I heard my sons
>> Who with me were, and asking after bread.
> Cruel indeed art thou, if yet thou grieve not,
>> Thinking of what my heart foreboded me,
>> And weep'st thou not, what art thou wont to weep at?
> They were awake now, and the hour drew nigh
>> At which our food used to be brought to us,
>> And through his dream was each one apprehensive;
> And I heard locking up the under door
>> Of the horrible tower; whereat without a word
>> I gazed into the faces of my sons.
> I wept not, I within so turned to stone;
>> They wept; and darling little Anselm mine
>> Said: "Thou dost gaze so, father, what doth ail thee?"
> Still not a tear I shed, nor answer made

> All of that day, nor yet the night thereafter,
>> Until another sun rose on the world.
> As now a little glimmer made its way
>> Into the dolorous prison, and I saw
>> Upon four faces my own very aspect,
> Both of my hands in agony I bit,
>> And, thinking that I did it from desire
>> Of eating, on a sudden they uprose,
> And said they: "Father, much less pain 'twill give us
>> If thou do eat of us; thyself didst clothe us
>> With this poor flesh, and do thou strip it off."
> I calmed me then, not to make them more sad.
>> That day we all were silent, and the next.
>> Ah! obdurate earth, wherefore didst thou not open.
> When we had come unto the fourth day, Gaddo
>> Threw himself down outstretched before my feet,
>> Saying, "My father, why dost thou not help me?"
> And there he died; and, as thou seest me,
>> I saw the three fall, one by one, between
>> The fifth day and the sixth; whence I betook me,
> Already blind, to groping over each,
>> And three days called them after they were dead;
>> Then hunger did what sorrow could not do.

Even in a cruel age, this deliberate starving to death of young children became notorious. But Dante has placed these two souls in one of the deepest parts of Hell because they had traitorously betrayed those to whom they had a duty to remain loyal. Dante sees the whole mix of wickedness as having reached the kinds of levels we see in the Old Testament, in which God decides to destroy whole communities for their corruption. To those of us living in comfortable modern societies, these groups seem simply wild. But in the twentieth century, we have seen tens and perhaps hundreds of millions of people killed in the name of political ideologies or ethnic hatreds. Dante's city-states practiced public evils on a smaller scale, but their spiritual roots may have been similar. Thus, when he declaims against Pisa, we would do well to think ourselves how some of our modern systems may look to a future observer:

> When he had said this, with his eyes distorted,
>> The wretched skull resumed he with his teeth,

> Which, as a dog's, upon the bone were strong.
> Ah! Pisa, thou opprobrium of the people
>> Of the fair land there where the Si doth sound,
>> Since slow to punish thee thy neighbours are,
> Let the Capraia and Gorgona move,
>> And make a hedge across the mouth of Arno
>> That every person in thee it may drown!
> For if Count Ugolino had the fame
>> Of having in thy castles thee betrayed,
>> Thou shouldst not on such cross have put his sons.

The mention of the cross here reminds us that it is precisely the betrayal and destruction of an innocent son, perhaps the most evil act in human history, that was required to redeem the full range of human evil.

But the poets still have to pass a few more degrees of such evil to see that:

> We passed still farther onward, where the ice
>> Another people ruggedly enswathes,
>> Not downward turned, but all of them reversed.
> Weeping itself there does not let them weep,
>> And grief that finds a barrier in the eyes
>> Turns itself inward to increase the anguish;
> Because the earliest tears a cluster form,
>> And, in the manner of a crystal visor,
>> Fill all the cup beneath the eyebrow full.

The punishment of this new set of souls, in other words, is that their very pain blocks the release of the pain as their tears freeze and stop up the shedding of further tears.

At this great depth, where no sun strikes, there should be no wind. But Dante, despite the loss of feeling in his face from the extreme cold, detects some motion in the air that puzzles him. Vergil tells him that he will soon see how this may be. But before they come to that Dante meets one last soul, one of those who were traitors to friends and guests. One item is worth remarking on. Dante disputes the account of this soul that he has died and come to this place, because he saw this person not long before still alive on earth. The soul explains:

> Know that as soon as any soul betrays
> As I have done, his body by a demon

> Is taken from him, who thereafter rules it,
> Until his time has wholly been revolved.
> Itself down rushes into such a cistern;
> And still perchance above appears the body
> Of yonder shade, that winters here behind me.

Such souls then literally turn into demons in this life.

Canto 34

But final evil still awaits and Dante begins an approach to it with
a properly ritualistic gesture. Vergil opens the final canto of the
Inferno with a variation on an Easter hymn:

> "Vexilla Regis prodeunt Inferni
> Towards us; therefore look in front of thee,"
> My Master said, "if thou discernest him."

The Latin here in the original hymn proclaims that the "banners
of the king come forth," but Vergil has altered them to say the
"king of Hell." When Dante looks ahead to see the source of
wind, he at first compares the vague outline to things with which
he is more familiar:

> As, when there breathes a heavy fog, or when
> Our hemisphere is darkening into night,
> Appears far off a mill the wind is turning,
> Methought that such a building then I saw;
> And, for the wind, I drew myself behind
> My Guide, because there was no other shelter.

Packed into this passage is an important allegory. Wind has tra-
ditionally been the symbol of the spirit and a windmill would be
a device turned by that spirit. Here, however, that is not the case,
because the wind is coming from the windmill, and he ducks
behind his guide, allegorically here Reason, as the only place to
hide from this ill wind.

In the meantime, he notices other souls:

> Now was I, and with fear in verse I put it,
> There where the shades were wholly covered up,
> And glimmered through like unto straws in glass.
> Some prone are lcing, others stand erect,

> This with the head, and that one with the soles;
> Another, bow-like, face to feet inverts.

The frozen state is the final condition of wicked souls who have removed themselves from the light, warmth, and breath of the universe. But there is still one degree further down even than this:

> When in advance so far we had proceeded,
> That it my Master pleased to show to me
> The creature who once had the beauteous semblance . . .

Readers of the Bible will detect the echo of the passage that describes Lucifer, the "light bearer," as having been the highest and most beautiful of the angels, now fallen to the lowest possible place in the universe. The book of Isaiah says:

> How art thou fallen from heaven, O Lucifer, who didst rise in the morning? How art thou fallen to the earth, that did wound the nations? And thou saidst in thy heart: I will ascend into heaven. I will exalt my throne above the stars of God. I will sit in the mountain of the covenant, in the sides of the north. I will ascend above the height of the clouds. I will be like the most High. But yet thou shalt be brought down to hell, into the depth of the pit. (14:12–15)

Dante, no doubt, expects us to be thinking of this passage as we journey to that very depth of the pit.

Many of us have experienced what is often called being "frozen" with fear or brought up short by some evil. Looking upon the purest and most absolute evil, Dante feels this same emotion carried to the highest possible pitch and describes it thus:

> He from before me moved and made me stop,
> Saying: "Behold Dis, and behold the place
> Where thou with fortitude must arm thyself."
> How frozen I became and powerless then,
> Ask it not, Reader, for I write it not,
> Because all language would be insufficient.
> I did not die, and I alive remained not;
> Think for thyself now, hast thou aught of wit,
> What I became, being of both deprived.

It is difficult to think of what it may be to be neither alive nor dead, but perhaps that suggests the state of soul of beings who have entirely sought to flee God and His universe: they cannot escape the only reality there is, but they continue to exist nominally.

Dante creatively uses traditional images of angels, mixed with their blasphemous inversion of meaning, to portray Satan:

> The Emperor of the kingdom dolorous
>> From his mid-breast forth issued from the ice,
>> And better with a giant I compare
> Than do the giants with those arms of his;
>> Consider now how great must be that whole,
>> Which unto such a part conforms itself.
> Were he as fair once, as he now is foul,
>> And lifted up his brow against his Maker,
>> Well may proceed from him all tribulation.
> O, what a marvel it appeared to me,
>> When I beheld three faces on his head!
>> The one in front, and that vermilion was;
> Two were the others, that were joined with this
>> Above the middle part of either shoulder,
>> And they were joined together at the crest;
> And the right-hand one seemed 'twixt white and yellow
>> The left was such to look upon as those
>> Who come from where the Nile falls valley-ward.

The three faces here are a wretched opposite to the Trinity; the angel that wanted to be like God is here turned into a caricature of the Faith, Hope, and Love that he rejected. A further torment for him is that, as in a Chinese handcuff, his very attempts to escape the Divine bind him forever in the most restrictive of settings:

> Underneath each came forth two mighty wings,
>> Such as befitting were so great a bird;
>> Sails of the sea I never saw so large.
> No feathers had they, but as of a bat
>> Their fashion was; and he was waving them,
>> So that three winds proceeded forth therefrom.
> Thereby Cocytus wholly was congealed.

> With six eyes did he weep, and down three chins
> Trickled the tear-drops and the bloody drivel.

Satan is thus condemned for all eternity to struggle to flee from what cannot be escaped and to fix himself still more by his struggling.

Dante believes some human souls have attempted analogous crimes, and he gives them, as usual, a fitting punishment:

> At every mouth he with his teeth was crunching
> A sinner, in the manner of a brake,
> So that he three of them tormented thus.
> To him in front the biting was as naught
> Unto the clawing, for sometimes the spine
> Utterly stripped of all the skin remained.
> "That soul up there which has the greatest pain,"
> The Master said, "is Judas Iscariot;
> With head inside, he plies his legs without.
> Of the two others, who head downward are,
> The one who hangs from the black jowl is Brutus;
> See how he writhes himself, and speaks no word.
> And the other, who so stalwart seems, is Cassius."

Judas, of course, betrayed Christ and has the greatest punishment of any human soul. Brutus and Cassius betrayed Julius Caesar, for Dante a figure of the proper earthly authority to which all owe a near-religious obedience. There is no need to linger over this sheer evil, however, and Vergil abruptly says:

> But night is reascending, and 'tis time
> That we depart, for we have seen the whole.

What an astonishing thing to be able to say that one has seen all the evil in the universe! But that was the intention of the poets as they set out, not to see evil for its own intrinsic interest, but as a necessary prelude to undertaking the opposite journey of purgation from evil and emergence into the light of salvation. And here at the very and literal bottom of the universe as Dante conceived of it, that ascent to light and truth begins by climbing over the very body of the devil himself.

Dante takes firm hold of his Guide and they proceed through a marvelous turnaround:

As seemed him good, I clasped him round the neck,
 And he the vantage seized of time and place,
 And when the wings were opened wide apart,
He laid fast hold upon the shaggy sides;
 From fell to fell descended downward then
 Between the thick hair and the frozen crust.
When we were come to where the thigh revolves
 Exactly on the thickness of the haunch,
 The Guide, with labour and with hard-drawn breath.
Turned round his head where he had had his legs,
 And grappled to the hair, as one who mounts,
 So that to Hell I thought we were returning.
"Keep fast thy hold, for by such stairs as these,"
 The Master said, panting as one fatigued,
 "Must we perforce depart from so much evil."
Then through the opening of a rock he issued,
 And down upon the margin seated me;
 Then tow'rds me he outstretched his wary step.
I lifted up mine eyes and thought to see
 Lucifer in the same way I had left him;
 And I beheld him upward hold his legs.
And if I then became disquieted,
 Let stolid people think who do not see
 What the point is beyond which I had passed.

The poets have passed through the center of the earth and what
formerly was the way down now is reversed and they will strug-
gle to climb back up. Dante asks Vergil to explain:

And he to me: "Thou still imaginest
 Thou art beyond the centre, where I grasped
 The hair of the fell worm, who mines the world.
That side thou wast, so long as I descended;
 When round I turned me, thou didst pass the point
 To which things heavy draw from every side,
And now beneath the hemisphere art come
 Opposite that which overhangs the vast
 Dry-land, and 'neath whose cope was put to death
The Man who without sin was born and lived.
 Thou hast thy feet upon the little sphere
 Which makes the other face of the Judecca
Here it is morn when it is evening there."

In Dante's symbolical geography, Jerusalem, the place of redemption, is on the side of Earth's sphere at the opposite to the point at which Satan fell. They have now passed to the other side of the Earth and, by continuing in the same direction they have been going, will now be able to retrace the path and ascend to the place from which Satan fell. A small stream descends through the channel that still remains there. We shall find out in *Purgatory* what this stream is and whence it comes. But having seen the evils of the world and ready now to ascend to a very different life, the poets climb briskly and come back to the light of promise:

> We mounted up, he first and I the second,
>> Till I beheld through a round aperture
>> Some of the beauteous things that Heaven doth bear;
> Thence we came forth to rebehold the stars.

Chapter 2

The Ascent of the Mountain

To run o'er better waters hoists its sail
  The little vessel of my genius now,
  That leaves behind itself a sea so cruel;
And of that second kingdom will I sing
  Wherein the human spirit doth purge itself,
  And to ascend to heaven becometh worthy.
Let dead Poesy here rise again,
  O holy Muses, since that I am yours . . .

After the spiritual cramp and suffering of the very bottom of
Hell, the opening of this second section of Dante's poem, the
Purgatory, comes with great relief. The image of Dante's genius as
a little boat hoisting its sail in bracing wind and water represents
a far more cheerful and open-ended atmosphere. In many ways,
the vision of evil has been only a preparation for the real journey
that must be made. It only taught by way of negative example
and energized the pilgrim for the ascent, which is now possible
since Dante is no longer simply blocked by unknown evil.

There are some echoes here of the first canto of the *Inferno*, but
transposed into a different key. Dante spoke in that place as well
of a cruel sea and a hill before him. The symbolism is transpar-
ent. Then he believed that the sun at the top of that hill was easy
to reach. Now Dante is far more humble about his own genius
and powers, calling them a "little vessel" in the lines above and
humbly invoking help from the divine Muses of poetry. Humility
will be a principal theme of the whole *Purgatory*, but it is espe-
cially important here because through humility we enter upon
the right path again.

One of the first fruits of humility is an appreciation of the beauty and joy in the world as opposed to the distortions and sorrows of Hell. Dante finds himself beneath a cloudless sky:

> Sweet colour of the oriental sapphire,
>   That was upgathered in the cloudless aspect
>   Of the pure air, as far as the first circle,
> Unto mine eyes did recommence delight
>   Soon as I issued forth from the dead air,
>   Which had with sadness filled mine eyes and breast.
> The beauteous planet, that to love incites,
>   Was making all the orient to laugh,
>   Veiling the Fishes that were in her escort.

In Dante's time, astrology was thought to be scientific, and his reference here is to Venus, the morning star, believed to influence love. Dante gently introduces the "influence" of love as immediately perceptible in this new realm. But there are other influences as well. Venus is in Pisces, the sign of the zodiac. In the Middle Ages it was believed that Venus occupied that position at the moment of Creation. Together with the reference to the resurgence of poetry in the previous passage quoted, all these details remind us that, in the larger time reference of the poem, Dante and Vergil have reemerged from Hell in Easter time 1300, the season commemorating Christ's resurrection and the new creation he brought forth.

This new birth entails still other new influences:

> To the right hand I turned, and fixed my mind
>   Upon the other pole, and saw four stars
>   Ne'er seen before save by the primal people.
> Rejoicing in their flamelets seemed the heaven.
>   O thou septentrional and widowed site,
>   Because thou art deprived of seeing these!

We can guess from what we know of Dante's thought that these four stars are the cardinal virtues: prudence, temperance, justice, and fortitude. In ancient philosophy and even in modern thinking about human virtue, these four qualities are what enable us to live a good earthly life. As such they are earthly manifestations of ordered love. When Dante says they have never been seen before except by the "primal people," he does not mean it literally. He knew that people lived at the equator and could see all the southern stars. He may even have heard from some traveler about the Southern Cross, which might have suggested to him the four stars here. But whatever Dante's sources, the symbolism is clear: perfect practice of the virtues only existed before the Fall. The "septentrional" site without these virtues refers to the Northern Hemisphere, where the Christian nations lie; this mountain of purgation is in the Southern Hemisphere.

Dante turns aside from looking at these heavenly bodies and sees:

> . . . an old man alone,
> Worthy of so much reverence in his look,
> That more owes not to father any son.
> A long beard and with white hair intermingled
> He wore, in semblance like unto the tresses,
> Of which a double list fell on his breast.
> The rays of the four consecrated stars
> Did so adorn his countenance with light,
> That him I saw as were the sun before him.

As soon becomes apparent, this man with the light of the virtues in his face is Cato, the virtuous Roman who resisted the loss of republican freedom to the dictatorship of the Caesars. By introducing this figure as the gatekeeper of Purgatory, Dante probably means us to understand that the cardinal virtues have immediate relevance to proper earthly behavior. As much as they depend on influences from above and lead to heights of the spirit that transcend them, the virtues acquired in this realm have a double effect that we have already discussed. They enable us to live the natural perfection of Earth and approach spiritual perfection in this life and the next. These, as we saw in the introduction, are explicitly mentioned in Dante's *On Monarchy* as the two perfections God has willed for the human race.

As the gatekeeper to these two perfections, Cato does not seem to understand how the two poets could possibly be coming to Purgatory from Hell:

> ". . . The laws of the abyss, are they thus broken?
> Or is there changed in heaven some council new,
> That being damned ye come unto my crags?"
> Then did my Leader lay his grasp upon me,

And with his words, and with his hands and signs, so
    Reverent he made in me my knees and brow:
Then answered him: "I came not of myself;
    A Lady from Heaven descended, at whose prayers
    I aided this one with my company.

.   .   .   .

How I have brought him would be long to tell thee.
    Virtue descendeth from on high that aids me
    To lead him to behold thee and to hear thee.
Now may it please thee to vouchsafe his coming;
    He seeketh Liberty, which is so dear,
    As knoweth he who life for her refuses."

"Virtue descendeth from on high that aids me," says Vergil, and this reminds us that Vergil, for all Dante's veneration of him as his poetic and philosophic master, also is a pagan. Like all of us who achieve some degree of discipline and ordered loves in this life, Vergil and Cato depend on powers beyond them. All good, in this universe, must come from above.

Vergil strikes another note that many in Dante's time and today might overlook: Dante seeks the discipline of ascending the mountain because "He seeketh Liberty." In the paradoxical ways of the spiritual life, liberty follows upon right restraint and habituation to right action. Cato can attest to how dear this liberty is because, as Dante knew, he committed suicide in 46 B.C., thus refusing life itself rather than fall into the future dictator Caesar's hands. It is somewhat odd that Dante gives this ancient suicide a high office in Purgatory; we have already seen that the suicides occupy the seventh circle in Hell. Apparently Dante believed that Cato's suicide did not belong in the same category with those who had merely thrown away their lives. Dante also thought that the Roman Empire was one of the instruments of Providence intended to help bring order into the world and facilitate the spreading of the Good News in the "fullness of time." That is why Brutus and Cassius, as plotters against Caesar, were being chewed horribly by Satan in Hell. For reasons not entirely clear, Cato seems to possess some virtues that transcend Dante's political and historical categories. Dante must have read the glowing stories of Cato's virtues in the Latin historians and poets. In some sources, Cato is portrayed as having killed himself after staying up almost the whole night reading the *Phaedo,* Plato's account of the noble death of Socrates. Whatever we are to think of Dante's reasoning, Cato's significance here involves something that every soul must sooner or later face: we must be willing to sacrifice everything, even life itself, to the pursuit of true liberty.

In this first canto, we also begin to see how human loves, even those honorable in their way, will gradually be replaced by divine ones. Vergil entreats Cato in memory of Marcia, his wife, whom he dearly loved and who occupies the classical Limbo with Vergil, to help the poets on their way. Cato replies with the mixture of affection and the sternness appropriate to this realm:

> "Marcia so pleasing was unto mine eyes
>> While I was on the other side," then said he,
>> "That every grace she wished of me I granted;
> Now that she dwells beyond the evil river,
>> She can no longer move me, by that law
>> Which, when I issued forth from there, was made.
> But if a Lady of Heaven do move and rule thee,
>> As thou dost say, no flattery is needful;
>> Let it suffice thee that for her thou ask me."

Then Cato instructs Vergil in how to begin the process of purgation. Purgatory is a mountain set on an island. Before they may rise, the poets have to descend to the shore:

> Go, then, and see thou gird this one about
>> With a smooth rush, and that thou wash his face,
>> So that thou cleanse away all stain therefrom,
> For 'twere not fitting that the eye o'ercast
>> By any mist should go before the first
>> Angel, who is of those of Paradise.
> This little island round about its base
>> Below there, yonder, where the billow beats it,
>> Doth rushes bear upon its washy ooze;
> No other plant that putteth forth the leaf,
>> Or that doth indurate, can there have life,
>> Because it yieldeth not unto the shocks.

Why is this here? Because the rush humbly bends with the waters

ISLAND OF PURGATORY

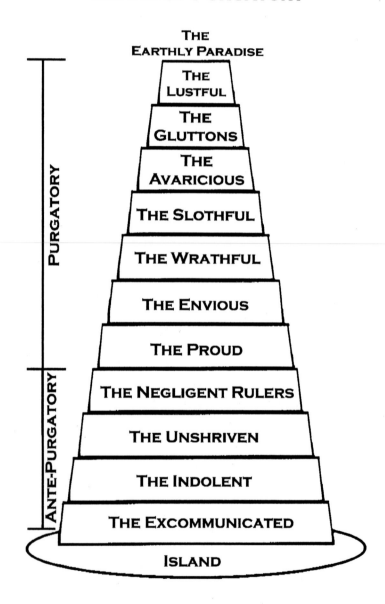

that constantly ebb and flow. Like the rushes, if we are not pliant to the movements of God in the world, we are soon broken down. And docility to the divine will is the ultimate lesson behind all the particular lessons of loosening wrong attachments and straightening the distorted human will in the terraces above. After these preparations, says Cato, do not return by the same path, but follow the sun and it will lead you to the entrance of the way.

So they set out in light and humility on their new journey:

> The dawn was vanquishing the matin hour
>> Which fled before it, so that from afar
>> I recognised the trembling of the sea
> Along the solitary plain we went
>> As one who unto the lost road returns,
>> And till he finds it seems to go in vain.
> As soon as we were come to where the dew
>> Fights with the sun, and, being in a part
>> Where shadow falls, little evaporates,
> Both of his hands upon the grass outspread
>> In gentle manner did my Master place;
>> Whence I, who of his action was aware,
> Extended unto him my tearful cheeks;
>> There did he make in me uncovered wholly
>> That hue which Hell had covered up in me.
> Then came we down upon the desert shore
>> Which never yet saw navigate its waters
>> Any that afterward had known return.
> There he begirt me as the other pleased
>> O marvellous! for even as he culled
>> The humble plant, such it sprang up again
> Suddenly there where he uprooted it.

"As one who unto the lost road returns, / And till he finds it seems to go in vain. . . ." Here Dante confirms that a new beginning has taken place. In the original Italian, this is further emphasized by the fact that Cato tells Vergil not simply to gird but to regird Dante. His first attempt to turn out of the Dark Wood from the lost way to the true one required two things. He first had to see all the forms of error and, next, find the humility to go beyond them. Now he enters definitively on the right way. The dew on the grass, a traditional symbol of divine grace, washes away the smoke of Hell. And the humble rush which prepares him for the journey, we discover, not only is flexible enough to withstand the sea's buffetings, but because humility itself comes from the spontaneous action of grace constantly offered to those prepared to bind themselves to it, these rushes also instantly replace themselves.

Canto 2

By the time the poets complete these preparations, the sun has already risen. The sun, a common symbol for God, must be visible, as we later learn, for the souls to ascend the mountain. At night, there is nothing to do but wait patiently. Like the dew and the rushes, this rule of Purgatory underscores that, in the Christian universe, we rise to God in cooperation with his grace, not by mere heroic will in the manner of the pagans. With the rising of the sun, the poets start to think about their way, when they are greeted with a marvelous sight:

> We still were on the border of the sea,
>> Like people who are thinking of their road,
>> Who go in heart and with the body stay;
> And lo! as when, upon the approach of morning,
>> Through the gross vapours Mars grows fiery red
>> Down in the West upon the ocean floor,
> Appeared to me—may I again behold it!—
>> A light along the sea so swiftly coming,
>> Its motion by no flight of wing is equalled.

At first, there is no indication of what this might be. But soon, Dante's own eyes tell him:

> . . . a small vessel, very swift and light,
>> So that the water swallowed naught thereof,
> Upon the stern stood the Celestial Pilot;
>> Beatitude seemed written in his face,
>> And more than a hundred spirits sat within.
> "In exitu Israel de Aegypto!"

> They chanted all together in one voice,
> With whatso in that psalm is after written.

This is the very psalm that in our introduction we saw Dante use to explain to his patron, Can Grande della Scala, about the four senses of Scripture commonly accepted in the Middle Ages. It tells of the exit of the Israelites from the bondage of Egypt to God's freedom, a reinforcement of the theme of liberty that appeared in the first canto of this *cantica*—the story of Cato. It is a fitting song for these souls to sing, since in coming to Purgatory, though still needing to cleanse themselves from past sins, they have passed over from this life to the realm that assures them they will eventually reach the total freedom and truth of Heaven. And it is a second reminder that in the poem's larger chronology, everything is taking place at the time when the world celebrated Passover, Holy Thursday in the Christian commemoration, and the new Passover of Easter.

For the moment, however, these souls, newly arrived on their shining boat, have no clue how to conduct themselves. They hasten to shore and begin looking around. Spotting Vergil and Dante, they ask:

> "If ye know,
> Show us the way to go unto the mountain."
> And answer made Virgilius: "Ye believe
> Perchance that we have knowledge of this place,
> But we are strangers even as yourselves.
> Just now we came, a little while before you;
> Another way, which was so rough and steep,
> That mounting will henceforth seem sport to us."

We have to correct our translation here. In the original, Vergil says, "we are pilgrims here as you are." This is the first use of the word "pilgrim" in the *Comedy*. The poets were never described as pilgrims in the *Inferno*, and with good reason. As Dante has made clear through other lines in these opening cantos, the poetic character Dante is now beginning the real pilgrimage for the first time. Hell was a preparation and a freeing of energy for the ascent; now he is about to move forward on the right way, like a pilgrim.

The souls notice that Dante is alive and, in gathering near to observe this curiosity, temporarily forget about their inquiry into how to climb the mountain. To Dante's great joy, one of these souls is a dear old friend, a musician named Casella, who had set several of Dante's poems to music. Their meeting is marked by both tenderness and frustration:

> One from among them saw I coming forward,
>   As to embrace me, with such great affection,
>   That it incited me to do the like.
> O empty shadows, save in aspect only!
>   Three times behind it did I clasp my hands,
>   As oft returned with them to my own breast!.

As is always the case in Dante, this inability to grasp a shade on the other side of death symbolically suggests that not only can we not hold on to a shade there, we should not even try, though love continues. The sequel confirms this:

> It made reply to me: "Even as I loved thee
> In mortal body, so I love thee free;
> Therefore I stop; but wherefore goest thou?"
>   "My own Casella! to return once more
>   There where I am, I make this journey," said I.
> . . . .
> . . ."If some new law take not from thee
>   Memory or practice of the song of love,
>   Which used to quiet in me all my longings,
> Thee may it please to comfort therewithal
>   Somewhat this soul of mine, that with its body
>   Hitherward coming is so much distressed."
> "Love, that within my mind discourses with me,"
>   Forthwith began he so melodiously,
>   The melody within me still is sounding.

"Love that within my mind discourses with me" is one of the poems that Dante wrote and commented on in his *Banquet*. As he mentions here, Casella's singing used to quiet all his longings and would be especially welcome now because Dante's soul and body are very weary and distressed from the rigors of the passage through Hell. Casella sings so sweetly that the poet, writing long after the event, still feels the sweetness of the melody.

Pausing from work or hardships for rest is a good thing at

appropriate moments in this life. In Purgatory, however, no delays should be indulged. The reason, as Dante underscores, is that there, and at times often here as well, even the highest artistry may distract us from other things more vital to our interests. Dante describes the problem precisely:

> My Master, and myself, and all that people
>> Which with him were, appeared as satisfied
>> As if naught else might touch the mind of any;

Dante was a lover of poetry, to which he had dedicated his life. At this very moment in which he hints at the problem of allowing poetry to so distract us "as if naught else might touch the mind," he is writing his great poem. But the *Comedy*, for all its poetic beauties and Dante's belief in the rightness of presenting truth in poetry, has to remind us that even the greatest poetry or other aesthetic pleasures should never distract us when our spiritual obligations present themselves. Cato arrives in a huff to stir up the immobilized group:

> "What is this, ye laggard spirits
> What negligence, what standing still is this?
>> Run to the mountain to strip off the slough,
>> That lets not God be manifest to you."
> Even as when, collecting grain or tares,
>> The doves, together at their pasture met,
>> Quiet, nor showing their accustomed pride,
> If aught appear of which they are afraid,
>> Upon a sudden leave their food alone,
>> Because they are assailed by greater care;
> So that fresh company did I behold
>> The song relinquish, and go tow'rds the hill,
>> As one who goes, and knows not whitherward;
> Nor was our own departure less in haste.

What "lets not God be manifest in you" is here left behind.

But though they scurry off, neither Dante and Vergil nor any of the other souls will move rapidly up the mountain. As we shall see in the following half-dozen cantos, there are many human impediments that either block or slow the entry into the way of repentance and purgation. Some spirits were excommunicated and must now spend thirty years for every one of excommunication in the ante-Purgatory before they will be allowed to enter Purgatory proper. Others were late in turning to God and therefore God justly is slow to admit them. Still others were indolent, among them some of the most powerful political figures on earth who had been entrusted with great power because great deeds needed doing. All of these figures remind us how much here, in our earthly life, we tarry, believing we have time to change or can neglect the important things.

Dante emphasizes the relevance of these spiritual problems to earthly life by a persistent literary device. In these cantos, the fact that his still living body casts a shadow on the mountain in the strong sunlight reminds us again and again that Dante's journey is not only about the other world. In addition, in this new hemisphere, he and Vergil are constantly discussing astronomy, the time differences between distant places like Rome, Jerusalem, and Purgatory. All of this too seems to suggest the temporal interrelatedness of all places on earth and Purgatory to the world, but from a perspective rarely experienced by anyone before Dante.

Canto 3

Furthermore, an even more important shift in perspective is occurring. On these lower slopes of Purgatory, Dante momentarily starts when he sees his own shadow, but not that of Vergil, because he thinks he has lost his guide. Vergil rebukes him for fearing abandonment after all they have been through and compares the mysterious transparency of his spirit body to the way God guides the planets through the heavens. Neither the one nor the other is graspable by human reason. Then this figure of Reason begins a theme that will echo throughout the *Purgatory*, the humility of the intellect before the mysteries of God:

> Insane is he who hopeth that our reason
> Can traverse the illimitable way,
> Which the one Substance in three Persons follow!
> Mortals, remain contented at the *Quia;*
> For if ye had been able to see all,
> "No need there were for Mary to give birth;

And ye have seen desiring without fruit,
   Those whose desire would have been quieted,
   Which evermore is given them for a grief.
I speak of Aristotle and of Plato,
   And many others";—and here bowed his head,
   And more he said not, and remained disturbed.

The "*quia*" in this passage means "because" in Latin, signifying
that our intellects often have to be satisifed with the explanation
that God did something a certain way "because" that was his
will. Human intellect cannot explain the revealed nature of the
divine nor its action. Vergil's reference to the great pagan phi-
losophers is also poignant because much of the *Purgatory* will fol-
low ancient systems of virtues and vices that go back to the great
pagans. Yet in the final analysis, these great virtues, as vigorously
as Dante will now climb toward them, retain a melancholy incom-
pleteness and lack of joy without the supernatural illumination
from which they stem.

Dante hints at other limitations of reason here. While Vergil
studies the path they should take without resolving the question,
Dante sees a group of souls moving along who, he suggests to
Vergil, may help, "If thou of thine own self can have it not." The
humility required for entering on this way is further reinforced
by the description of the souls they now encounter. We are con-
ditioned in the modern world to speak of people taking charge of
their lives and confidently asserting themselves. For the path
through Purgatory, however, Dante hints at the need to become
docile, like sheep, to the right outside guidance without in the
least becoming merely timid:

As sheep come issuing forth from out the fold
   By ones and twos and threes, and the others stand
   Timidly, holding down their eyes and nostrils,
And what the foremost does the others do,
   Huddling themselves against her, if she stop,
   Simple and quiet and the wherefore know not;
So moving to approach us thereupon
   I saw the leader of that fortunate flock,
   Modest in face and dignified in gait.

Canto 4

But in the meantime, there is little movement in this realm that is supposed to consist in an arduous climb to freedom. The "strait gate" by which we enter Purgatory proper—and by implication Paradise—suggests that the apparent difficulty in finding entry may have as much to do with a lack of will to undertake the task as it does with learning moral and spiritual strictness. When Dante and Vergil finally have the entry pointed out to them, it appears both homely and profound:

> A greater opening ofttimes hedges up
>   With but a little forkful of his thorns
>   The villager, what time the grape imbrowns,
> Than was the passage-way through which ascended
>   Only my Leader and myself behind him . . .
>   . . . here one needs must fly;
> With the swift pinions and the plumes I say
>   Of great desire, conducted after him
>   Who gave me hope, and made a light for me.
> We mounted upward through the rifted rock,
>   And on each side the border pressed upon us,
>   And feet and hands the ground beneath required.

Perhaps the closest modern approximation to the spiritual exertion Dante must make here is rock climbing, an activity very few people are in good enough condition to do. Though Dante follows behind Vergil's inspiration, the slope is steeper than forty-five degrees.

Dante would like to turn back from weariness, but Vergil encourages him to persist as far as one of the terraces just above them. There, as they rest, Dante asks about the mountain:

> . . . if it pleaseth thee, I fain would learn
>   How far we have to go; for the hill rises
>   Higher than eyes of mine have power to rise.
> . . . .
> And he to me: "This mount is such, that ever
>   At the beginning down below 'tis tiresome,
>   And aye the more one climbs, the less it hurts.
> Therefore, when it shall seem so pleasant to thee,
>   That going up shall be to thee as easy

> As going down the current in a boat,
> Then at this pathway's ending thou wilt be;
>   There to repose thy panting breath expect;
>   No more I answer; and this I know for true."

This describes a process familiar to all of us. When we begin some new regimen, whether a program to get into better physical condition or a new set of spiritual practices, the beginning is both difficult and discouraging. But if we persist in our disciplines, before long we are able to do things easily that earlier we could not do at all. Vergil, as Reason, knows that this internal development is true, but he cannot know the height of purgation from all sin, since that exceeds mere reason.

But before the poets climb further, they meet a figure who dramatizes much of the foregoing reflection:

> A voice close by us sounded: "Peradventure
> Thou wilt have need of sitting down ere that."
> At sound thereof each one of us turned round,
>   And saw upon the left hand a great rock,
>   Which neither I nor he before had noticed.
> Thither we drew; and there were persons there
>   Who in the shadow stood behind the rock,
>   As one through indolence is wont to stand.
> And one of them, who seemed to me fatigued,
>   Was sitting down, and both his knees embraced,
>   Holding his face low down between them bowed.

After another brief exchange, Dante recognizes this monumentally lazy soul:

> His sluggish attitude and his curt words
>   A little unto laughter moved my lips;
>   Then I began: "Belacqua, I grieve not
> For thee henceforth; but tell me, wherefore seated
>   In this place art thou? Waitest thou an escort?
>   Or has thy usual habit seized upon thee?"
> And he: "O brother, what's the use of climbing?
>   Since to my torment would not let me go
>   The Angel of God, who sitteth at the gate.
> First heaven must needs so long revolve me round
>   Outside thereof, as in my life it did,
>   Since the good sighs I to the end postponed,

Unless, e'er that, some prayer may bring me aid
    Which rises from a heart that lives in grace;
    What profit others that in heaven are heard not?"

This Belacqua is said to have been a maker of musical instruments in Florence and a man whose "usual habit" was to procrastinate. Since he postponed his repentance to the last moment, he justly must spend an equal time waiting before being admitted to the upper circles of Purgatory.

Canto 6

As this canto opens, Dante compares himself to someone who has won at gambling, and all the spectators follow him. Except in his case, the souls follow him enthusiastically asking not for money but for prayers when he returns to the world to speed them on their way. Dante names a number of famous and not so famous souls who accost him. But when he finishes with them he turns to Vergil and asks if it is not true that in the *Aeneid* the Roman poet had denied that prayers could bend the divine will. To us, this may seem a diversion. But Dante took pagan mythology seriously, even though he read it allegorically. Vergil answers that pagan prayers were not efficacious because they were separated from God. And, as usual, he advises Dante that another guide will be necessary for these matters that exceed human reason:

"Verily, in so deep a questioning
    Do not decide, unless she tell it thee,
    Who light 'twixt truth and intellect shall be.
I know not if thou understand; I speak
    Of Beatrice; her shalt thou see above,
    Smiling and happy, on this mountain's top."
And I: "Good Leader, let us make more haste,
    For I no longer tire me as before;
    And see, e'en now the hill a shadow casts."

Dante becomes eager even at the thought of seeing his dear Beatrice again, and this love will often keep him moving up the mountain. But there are constraints in this mountain, and they shall not be able to arrive at the summit in one day, says Vergil.

They can only ascend while the Sun, here symbolically the grace and strength provided by God, allows them to climb.

Canto 9

We have jumped over several cantos in which the poets have made little progress. All the delays and digressions and stories of long periods that souls must remain in ante-Purgatory before even being allowed to purge their remaining faults may seem excessive to us. We like to believe either that we can easily overcome our bad habits or that God simply forgets about them. Dante seems to think both attitudes mistaken; we know people who struggle with weaknesses their whole lives. He thinks that the struggle will be prolonged in the next life as well before we are ready to begin the ascent to perfection and joy. But he also believes that, while God does not forget, he is active in our salvation. In the fiction of the poem, we might expect that Dante, a living man with sins still on his head, would take quite a while to enter Purgatory as well. We are almost one-third of the way through this *cantica* and, while instructive, the overwhelming sense we have is of a clogged flow, of bright hope delayed, of an expectant lethargy that need not have been but, unfortunately for most souls, bars the way. Yet we are about to take an important step.

Night comes and Dante falls asleep:

> I, who something had of Adam in me,
>   Vanquished by sleep, upon the grass reclined,
>   There where all five of us already sat.
> Just at the hour when her sad lay begins
>   The little swallow, near unto the morning,
>   Perchance in memory of her former woes,
> And when the mind of man, a wanderer
>   More from the flesh, and less by thought imprisoned,
>   Almost prophetic in its visions is,
> In dreams it seemed to me I saw suspended
>   An eagle in the sky, with plumes of gold,
>   With wings wide open, and intent to stoop.
>
> . . . .

> Then wheeling somewhat more, it seemed to me,
>   Terrible as the lightning he descended,
>   And snatched me upward even to the fire.
> Therein it seemed that he and I were burning,
>   And the imagined fire did scorch me so,
>   That of necessity my sleep was broken.

Much is happening in this brief passage. Medieval people, like modern people since Freud, believed that dreams have a meaning. Indeed, they had an elaborate system of classification that enabled them to sort out dreams into various types. The kind of dream Dante speaks of here, the one just before morning, was thought to be the most clearly prophetic. The physical processes of digestion and rest are mostly completed; the body and mind are linked less closely than during activity; and the oncoming approach of day may impart a certain attentiveness. Indeed, prophetic dreams, though not a power of the soul in the sense that they are something we can control at will, were thought to be one of the signs of something immortal within us.

In this instance, the golden eagle is clearly a symbol of the divine that is leading Dante upward. But when he awakes he discovers something even more marvelous:

> "Be not intimidated," said my Lord,
>   "Be reassured, for all is well with us;
>   Do not restrain, but put forth all thy strength.
> Thou hast at length arrived at Purgatory;
>   See there the cliff that closes it around;
>   See there the entrance, where it seems disjoined.
> Whilom at dawn, which doth precede the day,
>   When inwardly thy spirit was asleep
>   Upon the flowers that deck the land below,
> There came a Lady and said: "I am Lucia;
>   Let me take this one up, who is asleep;
>   So will I make his journey easier for him."

St. Lucy, it will be recalled, was one of the three ladies—the Virgin Mary, Lucy, and Beatrice—who got Dante going on his way by sending Vergil to rescue him at the very beginning of the poem. And her appearance here signals a boost in Dante's pilgrimage toward his ultimate goal:

I saw a portal, and three stairs beneath,
   Diverse in colour, to go up to it,
   And a gate-keeper, who yet spake no word.
And as I opened more and more mine eyes,
   I saw him seated on the highest stair,
   Such in the face that I endured it not.
And in his hand he had a naked sword,
   Which so reflected back the sunbeams tow'rds us,
   That oft in vain I lifted up mine eyes.
"Tell it from where you are, what is't you wish?"
   Began he to exclaim; "where is the escort?
   Take heed your coming hither harm you not!"
"A Lady of Heaven, with these things conversant,"
   My Master answered him, "but even now
   Said to us, 'Thither go; there is the portal.'"
"And may she speed your footsteps in all good,"
   Again began the courteous janitor;
   "Come forward then unto these stairs of ours."
Thither did we approach; and the first stair
   Was marble white, so polished and so smooth,
   I mirrored myself therein as I appear.
The second, tinct of deeper hue than perse,
   Was of a calcined and uneven stone,
   Cracked all asunder lengthwise and across.
The third, that uppermost rests massively,
   Porphyry seemed to me, as flaming red
   As blood that from a vein is spirting forth.
Both of his feet was holding upon this
   The Angel of God, upon the threshold seated,
   Which seemed to me a stone of diamond.
Along the three stairs upward with good will
   Did my Conductor draw me, saying: "Ask
   Humbly that he the fastening may undo."
Devoutly at the holy feet I cast me,
   For mercy's sake besought that he would open,
   But first upon my breast three times I smote.
Seven P's upon my forehead he described
   With the sword's point, and, "Take heed that thou wash
   These wounds, when thou shalt be within," he said.

A cultured reader in Dante's time or anyone familiar with the
Bible and the Christian today will not have much difficulty in

deciphering these signs. The angel here guards the gate to Heaven, which, unlike the gate to Hell, is not an open, easy pass. The sword in his hand reminds us of the angels with the flaming swords that blocked Adam and Eve's return to Eden. And we shall find out later that the earthly Paradise will be regained at the top of this mountain. The three stairs Dante climbs appear to symbolize contrition, confession, and redemption through Christ's blood (red). And the seven P's stand for the seven deadly sins (*peccata* in Latin).

Several commentators have argued that the way of Dante the poet and pilgrim passing through Purgatory and the way of the other souls must diverge here. The seven P's inscribed on his forehead are not inscribed on other souls that we shall encounter. That is true. But clearly everyone from this point up until entry into the earthly Paradise is bearing, and therefore in need of cleansing, the ill effects of sin.

This dazzling angel with the blinding sword, however, also reminds us of humility in his clothing:

> Ashes, or earth that dry is excavated,
>> Of the same colour were with his attire,
>> And from beneath it he drew forth two keys.
> One was of gold, and the other was of silver;
>> First with the white, and after with the yellow,
>> Plied he the door, so that I was content.
> "Whenever faileth either of these keys
>> So that it turn not rightly in the lock,"
>> He said to us, "this entrance doth not open.
> More precious one is, but the other needs
>> More art and intellect ere it unlock,
>> For it is that which doth the knot unloose.
> From Peter I have them; and he bade me err
>> Rather in opening than in keeping shut,
>> If people but fall down before my feet."
> Then pushed the portals of the sacred door,
>> Exclaiming: "Enter; but I give you warning
>> That forth returns whoever looks behind."

It is important to understand what the angel is saying here. These souls on the mountain of Purgatory, through divine forgiveness, their own repentance, and now angelic protection cannot be lost again. But they can backslide. Dante will henceforth show a threefold scheme in explaining the purgations of Purgatory, and it may not be amiss to explain this warning in the same way. He will give an Old Testament, a New Testament, and a classical example in each of the circles above. The return to outside the gates for looking back here may be a triple reference to Lot's wife; Jesus' warning in Luke "No one, having put his hand to the plow and looking back, is fit for the kingdom of God"; and to the Orpheus and Eurydice legend as well. Dante thought all human wisdom—pagan, Jewish, and Christian—to be interrelated. And it seems that his weaving together here of various hints from the three cultures that formed his world is intended to reinforce the common notion that once we begin the spiritual advance we should not turn back.

The portals groan in opening, from so little use. Dante hears the hymn *Te Deum laudamus* ("We Praise You God"), one of the best known hymns in the Christian tradition, often sung when someone entered the religious life. Its appearance here, like the other Latin hymns earlier and those that are to follow, gives us a poetry and song that, unlike Dante's poem as performed by Casella, actually moves spirits along to their ultimate goal. Aesthetics too are being aligned with the synthesis of all human and divine goods.

Canto 10

> When we had crossed the threshold of the door
>   Which the perverted love of souls disuses,
>   Because it makes the crooked way seem straight,
> Re-echoing I heard it closed again;
>   And if I had turned back mine eyes upon it,
>   What for my failing had been fit excuse?
> We mounted upward through a rifted rock,
>   Which undulated to this side and that,
>   Even as a wave receding and advancing.

Dante is here playing with several notions. He reminds us that disordered love makes the crooked ways seem straight, as if by a kind of hypnosis or bewitchment, and then immediately presents himself as going through a zig-zag ascent ("undulated to this side and that") that is actually the right path. It may take, as we will hear above, what seems crookedness to straighten what has become crooked in us. And we detect that the traces of our habitual disordered loves are in his mind because a normal person would turn back on hearing a loud door slam. It is only the warning that has kept him from error.

Dante describes himself as coming through that "needle's eye" and then arriving at a terrace like a deserted mountain road with no safety rail. It measures perhaps eighteen feet from the drop to the wall. The interior wall is a marvel to Dante as he steps onto this path:

> Thereon our feet had not been moved as yet,
>> When I perceived the embankment round about,
>> Which all right of ascent had interdicted,
> To be of marble white, and so adorned
>> With sculptures, that not only Polycletus,
>> But Nature's self, had there been put to shame.
> The Angel, who came down to earth with tidings
>> Of peace, that had been wept for many a year,
>> And opened Heaven from its long interdict,
> In front of us appeared so truthfully
>> There sculptured in a gracious attitude,
>> He did not seem an image that is silent.
> One would have sworn that he was saying, "Ave";
>> For she was there in effigy portrayed
>> Who turned the key to ope the exalted love,
> And in her mien this language had impressed,
>> "Ecce ancilla Dei," as distinctly
>> As any figure stamps itself in wax.

As in a kind of motion picture in stone, the annunciation to Mary is sculpted on this marble, who says, "Behold the handmaid of the Lord." That affirmation turned the key to the gates of Heaven. We will soon learn why, but first Dante notes another moving bas-relief:

> There sculptured in the self-same marble were
>> The cart and oxen, drawing the holy ark . . .
>> . . . Preceded there the vessel benedight,

> Dancing with girded loins, the humble Psalmist,
> And more and less than King was he in this.

This is the famous scene when David ("the Psalmist"), king of Israel, danced for joy before the ark of the covenant. Dante, who in any age would be thought a grave figure, here seems to perceive in the joyful David a humility that, in its twofold nature, allows him to do this dance out of love for God, which scandalized the serious minds of his time. And in so stripping himself of the manners of a king to celebrate before the Lord, paradoxically, he becomes more than a king even as he becomes less because his worship carries him beyond all human honor. Finally, Dante concludes this series of living sculptures with a depiction of the Roman emperor Trajan humbly responding to the request of a humble woman. The pattern—Marian episode, Old Testament episode, and classical episode—will be repeated on every cornice where figures are depicted.

Humility as the expiation of pride is the lesson to be learned on this terrace. And so difficult is it to rid ourselves of the prideful preoccupation with ourselves that Dante, who has just given us moving examples of the greatness of humility, so to speak, now feels obligated to issue a rare warning:

> I wish not, Reader, thou shouldst swerve
>   From thy good purposes, because thou hearest
>   How God ordaineth that the debt be paid;
> Attend not to the fashion of the torment,
>   Think of what follows; think that at the worst
>   It cannot reach beyond the mighty sentence.
> "Master," began I, "that which I behold
>   Moving towards us seems to me not persons,
>   And what I know not, so in sight I waver."
> And he to me: "The grievous quality
>   Of this their torment bows them so to earth,
>   That my own eyes at first contended with it;
> But look there fixedly, and disentangle
>   By sight what cometh underneath those stones;
>   Already canst thou see how each is stricken."
> O ye proud Christians! wretched, weary ones!
>   Who, in the vision of the mind infirm
>   Confidence have in your backsliding steps,

Do ye not comprehend that we are worms,
  Born to bring forth the angelic butterfly
  That flieth unto judgment without screen?
Why floats aloft your spirit high in air?
  Like are ye unto insects undeveloped
  Even as the worm in whom formation fails!
As to sustain a ceiling or a roof,
  In place of corbel, oftentimes a figure
  Is seen to join its knees unto its breast,
Which makes of the unreal real anguish
  Arise in him who sees it, fashioned thus
  Beheld I those, when I had ta'en good heed.
True is it, they were more or less bent down,
  According as they more or less were laden;
  And he who had most patience in his looks
Weeping did seem to say, "I can no more!"

As is always the case in the *Comedy,* the mode of expiation fits the need. But these figures crushed under the weight of heavy rocks Dante compares to corbels, the ornamental figures in columns or buildings that seem to be bent over, holding up the great weight of the structure. It is a terrible corrective, but at least it will not last forever, like the torments in Hell.

The weight of pride is something we entirely decide to assume ourselves. When Jesus said that his yoke was easy and his burden light because he is meek and humble of heart, he was expressing not some mystical abstraction but the concrete truth that pride burdens us horribly, even if we do not recognize it. The spirits laboring at the very limit of their endurance here present us with a powerful warning about the way we create our own burdens through a false sense of importance about ourselves.

Canto 11

Our Father, thou who dwellest in the heavens,
  Not circumscribed, but from the greater love
  Thou bearest to the first effects on high,
Praised be thy name and thine omnipotence
  By every creature, as befitting is
  To render thanks to thy sweet effluence.

Come unto us the peace of thy dominion,
    For unto it we cannot of ourselves,
    If it come not, with all our intellect.
Even as thine own Angels of their will
    Make sacrifice to thee, Hosanna singing,
    So may all men make sacrifice of theirs.
Give unto us this day our daily manna,
    Withouten which in this rough wilderness
    Backward goes he who toils most to advance.
And even as we the trespass we have suffered
    Pardon in one another, pardon thou
    Benignly, and regard not our desert.
Our virtue, which is easily o'ercome,
    Put not to proof with the old Adversary,
    But thou from him who spurs it so, deliver.
This last petition verily, dear Lord,
    Not for ourselves is made, who need it not,
    But for their sake who have remained behind us.

The souls of the proud walk their circle of Purgatory with this philosophical variation on the Lord's Prayer. Their emphasis on the humility of waiting for grace and understanding that without grace "Backward goes he who toils most to advance," further underscores the dependency and openness of true life.

In earthly life, however, human beings have invented all sorts of reasons to think themselves better than one another. In Dante's time, noble birth was one such social classification that, however important in itself, has no importance in the eternal judgments indicated here. Dante, who, as we have seen, respects nobility of character even among the souls damned in Hell, meets a certain Omberto of the noble Aldobrandeschi family here who tells him:

The ancient blood and deeds of gallantry
    Of my progenitors so arrogant made me
    That, thinking not upon the common mother,
All men I held in scorn . . . .

We are usually aware of the kind of airs that people in exalted social positions give themselves, and this figure is entirely familiar. But Dante moves on to some others whose stories are equally worth recalling because pride is not merely a social sin, though it is sometimes that, but also a quality of soul.

Dante recognizes a painter he knew living, Oderisi of Gubbio, who reminds him of the pride and competitiveness among artists, which is just as grievous as the pride in the social or political sphere. Oderisi has a better perspective on all that now. He says that others painted better than himself, and that fame is something fickle that we foolishly try to make stay its course:

> In painting Cimabue thought that he
> > Should hold the field, now Giotto has the cry,
> > So that the other's fame is growing dim.
> So has one Guido from the other taken
> > The glory of our tongue, and he perchance
> > Is born, who from the nest shall chase them both.
> Naught is this mundane rumour but a breath
> > Of wind, that comes now this way and now that,
> > And changes name, because it changes side.

Just as the painters Cimabue and Giotto have in their times been regarded as the greatest, so too in poetry the Guidos mentioned here are two of Dante's predecessors. Dante clearly regards himself as the one now born "who from the nest shall chase them both" by becoming the top poet. But even that proper estimate is not to be taken seriously because for all of us, rumor or fame is nothing more than wind. Oderisi points out examples of those who humbly sought the good of others as having fame in eternity, where even a thousand years of earthly fame is the merest blink of an eye.

Canto 12

Dante has been walking bent over to converse with Oderisi and the other spirit, who are carrying weights so heavy that their faces nearly touch the ground. Now he notices that the pavement they are walking on is inscribed with scenes from the Bible and classical history reminding these souls of the burdens of pride. These figures are so vivid that the people who witnessed the actual events, says Dante, had no better view. And he counsels us here to look with equal clarity at our own pride in order to be freed from it. Dante himself is about to be freed from the rigors of this cornice, signaled by the fact that the two poets now

encounter another angel with a different office than the one
already met at the gates of Purgatory:

> Towards us came the being beautiful
>> Vested in white, and in his countenance
>> Such as appears the tremulous morning star.
>
> His arms he opened, and opened then his wings;
>> "Come," said he, "near at hand here are the steps,
>> And easy from henceforth is the ascent."
>
> At this announcement few are they who come!
>> O human creatures, born to soar aloft,
>> Why fall ye thus before a little wind?
>
> He led us on to where the rock was cleft;
>> There smote upon my forehead with his wings,
>> Then a safe passage promised unto me.
>
> As on the right hand, to ascend the mount.

These are cheering words to Dante, since for most of his journey
every step has been hard won. To lose pride is to lose the heaviest of weights indeed. But with his passing beyond the crushing
weight of pride, his spirit will change remarkably and the journey will become far easier:

> "Beati pauperes spiritu," voices
>> Sang in such wise that speech could tell it not.
>
> Ah me! how different are these entrances
>> From the Infernal! for with anthems here
>> One enters, and below with wild laments.
>
> We now were hunting up the sacred stairs,
>> And it appeared to me by far more easy
>> Than on the plain it had appeared before.
>
> Whence I: "My Master, say, what heavy thing
>> Has been uplifted from me, so that hardly
>> Aught of fatigue is felt by me in walking?"
>
> He answered: "When the P's which have remained
>> Still on thy face almost obliterate
>> Shall wholly, as the first is, be erased,
>
> Thy feet will be so vanquished by good will,
>> That not alone they shall not feel fatigue,
>> But urging up will be to them delight."

The beating wings of the angel, which touched Dante's forehead,
removed one of the P's, and that the heaviest, as pride always is.

Dante cannot see the change, perhaps suggesting that we do not have clear sight of our own recovery from sin. But both he and we know the experience of suddenly finding a troublesome habit gone and the pleasant recognition in our minds and hearts.

Canto 13

The pleasure in the transition from one realm of Purgatory to another underscores how different this journey is from the one through Hell. In a superficial sense, the successive cornices of Purgatory grow smaller because the mountain tapers toward the top, as Hell tapered toward the bottom. But the narrowing is actually a liberation, since what is being narrowed is the realm of sin in the soul. This becomes clear as the poets move into the next cornice, the circle of the envious:

> We were upon the summit of the stairs,
>> Where for the second time is cut away
>> The mountain, which ascending shriveth all
> There in like manner doth a cornice bind
>> The hill all round about, as does the first,
>> Save that its arc more suddenly is curved
> Shade is there none, nor sculpture that appears;
>> So seems the bank, and so the road seems smooth
>> With but the livid colour of the stone.
> "If to inquire we wait for people here,"
>> The Poet said, "I fear that peradventure
>> Too much delay will our election have."
> Then steadfast on the sun his eyes he fixed.
>> Made his right side the centre of his motion,
>> And turned the left part of himself about.
> "O thou sweet light! with trust in whom I enter
>> Upon this novel journey, do thou lead us,"
>> Said he, "as one within here should be led.
> Thou warmest the world, thou shinest over it;
>> If other reason prompt not otherwise,
>> Thy rays should evermore our leaders be!"

As we have seen earlier, this sun is the light of God that must lead docile souls upward. But here it takes on another dimension as well, as we learn about the necessary way of purging envy.

The cornice appears both unadorned and empty, being only an uninterrupted stretch of gray stone. But Vergil tells Dante to look more closely, and when he does he sees something he had not earlier: "shades with mantles / Not from the colour of the stone diverse." Their condition is so pitiful that Dante says:

> I do not think there walketh still on earth
>   A man so hard, that he would not be pierced
>   With pity at what afterward I saw.
> For when I had approached so near to them
>   That manifest to me their acts became,
>   Drained was I at the eyes by heavy grief.
> Covered with sackcloth vile they seemed to me,
>   And one sustained the other with his shoulder,
>   And all of them were by the bank sustained.
> Thus do the blind, in want of livelihood,
>   Stand at the doors of churches asking alms,
>   And one upon another leans his head
> So that in others pity soon may rise,
>   Not only at the accent of their words,
>   But at their aspect, which no less implores.
> And as unto the blind the sun comes not
>   So to the shades, of whom just now I spake,
>   Heaven's light will not be bounteous of itself;
> For all their lids an iron wire transpierces,
>   And sews them up, as to a sparhawk wild
>   Is done, because it will not quiet stay.

The sunlight imagery here reminds us of Vergil's earlier praise. These souls, like many of us, need to have their sight disciplined for a while since the things they saw in the divine light while they were still living moved them to envy. Dante compares them to the wild hawks that were favorites of hunters in the Middle Ages, which needed hoods over their eyes to calm them down when they were agitated. The necessity of curbing that free flight to a more narrow confine reminds us yet again that one portion of the soul must be reduced and eliminated here so that, in the end, the soul will be set free in its proper mode. The souls speak to Dante of their envies and how they let them disrupt the politics of Italy. They now recall Italy as a land through which they passed as pilgrims, not someplace they should have torn up through mutual hatreds. Now they "stoop to rise," one soul remarks.

Curiously, Dante confesses to his own sins at this point. He fears this circle less than the earlier one, pride being far more common in his soul than envy. A significant portion of the envy he has seen has to do with the growing political rivalry in Italy. After some discussion of how the whole valley of the Arno, with the cities Arezzo, Florence, and Pisa, is an accumulation of envy and bestiality, Dante is surprised by the shouts of some of these poor spirits about examples of envy drawn from Scripture and classical mythology. Such examples should be a word of warning to human beings:

> That was the hard curb
> That ought to hold a man within his bounds;
> But you take in the bait so that the hook
> Of the old Adversary draws you to him,
> And hence availeth little curb or call.
> The heavens are calling you, and wheel around you,
> Displaying to you their eternal beauties,
> And still your eye is looking on the ground;
> Whence He, who all discerns, chastises you."

Canto 15

Vergil continues, clarifying things for Dante. As he does so, he speaks in terms of light, a created thing that will become more and more important as Dante rises toward the Heavens. Just as the growing darkness accompanied the descent into Hell, a growing light and understanding accompany the poets on their ascent to divine things. The very first of such things is another angel at the entrance to the next level, and Vergil comments:

> "Marvel thou not, if dazzle thee as yet
> The family of heaven," he answered me;
> "An angel 'tis, who comes to invite us upward.
> Soon will it be, that to behold these things
> Shall not be grievous, but delightful to thee
> As much as nature fashioned thee to feel."
> When we had reached the Angel benedight,
> With joyful voice he said: "Here enter in

> To stairway far less steep than are the others."
> We mounting were, already thence departed,
>   And "Beati misericordes" was
>   Behind us sung, "Rejoice, thou that o'ercomest!"

As the poets climb to the next circle, however, Dante requests an explanation for how it is that by setting their sights on heavenly things people are more satisfied. Vergil responds:

> Because thou fixest still
> Thy mind entirely upon earthly things,
> Thou pluckest darkness from the very light.
> That goodness infinite and ineffable
>   Which is above there, runneth unto love,
>   As to a lucid body comes the sunbeam.
> So much it gives itself as it finds ardour,
>   So that as far as charity extends,
>   O'er it increases the eternal valour.
> And the more people thitherward aspire,
>   More are there to love well, and more they love there,
>   And, as a mirror, one reflects the other.
> And if my reasoning appease thee not,
>   Thou shalt see Beatrice; and she will fully
>   Take from thee this and every other longing.
> Endeavour, then, that soon may be extinct,
>   As are the two already, the five wounds
>   That close themselves again by being painful.

Reflections of this kind on light and the division of love and grace that God sends each soul according to its desire will be further treated of in the *Paradiso*. But what Vergil is doing here is beginning the process by which Dante will be accustomed to a greater and different kind of light of understanding. The patience and willingness to remain without complete explanation at this stage are typical of the kinds of spiritual progress we make as we begin to get inklings into a larger world. But we must follow our intentions vigorously if we expect to arrive at full comprehension of the light granted to us.

And, in fact, as Dante climbs into the next circle, his sight is now prepared to receive visions that will lead him further upward. In succession, he has a vision of Mary and Joseph discovering Jesus in the Temple; of an Athenian leader, Pisistratus, practicing mildness; and of St. Stephen, forgiving the anger of those who stoned him as he is martyred. These examples of mildness appear here because the sin purged in this circle is anger. But in addition to this lesson on a moral plane, Vergil teaches Dante something important about the response of the soul, what the medievals would have called an anagogic point. Dante has just seen "not false" visions, or something unreal. He has enough illumination in his mind now to distinguish clearly between the not-real, but edifying, and reality. But Vergil chides him for allowing the illumination he is now receiving to slacken his steps toward full liberation:

> What thou hast seen was that thou mayst not fail
>   To ope thy heart unto the waters of peace
>   Which from the eternal fountain are diffused.
> I did not ask, "What ails thee?" as he does
>   Who only looketh with the eyes that see not
>   When of the soul bereft the body lies,
> But asked it to give vigour to thy feet;
>   Thus must we needs urge on the sluggards, slow
>   To use their wakefulness when it returns.

We are familiar with the situations in which depression or sluggishness of vision impedes our spiritual advance; this is a good warning that graces granted, by their very excess of stimulation, may distract us from keeping to the vigorous path they are meant to spur us along.

Canto 16

The poets, however, are soon moving on around this cornice, when they are surprised by another new phenomenon that we would not have expected after all the action of light and spiritual illumination in this region:

> Darkness of hell, and of a night deprived
>   Of every planet under a poor sky,
>   As much as may be tenebrous with cloud,
> Ne'er made unto my sight so thick a veil,
>   As did that smoke which there enveloped us,
>   Nor to the feeling of so rough a texture;

> For not an eye it suffered to stay open;
>> Whereat mine escort, faithful and sagacious,
>> Drew near to me and offered me his shoulder.
> E'en as a blind man goes behind his guide,
>> Lest he should wander, or should strike against
>> Aught that may harm or peradventure kill him,
> So went I through the bitter and foul air,
>> Listening unto my Leader, who said only,
>> "Look that from me thou be not separated."

Vergil, as Reason, is Dante's sure guide through this fog. But the fog itself serves a purpose in that it purges wrath by reproducing the kind of effect wrath has on the soul: by its fiery passion, it envelops up in a kind of smoke that obscures the light of God's grace and the created order he has provided to us.

The wayfarers come upon a soul named Marco Lombardo, who laments that the world of Dante's time is without virtue. We are now in canto 16 of the *Purgatory*. Fifty cantos (thirty-four of Hell plus sixteen of Purgatory) lie behind us, fifty more lie ahead (seventeen of Purgatory plus thirty-three of Paradise). Dante never neglects these structural turning points and neither should we. For him, the structure reflects both a literal and an allegorical meaning. We are literally nearing the midpoint of the journey, and allegorically we may expect that something of a turnaround is about to occur. Dante asks Lombardo why the world is corrupt. Is the cause in the Heavens? In the remainder of this canto, Lombardo explains how free will persists despite all things. In the next canto, Vergil will explain to Dante a general theory about the love in the universe and how it is embodied in the structure of Purgatory. It is worth keeping this larger context in mind as we turn to each of these two arguments.

In modern terms, what Marco is addressing here is the age-old question of free will versus determinism. In Dante's day, the determinism came from the astrological influence of the stars. Just as we look to physics and biology for explanations of large parts of our universe, the medievals looked to the overwhelming physical influence of the heavenly bodies. But Marco denies that this is all there is to say about the issue. God, working both directly and through secondary causes, has also put into us something free that can never be controlled even by the powerful heavens.

This fact has consequences, not only for private behavior but also for the general condition in which we find our public world: "Hence, if the present world doth go astray, / In you the cause is, be it sought in you," says Marco.

Church and empire, pope and king, were given to us by God to help guide us on our way. But in Dante's view, these "two suns" who should illuminate us are not functioning. The emperors have refused to assume their proper authority, and the popes have wrongly usurped what belongs to the secular power:

> Clearly canst thou perceive that evil guidance
>> The cause is that has made the world depraved,
>> And not that nature is corrupt in you.
> Rome, that reformed the world, accustomed was
>> Two suns to have, which one road and the other,
>> Of God and of the world, made manifest.
> One has the other quenched, and to the crosier
>> The sword is joined, and ill beseemeth it
>> That by main force one with the other go,
> Because, being joined, one feareth not the other.

The confusion and anarchy that have resulted have spilled over into both the spiritual and the political realm, so that the typical vices of individuals are not checked by the proper political authorities, and the spiritual authorities soil their hands with trying to do profane actions. Significantly, given that this discussion is taking place in a dark cloud—darker than anything Dante encountered in Hell though its effects are for good—Dante is told that these two powers must be as two suns.

Canto 17

And shortly after, a kind of illumination begins to pierce the darkness:

> Remember, Reader, if e'er in the Alps
>> A mist o'ertook thee, through which thou couldst see
>> Not otherwise than through its membrane mole,
> How, when the vapours humid and condensed
>> Begin to dissipate themselves, the sphere
>> Of the sun feebly enters in among them,

> And thy imagination will be swift
>   In coming to perceive how I re-saw
>   The sun at first, that was already setting.

Something curious then happens. Just as we might expect Dante
to turn toward this light, instead he begins to have another
vision. This would be inexplicable if we thought what he was
doing was turning away, as the wrathful had, into a world closed
on itself by the passions in his soul. But in fact what might seem
a casual episode in the pilgrimage should lead us to reflect back
on Marco's words about the part in us that is free, whatever our
surroundings. Dante's current surroundings are still mostly
smoke, pierced by light. He sees some examples of wrath from
classical and biblical history. But more important than that, he
senses that something else lies behind the imagining:

> O thou, Imagination, that dost steal us
>   So from without sometimes, that man perceives not,
>   Although around may sound a thousand trumpets,
> Who moveth thee, if sense impel thee not?
>   Moves thee a light, which in the heaven takes form,
>   By self, or by a will that downward guides it.

The visions intervene at this point and need not detain us. But
when Dante returns to reflection, we see the relevance of his ear-
lier emphasis on heavenly light moving the imagination to
understanding:

> As sleep is broken, when upon a sudden
>   New light strikes in upon the eyelids closed,
>   And broken quivers ere it dieth wholly,
> So this imagining of mine fell down
>   As soon as the effulgence smote my face,
>   Greater by far than what is in our wont.
> I turned me round to see where I might be,
>   When said a voice, "Here is the passage up;"
>   Which from all other purposes removed me,
> And made my wish so full of eagerness
>   To look and see who was it that was speaking,
>   It never rests till meeting face to face;
> But as before the sun, which quells the sight,
>   And in its own excess its figure veils,
>   Even so my power was insufficient here.

"This is a spirit divine, who in the way
  Of going up directs us without asking
  And who with his own light himself conceals.
He does with us as man doth with himself;
  For he who sees the need, and waits the asking,
  Malignly leans already tow'rds denial."

This is a very rich passage in the context. The angel is so bright, his very excess of light, of things to see, conceals him. Yet it is his nature, now that we are passing away from the sin of wrath, to act with others as he would toward himself, without waiting to be asked.

Further energized by this encounter, the poets hasten to climb higher while there is still light. Dante feels the brush of wings and hears "Blessed are the peacemakers," which encourages him further, but night quickly falls and his legs will not carry him a step further—in the allegory of the poem, God's grace for the ascent being temporarily suspended. Rather than waste the time, Dante asks Vergil where they now have arrived. He will learn that it is the cornice of the slothful, those who take laziness and the neglect of the good to the point of sinfulness. It is fitting that this circle and discussion occur right near the central point of the whole poem because after this there will be no slackness or neglect of love. Vergil describes this level of Purgatory and the theory of love, which we looked at briefly in the introduction.

"Neither Creator nor a creature ever,
  Son," he began, "was destitute of love
  Natural or spiritual; and thou knowest it."

It is worth looking back at our earlier discussion of this material for what is to follow. Vergil takes the cosmic points further into concrete sin:

Hence if, discriminating, I judge well,
  The evil that one loves is of one's neighbour,
  And this is born in three modes in your clay.
There are, who, by abasement of their neighbour,
  Hope to excel, and therefore only long
  That from his greatness he may be cast down;
There are, who power, grace, honour, and renown
  Fear they may lose because another rises,

> Thence are so sad that the reverse they love;
> And there are those whom injury seems to chafe,
>   So that it makes them greedy for revenge,
>   And such must needs shape out another's harm.

The last nine lines divide so as to describe each of the faults in three lines apiece—the pride, envy, and wrath we have already encountered in Purgatory:

> This threefold love is wept for down below;
>   Now of the other will I have thee hear,
>   That runneth after good with measure faulty.
> Each one confusedly a good conceives
>   Wherein the mind may rest, and longeth for it;
>   Therefore to overtake it each one strives.
> If languid love to look on this attract you,
>   Or in attaining unto it, this cornice,
>   After just penitence, torments you for it.
> There's other good that does not make man happy;
>   'Tis not felicity, 'tis not the good
>   Essence, of every good the fruit and root.
> The love that yields itself too much to this
>   Above us is lamented in three circles;
>   But how tripartite it may be described,
> I say not, that thou seek it for thyself.

As we shall learn, the excessive loves of things that are good in themselves, but not in the way the penitent souls loved them on earth, are avarice, gluttony, and lust. Vergil, as human Reason, does not anticipate here, judging that it is better for the wayfarer to learn of these things himself through experience rather than mere abstract knowledge. This too inaugurates the coming of a different approach in this second half of the pilgrimage, where the rapidly burgeoning power and freed love in the soul will need fewer outside helps and, coming into its own proper and ordered powers of love, will be moved by natural energies toward the culminating vision.

Canto 18

Though we have already had a substantial discourse on the nature of love, Dante is still eager to know more, and more

precisely, this mainspring of his whole universe. So he turns
again to his dear Vergil:

> "Direct," he said, "towards me the keen eyes
>   Of intellect, and clear will be to thee
>   The error, of the blind, who would be leaders.
> The soul, which is created apt to love,
>   Is mobile unto everything that pleases,
>   Soon as by pleasure she is waked to action.
> Your apprehension from some real thing
>   An image draws, and in yourselves displays it
>   So that it makes the soul turn unto it.
> And if, when turned, towards it she incline,
>   Love is that inclination; it is nature,
>   Which is by pleasure bound in you anew
> Then even as the fire doth upward move
>   By its own form, which to ascend is born,
>   Where longest in its matter it endures,
> So comes the captive soul into desire,
>   Which is a motion spiritual, and ne'er rests
>   Until she doth enjoy the thing beloved.
> Now may apparent be to thee how hidden
>   The truth is from those people, who aver
>   All love is in itself a laudable thing,
> Because its matter may perchance appear
>   Aye to be good; but yet not each impression
>   Is good, albeit good may be the wax."

Vergil is continuing here the deep appreciation for the roots of
love that are built into the very nature of the human person and,
in different fashions, into all things by God. But we are made in
a way different from the creatures that merely follow the first
impulses of their own natures. Dante is unclear about this dis-
tinction, because it seems that an innocent soul would simply
follow these leadings of nature without any other power inter-
vening. He puts the case for this immediate impulse in a way that
many people might applaud:

> For if love from without be offered us,
>   And with another foot the soul go not,
>   If right or wrong she go, 'tis not her merit.

We are approaching here a mystery whose nature reason can only begin to glimpse. Vergil's answer, like many of those that will now follow as we approach the supernatural realm proper, is cautious about what reason is able to affirm, and what it must wait for a higher illumination to clarify:

> And he to me: "What reason seeth here,
>   Myself can tell thee; beyond that await
>   For Beatrice since 'tis a work of faith.
> Every substantial form, that segregate
>   From matter is, and with it is united,
>   Specific power has in itself collected,
> Which without act is not perceptible,
>   Nor shows itself except by its effect,
>   As life does in a plant by the green leaves.
> But still, whence cometh the intelligence
>   Of the first notions, man is ignorant,
>   And the affection for the first allurements,
> Which are in you as instinct in the bee
>   To make its honey; and this first desire
>   Merit of praise or blame containeth not.
> Now, that to this all others may be gathered,
>   Innate within you is the power that counsels,
>   And it should keep the threshold of assent.
> This is the principle, from which is taken
>   Occasion of desert in you, according
>   As good and guilty loves it takes and winnows.
> Those who, in reasoning, to the bottom went,
>   Were of this innate liberty aware,
>   Therefore bequeathed they Ethics to the world.
> Supposing, then, that from necessity
>   Springs every love that is within you kindled,
>   Within yourselves the power is to restrain it.
> The noble virtue Beatrice understands
>   By the free will; and therefore see that thou
>   Bear it in mind, if she should speak of it."

To follow up these hints here would take us far away from the main theme of the spiritual pilgrimage. But it is worth noting that in this passage Vergil affirms six or seven central points. First, human beings are a composite nature of a spiritual form and a physical body. Next, the spiritual form cannot be known except through its operations, just as we know that a plant is living by the fact that it puts forth new shoots, grows, and so forth. Third, the nature of this living quality, though revealed by its acts, is also hidden because it is not immediately open to inspection by our senses. So the ultimate source of the various kinds of love that arise in the human soul is a mystery. That we have the power to allow those desires to pursue their objects or refuse assent is noted even by the pagan philosophers who saw deepest and created the discipline we know as ethics. But Dante will have to wait for Beatrice to explain more about these mysteries.

As the poets speak, the moon is rising overhead. Dante begins to become drowsy, but his sleep is interrupted by a band of souls who are running around the mountain, even at night, to rid themselves of their former sloth in pursuing the good. For many of us in frenetic modern societies, the spiritual life is something that we regard as a kind of relaxation and quiet contemplation. Dante is not rejecting that notion here. That kind of contemplative stillness will emerge ever more strongly as he ascends toward the Heavens. What he is warning about here is a slackness in the cultivation of the various loves in the soul that should lead us up to the higher modes of contemplation. Many people, for instance, find spiritual peace and progress in certain religious practices or moral disciplines, but allow the cares of the world and the burdens of mere physical existence to divert them from pursuing those goods further. These souls are a reminder that we need great efforts in our spiritual lives to overcome the inertia that seems to weigh down the average person, which in the last analysis is "little love:"

> Full soon they were upon us, because running
>   Moved onward all that mighty multitude,
>   And two in the advance cried out, lamenting,
> "Mary in haste unto the mountain ran,
>   And Caesar, that he might subdue Ilerda,
>   Thrust at Marseilles, and then ran into Spain."
> "Quick! quick! so that the time may not be lost
>   By little love!" forthwith the others cried,
>   "For ardour in well-doing freshens grace!"

Continuing the parallel between sacred and profane history, a little further on the souls recall how the Israelites who did not persist never entered the Promised Land and how not all those who followed Aeneas from Troy to found Rome, as recounted in Vergil's *Aeneid,* were persistent enough to participate in an event that reshaped the world. But these souls soon speed past, and their passing both stimulates Dante to new thoughts and lulls him into yet another significant dream.

Canto 19

Dreams and visions are coming more frequently now as imagination and vision are purified and free. By the time we reach the summit of Purgatory, Dante will have something like a vision that is literally true. At this stage his dream flows directly from the earlier conversation about true and false loves. Dante will see concretely how it is that appearances that seem attractive, even fascinating, may in fact mislead us if we do not know how to look further into what lies behind them and where they fit into the larger reality of God's world:

> There came to me in dreams a stammering woman
>> Squint in her eyes, and in her feet distorted,
>> With hands dissevered and of sallow hue.
> I looked at her; and as the sun restores
>> The frigid members which the night benumbs,
>> Even thus my gaze did render voluble
> Her tongue, and made her all erect thereafter
>> In little while, and the lost countenance
>> As love desires it so in her did colour
> When in this wise she had her speech unloosed,
>> She 'gan to sing so, that with difficulty
>> Could I have turned my thoughts away from her
> "I am," she sang, "I am the Siren sweet
>> Who mariners amid the main unman
>> So full am I of pleasantness to hear
> I drew Ulysses from his wandering way
>> Unto my song, and he who dwells with me
>> Seldom departs so wholly I content him."
> Her mouth was not yet closed again, before

> Appeared a Lady saintly and alert
>> Close at my side to put her to confusion.
> "Virgilius, ah Virgilius! who is this?"
>> Sternly she said; and he was drawing near
>> With eyes still fixed upon that modest one.
> She seized the other and in front laid open,
>> Rending her garments, and her belly showed me;
>> This waked me with the stench that issued from it.
> I turned mine eyes, and good Virgilius said:
>> "At least thrice have I called thee; rise and come;
>> Find we the opening by which thou mayst enter."

Dante has actually erred here, because, as we saw in *Inferno*, he has no accurate knowledge of the *Odyssey*. The Siren did not succeed in deceiving Ulysses. But his point is nonetheless correct. All pleasures may be a type of Siren, enchanting and diverting us. Even more seriously, however, unless we receive and give heed to divine grace and the motions of reason that such grace induces in us, we will not rip aside the veil to see the reality. Now that he has been awakened and the sun has risen, Dante is in a condition to make use of what has been revealed to him and move ever higher on his journey. His dream remains with him, even as he goes, and he is bent over in thought as he walks behind Vergil:

> Following behind him, I my forehead bore
>> Like unto one who has it laden with thought,
>> Who makes himself the half arch of a bridge,
>
> When I heard say, "Come, here the passage is,"
>> Spoken in a manner gentle and benign,
>> Such as we hear not in this mortal region.

With this image, perhaps something in Dante has become like a bridge that meets halfway, the invitation to an understanding of the new circle to which he has now come. Even more than Dante, who had previously been half bent over, the souls on this cornice are fixed face-down to the ground as a means of purging their too great attachment in their former life to the things of this earth through avarice. Dante begins speaking with one of the souls there and is surprised to learn that it is the shade of the Pope Adrian V. "Know that I was the successor of Peter," says Adrian in the Latin fitting to the former head of the church. Though pope, this man reveals that he had to undergo a conversion from his avarice late in life. And as he explains, avarice entails a loss of other loves:

> "As avarice had extinguished our affection
>   For every good, whereby was action lost,
>   So justice here doth hold us in restraint,
> Bound and imprisoned by the feet and hands;
>   And so long as it pleases the just Lord
>   Shall we remain immovable and prostrate."
> I on my knees had fallen, and wished to speak;
>   But even as I began, and he was 'ware,
>   Only by listening, of my reverence,
> "What cause," he said, "has downward bent thee thus?"
>   And I to him: "For your own dignity,
>   Standing, my conscience stung me with remorse."
> "Straighten thy legs, and upward raise thee, brother,"
>   He answered: "Err not, fellow-servant am I
>   With thee and with the others to one power."

At these heights, mere human respect of offices is no longer operative. The souls that are eminent are those that forgo their attachment to lesser things and serve what is above.

Dante underscores this point by a meeting in the next canto with a leader from the secular world. His preparation for this encounter is to recall one of the beasts who blocked his way forward in the opening canto of the whole poem, the she-wolf, who, we remember, represented avarice. And Dante makes his old complaint that the world awaits the political leader, the greyhound we also met earlier, who will drive back this wolf, politics and the spiritual life mutually reinforcing each other.

Canto 20

> Accursed mayst thou be, thou old she-wolf,
>   That more than all the other beasts hast prey,
>   Because of hunger infinitely hollow!
> O heaven, in whose gyrations some appear
>   To think conditions here below are changed,
>   When will he come through whom she shall depart?

And in subsequent cantos, Dante describes the purgation from false hunger that not only the avaricious, but the gluttonous must undergo. Nothing on earth can satisfy the longings of the human heart, which will naturally look to some further fulfillment.

Canto 25

Nowhere does that become clearer than in the circle we have now entered, which deals with the disordered love between men and women that we call lust. As the poets climb, they engage in a long discussion of how generation occurs and how it is that souls after death can display the ghostly bodies that Dante has seen in Purgatory and Hell. Though interesting in themselves, these points provide a silent witness to the cosmic purposes of sexuality in bringing forth human beings on Earth and then souls for Heaven after death. But as the poets emerge on the new terrace, they behold a new situation:

> There the embankment shoots forth flames of fire,
> And upward doth the cornice breathe a blast
> That drives them back, and from itself sequesters.
> Hence we must needs go on the open side,
> And one by one; and I did fear the fire
> On this side, and on that the falling down.
> My Leader said: "Along this place one ought
> To keep upon the eyes a tightened rein,
> Seeing that one so easily might err."
> "Summae Deus clementiae," in the bosom
> Of the great burning chanted then I heard,
> Which made me no less eager to turn round;
> And spirits saw I walking through the flame;
> Wherefore I looked, to my own steps and theirs
> Apportioning my sight from time to time.

This may be the most precarious point in the entire journey so far. Fire on the one hand, a steep precipice on the other: it does not take much imagination to sense that Dante is trying to show the narrow way of self-control that will have to be traversed to get through this last of the purgations. As with earlier sins, the mode of recovery is similar to the mode of transgression. Lust has often been compared to a fire in both secular and sacred literature. In addition, Moses encountered the Almighty in a burning bush, and the Holy Spirit itself came to the apostles in the form of tongues of fire. The fire of passion as we have seen elsewhere along the way is a very great good when it leads into the right ways. But its very power is what makes handling it such a difficult and delicate process. As the modern poet T. S. Eliot put it in his *Four Quartets,* in a passage inspired both by the biblical tradition and by Dante:

> The dove descending breaks the air
> With flame of incandescent terror
> Of which the tongues declare
> The one discharge from sin and error.
> The only hope, or else despair
>   Lies in the choice of pyre or pyre—
>   To be redeemed from fire by fire.
>
> Who then devised the torment? Love.
> Love is the unfamiliar Name
> Behind the hands that wove
> The intolerable shirt of flame
> Which human hands cannot remove.
>   We only live, only suspire
>   Consumed by either fire or fire.

Or as Dante puts it more briefly:

> And I believe that them this mode suffices,
>   For all the time the fire is burning them;
>   With such care is it needful, and such food,
> That the last wound of all should be closed up.

Canto 26

Yet reason will guide us to a point that will exceed reason, and Vergil warns Dante at the beginning of this canto, "Take thou heed! suffice it that I warn thee." Led by Vergil, Dante walks carefully outside the wall of fire. The souls purging their lust in the flames notice that Dante's body breaks the sunlight and inquire of him how that is possible at this altitude. Before he can reply, however, he sees a second group of souls who draw his attention:

> For through the middle of the burning road
> > There came a people face to face with these,
> > Which held me in suspense with gazing at them.
> There see I hastening upon either side
> > Each of the shades, and kissing one another.
> > Without a pause, content with brief salute.
> Thus in the middle of their brown battalions
> > Muzzle to muzzle one ant meets another
> > Perchance to spy their journey or their fortune.
> No sooner is the friendly greeting ended,
> > Or ever the first footstep passes onward,
> > Each one endeavours to outcry the other;
> The new-come people: "Sodom and Gomorrah!"
> > The rest: "Into the cow Pasiphae enters,
> > So that the bull unto her lust may run!"

It is obvious that this brief encounter is meant to reflect the "holy kiss" of Christian brothers and sisters rather than the passionate embraces of the past. The references at the end may seem obscure, but we soon learn that they refer to those who have sinned through homosexual lust ("Sodom and Gomorrah!") and those who were heterosexual but sinned by a bestial (Pasiphae) indulgence of their appetites outside of marriage. Dante remarks to these souls, whom he reminds are secure now of finding peace someday, that he is still in his flesh and that "A Lady is above, who wins this grace." Some think this refers to the Virgin Mary, but most commentators see here a reference to Dante's Beatrice. The condition of his still being in the flesh and being rightly inspired by a lady is surely not lost upon these souls. Dante desires to know, however, who these souls are, and the one who first approached him tells him that he is Guido Guinicelli, one of Dante's eminent poetic predecessors. Dante cannot embrace this poetical father because of the fire that envelops him. But he shows his affection all the same. And Guido, referring to Lethe, the river of forgetfulness of sins that we shall soon encounter, says he has heard that Dante's work is such that Lethe itself will not wash away its fame. This is a tacit indication that Dante's work does not

partake of the sinful form of love here being expiated. Still, Dante
tells Guido how dear the very ink of his work has been to all poets
who have come after him. Guido replies humbly:

> "O brother," said he, "he whom I point out,"
>   And here he pointed at a spirit in front,
>   "Was of the mother tongue a better smith.
> Verses of love and proses of romance,
>   He mastered all . . ."

This soul is Arnaut Daniel, one of the great poets from the French
region of Provence, a troubadour and therefore poet in his own
right. Guido leaves the two of them with the request to Dante
that when he comes into Heaven to

>   repeat for me a Paternoster,
>   So far as needful to us of this world,
>   Where power of sinning is no longer ours.

Daniel steps forward and, in homage Dante pays no other figure
except for a line or two in Latin here and there, he is allowed to
speak in his own tongue, a Latin dialect related to French and
Italian, but quite different from each. In his "On the Vulgar
Tongue," Dante called Daniel the greatest singer of love, one of
the three great subjects for poetry, the other two being valor in
arms and high moral action. His tribute to Daniel then is to have
him say:

> I am Arnaut, who weep and singing go;
>   Contrite I see the folly of the past
>   And joyous see the hoped-for day before me.
> Therefore do I implore you, by that power
>   Which guides you to the summit of the stairs
>   Be mindful to assuage my suffering!
>
> Then hid him in the fire that purifies them.

The word that is translated as "purify" here has the sense of
purification that occurs when metals are heated to high temper-
atures to separate the pure liquid metal from the other elements.
And it is a heating of that kind that Dante himself must now pro-
ceed to face.

Canto 27

He sees the final angel guardian at the final gate.

> Outside the flame he stood upon the verge,
>> And chanted forth, "Beati mundo corde,"
>> In voice by far more living than our own.
> Then: "No one farther goes, souls sanctified,
>> If first the fire bite not; within it enter,
>> And be not deaf unto the song beyond."
> Wherefore e'en such became I, when I heard him,
>> As he is who is put into the grave.
>> Upon my clasped hands I straightened me,
> Scanning the fire, and vividly recalling
>> The human bodies I had once seen burned.
>> Towards me turned themselves my good Conductors,
> And unto me Virgilius said: "My son,
>> Here may indeed be torment, but not death.
>> Remember thee, remember! and if I
> On Geryon have safely guided thee,
>> What shall I do now I am nearer God?
>> Believe for certain, shouldst thou stand a full
> Millennium in the bosom of this flame,
>> It could not make thee bald a single hair.
>> And if perchance thou think that I deceive thee,
> Draw near to it, and put it to the proof
>> With thine own hands upon thy garment's hem.
>> Now lay aside, now lay aside all fear,
> Turn hitherward, and onward come securely."

The Latin of the angel reminds us of the beatitude, "Blessed are the pure of heart, for they shall see God." We are coming to the point where direct seeing will replace the elaborate preparation and purgation that have occupied us until now. But despite this recollection by Vergil of everything he has done for Dante along the entire journey, Dante cannot move a step forward. At first it may appear that this is mere human fear, but the fire is clearly meant to represent the wall of fire that several medieval theologians believed God had interposed between us and the Garden of Eden after the Fall. This last step, though small, is the biggest of all since it means leaving behind all our mistaken ways and false consolations of human life and finally entering back into true rest and real life.

For the moment, Dante sees only the fire, and his reason, even at Vergil's urging, is of no avail. But Vergil invokes someone who motivates Dante beyond his own fear and doubt: "Now look thou, Son, / 'Twixt Beatrice and thee there is this wall":

> I turned to my wise Guide, hearing the name
> That in my memory evermore is welling.
> Whereat he wagged his head, and said: "How now?
> Shall we stay on this side?" then smiled as one
> Does at a child who's vanquished by an apple.
> Then into the fire in front of me he entered
>
> . . . .
>
> When I was in it, into molten glass
> I would have cast me to refresh myself,
> So without measure was the burning there!
> And my sweet Father, to encourage me,
> Discoursing still of Beatrice went on,
> Saying: "Her eyes I seem to see already!"
> A voice, that on the other side was singing,
> Directed us, and we, attent alone
> On that, came forth where the ascent began.
> "Venite, bendicti Patris mei."

This last line recalls Christ's account in Matthew 25 of the words that will be addressed to the righteous at the last judgment: "Then shall the King say unto them on his right hand, Come ye blessed of my father, inherit the kingdom prepared for you from the foundation of the world."

But night is falling as the poets reach the final stair. Dante paints a kind of quiet pastoral scene as he experiences the last instants outside the earthly Paradise. In that setting, everything becomes more intense and now leads to anticipations of fulfillment:

> I beheld the stars
> More luminous and larger than their wont.
> Thus ruminating, and beholding these,
> Sleep seized upon me,—sleep, that oftentimes
> Before a deed is done has tidings of it.

It was the hour, I think, when from the East
First on the mountain Citherea beamed,
　Who with the fire of love seems always burning;
　Youthful and beautiful in dreams methought
I saw a lady walking in a meadow,
　Gathering flowers; and singing she was saying:
　"Know whosoever may my name demand
That I am Leah, and go moving round
　My beauteous hands to make myself a garland.
　To please me at the mirror, here I deck me,
But never does my sister Rachel leave
　Her looking-glass, and sitteth all day long.
　To see her beauteous eyes as eager is she,
As I am to adorn me with my hands;
　Her, seeing, and me, doing satisfies."
　And now before the antelucan splendours
That unto pilgrims the more grateful rise,
　As, home-returning, less remote they lodge,
　The darkness fled away on every side,
And slumber with it; whereupon I rose . . . .

In his prophetic dream, Dante has seen the two classical images
of the active life and the contemplative life, the two daughters of
Laban whom Jacob had wooed, Leah and Rachel. Elsewhere in
Dante, we find that he believed that God had basically laid out
two forms of beatitude for human beings, one through activity in
the things of this world, the other in detachment and contempla-
tion. Like the Martha and Mary of the Gospels, the contemplative
life is superior to the active, but the active too is good and neces-
sary because without it, at the very least, life itself and contem-
plation with it would simply perish.

At the end of this passage, Dante compares himself to the pil-
grims who, as they return home, find themselves lodging closer
and closer to their destination. And Vergil now adds that he is
about to enjoy the fruit of all his wandering:

"That apple sweet, which through so many branches
The care of mortals goeth in pursuit of,
　To-day shall put in peace thy hungerings."
　Speaking to me, Virgilius of such words
As these made use; and never were there guerdons
　That could in pleasantness compare with these.

Such longing upon longing came upon me
To be above, that at each step thereafter
　For flight I felt in me the pinions growing
　When underneath us was the stairway all
Run o'er, and we were on the highest step,
　Virgilius fastened upon me his eyes,
　And said: "The temporal fire and the eternal,
Son, thou hast seen, and to a place art come
　Where of myself no farther I discern.
　By intellect and art I here have brought thee;
Take thine own pleasure for thy guide henceforth;
　Beyond the steep ways and the narrow art thou.
　Behold the sun, that shines upon thy forehead,
Behold the grass, the flowerets, and the shrubs
　Which of itself alone this land produces.
　Until rejoicing come the beauteous eyes
Which weeping caused me to come unto thee,
　Thou canst sit down, and thou canst walk among them.
　Expect no more or word or sign from me;
Free and upright and sound is thy free-will,
　And error were it not to do its bidding;
　Thee o'er thyself I therefore crown and mitre!"

We human beings seek this final fruition in various goods that are either idolatrously taken for our heart's desire or pursued, as we learned below, with too much or too little desire. Dante's soul, however, is restored to wholeness now, and Vergil's very words increase the desire in him to rise toward the true good. He has seen the eternal fire of punishment (Hell), and the temporary fire that purges sins in Purgatory. Soon he will go on to find his way among the eternal fires of the Heavens. But together with the joy of this achievement, Vergil's fatherly care now comes to an end.

Dante may now follow his own pleasure in the light of God. Many people in every age think that following pleasure is the path to happiness. But our whole journey has shown us how complicated and demanding and exacting a task it is for us in our usual conditions to arrive back at the original nature that God intended for us. For most of us many lifetimes are insufficient to achieve that innocence, and it shall be our possession again only after long spiritual reformation here and hereafter. Then our wills will be free again, upright, and healthy. Then we will have the kingly crown given to us over temporal affairs and the bishop's miter that makes us sovereign over spiritual affairs as well. Then we shall be our own kings and bishops. But only then, after we have been restored to the fullness of our nature. And anyone who desires this fulfillment rather than the many simulacra that counterfeit it must be prepared to abandon self and to undertake the journey that literally spans heaven and earth. Dante has now completed that preliminary pilgrimage and is about to enter realms most of us have a great deal of difficulty even imagining. The first realm we need to familiarize ourselves with is the earthly Paradise, the Garden of Eden, which we forfeited with original sin. It will only be a foretaste of Paradise itself. In the remaining six cantos of *Purgatory,* Dante will rediscover what could have been ours all along had we remained faithful to our divine call.

Canto 28

Eager already to search in and round
　The heavenly forest, dense and living-green,
　Which tempered to the eyes the new-born day,
Withouten more delay I left the bank,
　Taking the level country slowly, slowly
　Over the soil that everywhere breathes fragrance.
A softly-breathing air, that no mutation
　Had in itself, upon the forehead smote me
　No heavier blow than of a gentle wind,
Whereat the branches, lightly tremulous,
　Did all of them bow downward toward that side
　Where its first shadow casts the Holy Mountain.

Dante continues on in this vein about the gentle pleasantness of the earthly Paradise, wherein the birds sing and, along with the sound of the wind, a virtual symphony is heard while sight and hearing are gratified in other ways. This is a "divine forest," as we shall learn, because it was the place God had originally created for us to live in before the Fall. Nothing here is harsh, not even the sunlight, the symbol of God's grace; here it is tempered. All of this is meant to connect back with the rigors of the way up

until now and to show how human life could have been differ-
ent. In fact, the forest at this point may be intended to remind us
of the "dark wood" in which Dante first set out. Now that very
natural surrounding mediates God's bounty as earlier it threat-
ened his absence:

> Already my slow steps had carried me
> > Into the ancient wood so far, that I
> > Could not perceive where I had entered it
> And lo! my further course a stream cut off,
> > Which tow'rd the left hand with its little waves
> > Bent down the grass that on its margin sprang
> All waters that on earth most limpid are
> > Would seem to have within themselves some mixture
> > Compared with that which nothing doth conceal.

We notice that after a few steps—slow steps unlike the striving
course until now—Dante forgets the "way" he has taken, another
echo of the first canto of the *Inferno*. There, it will be recalled,
Dante had lost the "right way" as well. Now he has arrived; even
to rethink how he entered this blessedness would only distract
him from what is before him. There he says he did not recall how
he had entered because he was "so full of sleep"; here he loses
sight of his entry point because he is fully awake and delighted
by everything around him. But an even greater delight comes to
add even higher satisfaction upon that already received:

> A lady all alone, who went along
> > Singing and culling floweret after floweret,
> > With which her pathway was all painted over.
>
> .   .   .   .
>
> As turns herself, with feet together pressed
> > And to the ground, a lady who is dancing,
> > And hardly puts one foot before the other,
> On the vermilion and the yellow flowerets
> > She turned towards me, not in other wise
> > Than maiden who her modest eyes casts down.
>
> .   .   .   .
>
> I do not think there shone so great a light
> > Under the lids of Venus, when transfixed
> > By her own son, beyond his usual custom!

This is Matelda, a figure of the active life, who may refer to some-
one who actually lived around Dante's time, though there has
been no convincing case made for anyone in particular. In any
event, she is the actual culmination of an ease in the world that
poets and others have intuited since the beginning of history as
somehow part of the patrimony of the human race. Many have
tried to achieve this state through a return to the simple life. But
it is Dante's contention that this simple life is only achieved after
the most complex purification of motives and understanding.
The paradox, however, does not negate the reality.

The river that separates Dante from this figure makes him
think of examples from ancient history, a suggestion that we have
not moved from the human to the superhuman just yet. Dante
sees this river as like the Hellespont, the water that separates
Europe from Asia in modern Turkey. In ancient times, it pre-
sented an obstacle to the armies of Xerxes, who was crossing to
invade ancient Greece. It was also the body of water that, in the
myth of Hero and Leander, separated two lovers, forcing one of
them to swim back and forth each night. All of this imagery sug-
gests to us that crossing this little stream will have momentous
consequences. Specifically it will sieve out the kind of earthly
strife the Xerxes reference reminds us about and will unite two
lovers separated by various factors until now.

Matelda explains that this place does not suffer changes of
weather and brings forth different kinds of plants and fruits. But
more important from the standpoint of spiritual progress, she
explains the origins of the stream. Since there is no rain or con-
densation of moisture at this altitude, the stream derives directly
from the divine will for two purposes:

> Upon this side with virtue it descends,
>> Which takes away all memory of sin;
>> On that, of every good deed done restores it.
> Here Lethe, as upon the other side
>> Eunoe, it is called; and worketh not
>> If first on either side it be not tasted.

We may recall that in Hell Dante learned that the river Lethe, one
of the rivers of the underworld according to classical mythology,
flowed down from above. Here we see that it carries all memory

of sin down the mountain of Purgatory and into Hell, where it winds up frozen by the cold blasts from Satan's wings in Cocytus. But Dante also names another stream, Eunoe, really a portion of a single stream with two sides, which restores memories of good deeds. Combined, these waters carry out a process that is necessary for the entry into Heaven. Memory of evil—at least as such—would be inappropriate in Heaven. But if that memory is restored as an occasion for divine grace to work or human repentance to take place, it shifts the understanding of the fault from an imperfection to be lamented to an occasion of spiritual advancement.

The use of classical images here again reminds us that we are still on the border between the highest achievement of human nature without divine grace and the realm of grace proper, which is yet to come.

Matelda underscores this point, paying a final compliment to the things that human wisdom was able to achieve in the ancient world by citing what Dante, in his *Letter to Can Grande*, once called the "scripture of the pagans." Those scriptures were an anticipation—through intuition—of a reality that would become clear only later in history:

> Those who in ancient times have feigned in song
>   The Age of Gold and its felicity,
>   Dreamed of this place perhaps upon Parnassus.
> Here was the human race in innocence;
>   Here evermore was Spring, and every fruit;
>   This is the nectar of which each one speaks.

Canto 29

Matelda walks along the bank and Dante mirrors her motions, hinting at some connection between her as figure of natural rightness and the state in which he now finds himself. But they had not gone a hundred paces when she turned to him and said, "Brother, look and listen!'" What then emerges is one of the most symbolically rich episodes in the entire *Comedy* and warrants some careful attention. First, Dante becomes aware of blinding light:

And lo! a sudden lustre ran across
On every side athwart the spacious forest,
Such that it made me doubt if it were lightning.
But since the lightning ceases as it comes,
And that continuing brightened more and more,
Within my thought I said, "What thing is this?"
And a delicious melody there ran
Along the luminous air, whence holy zeal
Made me rebuke the hardihood of Eve.

. . . .

In front of us like an enkindled fire
Became the air beneath the verdant boughs,
And the sweet sound as singing now was heard.

Dante is so overwhelmed by this vision that he begs the Muses, if ever he labored to follow their inspiration, that they now inspire him to be able to give a good account of what he saw. The first things to emerge are so large that they appear to be seven trees. But as they approach, Dante is able to see that they are actually seven golden candlesticks. Matelda bids him look behind them:

Then saw I people, as behind their leaders,
Coming behind them, garmented in white,
And such a whiteness never was on earth.

This pageant is remarkable enough itself in its color and power. But things almost supernatural also begin to occur. For one thing, the seven candlesticks leave seven lines of color in the sky like a rainbow of pennons over the procession. It is almost as if the candles are paint brushes. All of this follows images in the book of Revelation where the sevenfold spirit of God encompasses everything and twenty-four elders are described as occupying the Heavens:

They all of them were singing: "Blessed thou
Among the daughters of Adam art, and blessed
For evermore shall be thy loveliness."

This procession clearly portends the coming of something still greater, and every detail finds an echo in Scripture or in the Christian tradition. In addition to the sevenfold spirit of God in the Heaven above, the streaks left may suggest the seven sacraments or the gifts of the Holy Spirit, which according to Isaiah are wisdom, understanding, counsel, might, knowledge, pity, and fear of the LORD (11:2–3). The twenty-four elders here are meant to represent the books of the Old Testament, as those were counted by certain authorities during the Middle Ages (we divide some of those and count them differently today). Furthermore, these seem to be identified with the figures mentioned in Revelation 4:4: "And round about the throne were four and twenty seats; and upon the seats I saw four and twenty elders sitting, clothed in white raiment; and they had on their heads crowns of gold." Their song embroiders on the angel Gabriel's annunciation to Mary, and perhaps something more as well. In any event, the immediate sequel to Dante's arrival at the state of restored justice, almost an automatic addition to this state, reflecting its natural openness to transcendence, is the manifestation of the fullness of God, the history of revelation down to the annunciation. And this is just the beginning.

Yet Dante suggests the naturalness of this appearance of the supernatural with appropriate imagery:

> Even as in heaven star followeth after star,
> There came close after them four animals,
> Incoronate each one with verdant leaf.
> Plumed with six wings was every one of them,
> The plumage full of eyes; the eyes of Argus
> If they were living would be such as these.

These four beasts—man, lion, ox, and eagle—were traditionally associated with Matthew, Mark, Luke, and John. Dante's readers would have immediately recognized that reference and the fact that the green crowns on their head symbolize the theological virtue of hope. For us, it is well to note that these four beasts have a far different effect than the three beasts that blocked the way at the beginning of the poem. Just as those induced emotions that prevented Dante from going on, here the sight of such marvels fills him with an expectation to look further into the unfolding revelation of things beyond him.

And what then appears is, if anything, even more symbolically charged than what has gone before:

> The interval between these four contained
>> A chariot triumphal on two wheels,
>> Which by a Griffin's neck came drawn along;
> And upward he extended both his wings
>> Between the middle list and three and three,
>> So that he injured none by cleaving it
> So high they rose that they were lost to sight;
>> His limbs were gold, so far as he was bird,
>> And white the others with vermilion mingled.

The chariot is the church and the Griffin that draws it, being a compound of two natures (eagle and lion), is an image of Christ, who is both divine and human. The wings extend between the bands of color above and are lost to sight just as the heights of Christ's nature extend beyond our vision. The golden limbs of the bird show his divine nature, and the vermilion his human nature.

Amidst all this imagery it is good to keep clear about where it is all leading. We might have expected the procession to end with Christ himself as the Redeemer. But in fact Dante has chosen to make all of sacred history something of a piece that will then recapitulate his own personal mode of realizing the truth. But there are still a few more essential beings to get into the procession before we turn to Dante's particular position in this great divine movement.

> ` . . . Three maidens at the right wheel in a circle
>> Came onward dancing; one so very red
>> That in the fire she hardly had been noted.
> The second was as if her flesh and bones
>> Had all been fashioned out of emerald;
>> The third appeared as snow but newly fallen.
> And now they seemed conducted by the white,
>> Now by the red, and from the song of her
>> The others took their step, or slow or swift.
> Upon the left hand four made holiday
>> Vested in purple, following the measure
>> Of one of them with three eyes in her head.

Anyone familiar with the color symbolism of the church will recognize here the three theological virtues: red for charity, green for hope, and white for faith, followed by the four cardinal virtues (prudence, justice, temperance, fortitude) vested in purple because they are no longer merely natural virtues but infused by charity. Prudence, or wisdom, has three eyes in her head because she has to look out for the proper use of all the rest. And to round out the books of Scripture, we see Luke, the physician, writer of the Acts of the Apostles, and Paul, writer of epistles, with the sharp sword. Then the four writers of personal epistles: Peter, John, James, and Jude, followed by John as writer of the last book of the Bible, the Apocalypse.

And now we have seen pass before us the entirety of the sacred pageant. Dante remains a few feet across the river, on the bank, still separated from all this by a gentle stream of water. Everything until this point belongs to the universal vehicle of salvation for the entire human race. But as salvation is a special event for every person, so shall Dante's final transition across the water be tailored to his life in the world. Great expectation hangs in the air as he observes:

> And when the car was opposite to me
>   Thunder was heard; and all that folk august
>   Seemed to have further progress interdicted,
> There with the vanward ensigns standing still.

Canto 30

And so the stage is set for a great apparition. If Dante were writing simply of this pilgrimage as the general movement toward God of all Christians, Everyman as the medieval book named after him, then we might have expected Christ to appear at this point as the Savior of the Race. But as we have seen from the very outset, Dante is also telling the story of his own personal path toward salvation. The universal means are available to all, but each of us, as time-bound beings, has the message of salvation mediated to us not only through the direct appearance of Christ, but through his church, through parents, relatives, friends, clergy, historical events, and many other ways. What Dante is about to show us here scandalized and continues to scandalize some people, as if typical human interactions were not a channel of divine grace and salvation. And, in fact, his story is also the story of Everyman in the sense that each of us in reality comes to revelation by means of quite personal occurrences. Each of us must learn to notice and appreciate those particulars and to value them in the right way if we are to get the fullness we are meant to acquire from them.

Dante took a long time to "get it," even though he had been led by strong impulses along the path at quite an early age. And it is to the divine reading of Dante's own personal history that the pageant and the whole story of the pilgrimage now have delivered us. Dante says that the seven candlesticks with their flames are like the seven stars of the Big Dipper in that they provide a point of navigation in the heavens the way the constellation provides an indication of the unchanging north on Earth. The difference between the two, however, is that clouds may sometime veil the stars; not so with these lights.

The procession begins a second phase:

> Motionless halted the veracious people,
> > That came at first between it and the Griffin,
> > Turned themselves to the car, as to their peace.
> And one of them, as if by Heaven commissioned,
> > Singing, "Veni, sponsa, de Libano"
> > Shouted three times, and all the others after.
> Even as the Blessed at the final summons
> > Shall rise up quickened each one from his cavern,
> > Uplifting light the reinvested flesh.
> So upon that celestial chariot
> > A hundred rose ad vocem tanti senis,
> > Ministers and messengers of life eternal.
> They all were saying, "Benedictus qui venis,"
> > And, scattering flowers above and round about,
> > "Manibus o date lilia plenis."

The peace to which they turn can only be the salvation of God. And we get several indications of what that means by the singing of the verse, "Come with me from Lebanon, my spouse. . . ." This is from the Song of Solomon and, as we noted in the introduction of the present volume, that biblical text is one of the few that parallels Dante's vision in its view of the beloved as a type of the passionate relationship between God and the soul. Shortly after this verse, the same book asks, "Who is she that comes forth like the morning rising, as beautiful as the moon, as bright as the sun, as awe-inspiring as an army in battle array?" We may find a comparison of the beloved to an army a bit forced, but the overwhelming power of a true love and its capacity to conquer the weaker motions of body and spirit are themes that Dante will invoke from this point until the very end of the *Purgatory*.

The spirits that rise up, like those who shall rise from the dead on the last day, are also singing, "Blessed is he who comes in the name of the Lord!"—a reference to the cries of the crowd upon Christ's triumphal entry into Jerusalem just before his passion and death. Dante keeps the masculine form *"Benedictus"* here when he could have made it feminine had he wished to. And this alerts us to the fact that he is presenting an analogical relationship between the original, masculine Christ who came to save all and the feminine figure through whom that Christ was made manifest to him. And further drama is provided by the citation of a single line from Vergil, "O scatter lilies with full hands!" That line is the last spoken during Aeneas's visit to the other world by his father, Anchises, who is prophesying the future of the Roman Empire. As usual, Dante sees the culmination of his journey as the twin culminations of the Old/New Testament story and the secular history of Rome.

And so, like the sunrise amidst the mists, another source of light now appears to him:

> Thus in the bosom of a cloud of flowers
>> Which from those hands angelical ascended,
>> And downward fell again inside and out,
> Over her snow-white veil with olive cinct
>> Appeared a lady under a green mantle,
>> Vested in colour of the living flame.
> And my own spirit, that already now
>> So long a time had been, that in her presence
>> Trembling with awe it had not stood abashed,
> Without more knowledge having by mine eyes,
>> Through occult virtue that from her proceeded
>> Of ancient love the mighty influence felt.

The apparition so far remains only something intuited rather than fully known. Whoever she is, she is dressed in the colors of the three theological virtues: white veil for faith, green mantle for hope, and living flame (red) for charity. And the cincture of olive around her head and outside the veil indicates her connection with Minerva and therefore with both poetry and wisdom. It is interesting to note as well that, playing on the mystical significance of numbers that was common in his day, Dante has this lady appear in canto 30 and exactly at lines 30–33, reflecting trinitarian significance among the other meanings. The "occult," which is to say, hidden virtue, of this figure shall now become manifest while another beloved figure departs:

> As soon as on my vision smote the power
> Sublime, that had already pierced me through
> Ere from my boyhood I had yet come forth,
> To the left hand I turned with that reliance
> With which the little child runs to his mother,
> When he has fear, or when he is afflicted,
> To say unto Virgilius: "Not a drachm
> Of blood remains in me, that does not tremble;
> I know the traces of the ancient flame."
> But us Virgilius of himself deprived
> Had left, Virgilius, sweetest of all fathers,
> Virgilius, to whom I for safety gave me . . .
> "Dante, because Virgilius has departed
> Do not weep yet, do not weep yet awhile;
> For by another sword thou need'st must weep."

"I know the traces of the ancient flame," a last citation from the beloved Vergil before Dante notices his absence. And as it must be, the arrival of the Christian dispensation does not obliterate but must rise beyond his scope as the representative of even the most fully human things. Dante rightly feels sorrow that this dear guide cannot continue along further with him. Yet he is immediately moved on to other concerns. To begin with, Dante's name is here mentioned—the only time such a thing occurs in the whole *Comedy*—but a fitting first word to be addressed to him by this lady. We often say God knows each of us by name, but the use of Dante's name, which, he says, "of necessity is here recorded," apparently to document the fact that this was a personal address rather than the general Christian call, leads right on to personal business:

> Look at me well; in sooth I'm Beatrice!
> How didst thou deign to come unto the Mountain?
> Didst thou not know that man is happy here?

Another surprise. We might have expected words of consolation and welcome at this point. But in keeping with the whole story of Dante's love for Beatrice and the vicissitudes of that attachment, Beatrice is still a high-spirited lady who puts embarrassing questions to a man who fell short of what he was capable of having done. We do not know yet what Dante is guilty of, though from his *New Life* we may recall infidelities of a philosophical, theological, or perhaps even amorous sort. But whatever the faults, they make Dante ashamed to confront himself:

> Mine eyes fell downward into the clear fountain,
> But, seeing myself therein, I sought the grass,
> So great a shame did weigh my forehead down.
> As to the son the mother seems superb,
> So she appeared to me; for somewhat bitter
> Tasteth the savour of severe compassion.

"Severe" and "compassion" are not normally words we put together like this. But unless the severity provokes personal contrition, the forgiveness of the fault, as the church teaches about the requirements for the sacrament of Penance, cannot effectively be given. Dante says he felt like the frozen snows in the mountains during what followed. Nothing stirred inside of him until a change occurs in the songs of the other figures across the stream:

> But when I heard in their sweet melodies
> Compassion for me, more than had they said,
> "O wherefore, lady, dost thou thus upbraid him?"
> The ice, that was about my heart congealed,
> To air and water changed, and in my anguish
> Through mouth and eyes came gushing from my breast.

And while Dante weeps for his past faults, Beatrice begins a long explanation to those present how it is that the whole of heavenly influences had made a good beginning in Dante (the "new life" in the following line refers both to his early age and the book Dante gave that name), but that they were thwarted by his own weakness and misguided will:

Such had this man become in his new life
   Potentially, that every righteous habit
   Would have made admirable proof in him;
But so much more malignant and more savage
   Becomes the land untilled and with bad seed,
   The more good earthly vigour it possesses.
Some time did I sustain him with my look;
   Revealing unto him my youthful eyes,
   I led him with me turned in the right way.
As soon as ever of my second age
   I was upon the threshold and changed life,
   Himself from me he took and gave to others.
When from the flesh to spirit I ascended,
   And beauty and virtue were in me increased,
   I was to him less dear and less delightful;
And into ways untrue he turned his steps,
   Pursuing the false images of good,
   That never any promises fulfil;
Nor prayer for inspiration me availed,
   By means of which in dreams and otherwise
   I called him back, so little did he heed them.
So low he fell, that all appliances
   For his salvation were already short,
   Save showing him the people of perdition.
For this I visited the gates of death,
   And unto him, who so far up has led him,
   My intercessions were with weeping borne.
God's lofty fiat would be violated,
   If Lethe should be passed, and if such viands
   Should tasted be, withouten any scot
Of penitence, that gushes forth in tears.

So here we have it openly. As a soul about to enter the celestial realms, Dante needs to taste the waters of Lethe to forget the evil in his sins. No soul may do so that does not first show penitence through tears. Beatrice was the instrument that rescued him in his deepest moment, which is to say, divine grace pursues us and will not abandon us until we turn back toward it even amidst the consequences of our sins. So she now has the role of encouraging him to the final step of full contrition and entry into the happiness of the life beyond the stream. Divine justice, "God's lofty fiat," requires that this last price be paid.

Canto 31

Beatrice continues pressing this personal examination in the same vein until finally:

> Confusion and dismay together mingled
>> Forced such a Yes! from out my mouth, that sight
>> Was needful to the understanding of it.

As we know when confronted with our own need to confess some shameful episode, it is hard. Dante's admission was so weak that it could be seen better than it could be heard. But even this weak admission has far-reaching effects; confession of wrongdoing in the Christian cosmos brings about forgiveness. God already knows our sins; it is when we acknowledge them and the guilt they naturally incur that God's mercy and salvation can come more fully into play. But Beatrice is not content with a general confession. She rubs Dante's nose in it for a while, first pointing out what should have been his behavior after her death and then hinting at some personal particulars so that Dante (who, after all, will be returning to the world and will face fresh temptations, as we all do) will be better prepared for the future:

> "In those desires of mine
>> Which led thee to the loving of that good,
>> Beyond which there is nothing to aspire to,
> What trenches lying traverse or what chains
>> Didst thou discover, that of passing onward
>> Thou shouldst have thus despoiled thee of the hope?
> And what allurements or what vantages
>> Upon the forehead of the others showed,
>> That thou shouldst turn thy footsteps unto them?"
> After the heaving of a bitter sigh,
>> Hardly had I the voice to make response,
>> And with fatigue my lips did fashion it
> Weeping I said: "The things that present were
>> With their false pleasure turned aside my steps,
>> Soon as your countenance concealed itself."

Beatrice already knows all this and both to purify him and to warn him for the future makes herself a lesson:

> . . . Never to thee presented art or nature
>> Pleasure so great as the fair limbs wherein

> I was enclosed, which scattered are in earth.
> And if the highest pleasure thus did fail thee
>> By reason of my death, what mortal thing
>> Should then have drawn thee into its desire?

Dante is too old and wise a bird to be taken by simple tricks, and he feels the sting to his manhood in her final rebuke to him to lift up his "beard":

> "If thou
> In hearing sufferest pain, lift up thy beard
> And thou shalt feel a greater pain in seeing". . .
> So pricked me then the thorn of penitence,
>> That of all other things the one which turned me
>> Most to its love became the most my foe.
> Such self-conviction stung me at the heart
>> O'erpowered I fell, and what I then became
>> She knoweth who had furnished me the cause.

Now that Dante is returning to the fullness of his right relation to Beatrice and, as shall soon become apparent, to Christ, arguments are less forceful than what he can see. Thus, what causes him to love becomes his "foe" in the sense that it convicts him of having used much lesser things to try to assuage his lack of Beatrice, when the memory and reality of her should have stayed with him. He faints and wakes up to find himself in the water of the stream with the lady Matelda, who is saying, "Hold me, hold me." This figure of natural innocence will now take him through the last step of his liberation from his misguided past:

> Up to my throat she in the stream had drawn me,
>> And, dragging me behind her, she was moving
>> Upon the water lightly as a shuttle.
> When I was near unto the blessed shore,
>> "Asperges me," I heard so sweetly sung,
>> Remember it I cannot, much less write it
> The beautiful lady opened wide her arms,
>> Embraced my head, and plunged me underneath,
>> Where I was forced to swallow of the water.

Having drunk of Lethe, the water that removes the sting of past evil deeds, Dante is led by a group of nymphs to see the emerald green eyes of Beatrice in which divine light is reflected. Many poets, echoing Dante's discovery, have sung of seeing God in the beloved's eyes. Dante will show how, at least in his own case, this mediation of universal salvation through his beloved is quite literally, if mysteriously, true:

> "We here are Nymphs, and in the Heaven are stars;
>   Ere Beatrice descended to the world,
>   We as her handmaids were appointed her.
> We'll lead thee to her eyes; but for the pleasant
>   Light that within them is, shall sharpen thine
>   The three beyond, who more profoundly look."
> Thus singing they began; and afterwards
>   Unto the Griffin's breast they led me with them,
>   Where Beatrice was standing, turned towards us.
> "See that thou dost not spare thine eyes," they said;
>   "Before the emeralds have we stationed thee,
>   Whence Love aforetime drew for thee his weapons."
> A thousand longings, hotter than the flame,
>   Fastened mine eyes upon those eyes relucent,
>   That still upon the Griffin steadfast stayed.
> As in a glass the sun, not otherwise
>   Within them was the twofold monster shining,
>   Now with the one, now with the other nature.

Beatrice's eyes here are literally a mirror for the divine reality that is both human and superhuman. Dante's imagery is quite striking: he might still be able to discern this Griffin, Christ, without Beatrice, but he would already have had to undertake quite a journey to encounter him. His personal history—and the history of almost all of us who arrive at a belief in God through human vessels—is to see the two natures in one person reflected in a specific person on Earth. And the Nymphs now entreat Beatrice, since Dante has confessed and drunken of the waters that heal even the memory of the past, that she turn her eyes on this wayward, yet—finally—faithful admirer "Who has to see thee ta'en so many steps." Dante has now received absolution and crossed over the last divide between him and his lady. The whole of Purgatory has been traversed. His pilgrimage through the earthly realms draws to an end. But there are two cantos remaining in which certain visions are granted to him before he passes into Paradise proper. These visions are also highly symbolic, as the pageant in the earthly Paradise has been. Reading them in their entirety is the best way to appreciate Dante's genius as both a poet and a spiritual guide. Here, however, we shall only touch on the major points of a much richer and more wide-ranging vision.

Canto 32

Vision in itself here begins to be a central subject of the poem. In the *Paradise*, Dante will gradually have to accustom his eyes to the excess of light, beyond our mortal power to bear, just as in Hell he had to accustom himself to foul odors and cries of overwhelming evil. We get a foretaste of the overwhelming light at the very beginning of the next canto, when the pilgrim, who had waited ten years since Beatrice's death for this chance to see her again, stares too much upon the lady in his newly purified state and finds himself momentarily blinded by the divine light he sees reflected from her.

A curious vision then ensues, and the best commentators on Dante regard it as a symbolic representation of the plight of the world in Dante's time, bringing the salvation story down from Christ's day to Dante's own time. First, the procession reverses itself in a kind of wheeling military maneuver, a hint at what is often called the Church Militant, the church that must do battle with the various evil forces in the world that seek to corrupt or destroy it. The Griffin (Christ) draws the chariot (church) near a tree, the forbidden tree of the knowledge of good and evil that was involved in the Fall. But the Griffin, as restored man, does not seek the fruit of this tree and by obeying where Adam disobeyed redeems the race. The attendants sing:

> "Blessed art thou, O Griffin, who dost not
>   Pluck with thy beak these branches sweet to taste,
>   Since appetite by this was turned to evil."
> After this fashion round the tree robust
>   The others shouted; and the twofold creature:
>   "Thus is preserved the seed of all the just."

The words of the Griffin recorded here reinforce that doing right preserves the just. But in added significance, he harnesses the pole of the chariot, which Dante's readers would have known was in the form of a cross, to the tree. The symbolism here is worth noting: Christ draws the church through the cross and the tree of the cross, as was sometimes argued during the Middle Ages, must be related to the tree that caused the Fall, so that the original error, turned back against itself, might restore God's original intention for the human race.

When these two "trees" are united, Dante is overcome by what may be a kind of sleep of the just, but his brief slumber alerts us that something quite unprecedented will follow. First, he hears the figures sing a hymn never before heard on Earth; then he begins to drift. But a bright light and someone calling him awaken him, and he is like the three apostles blinded by Christ's transfiguration.

He awakens to see Beatrice sitting on the root of this tree with her seven handmaids, in the symbolic language of Dante's day, clearly a figure of earthly Wisdom with the seven virtues. And the fact that the Griffin is ascending into the heavens with the other figures we have previously encountered indicates that Beatrice is the wisdom left with the church as Christ ascended and left behind the record of revelation and the human ability to make use of it. Beatrice directs Dante's attention to the vision that is about to unfold and, unusually, tells him to make sure to write of it when he returns—Wisdom, perhaps, wishing to record a cautionary history for the sake of those struggling with various difficulties:

> Short while shalt thou be here a forester,
>> And thou shalt be with me for evermore
>> A citizen of that Rome where Christ is Roman.
> Therefore, for that world's good which liveth ill,
>> Fix on the car thine eyes, and what thou seest,
>> Having returned to earth, take heed thou write.

The mention of Rome alerts us that Dante will be writing a political as well as a religious vision. Immediately there begins a series of seven calamities that have overtaken the church and that call for redress. We shall go through them schematically for what they tell us about Dante's views of history.

First, an image appears of the depredations of the Roman Empire (eagle) against the church during the early persecutions.

With this Dante returns to an old theme with him: the incursions by the temporal power against the spiritual, which has taken many odd twists throughout the Christian era. Second, he sees the church besieged by heretics, whom St. Augustine had compared to foxes in their craftiness at deluding those within with what appear to be authentically Christian words. As Wisdom, Beatrice takes an active role here in defense of the church against the foxes. Third, the eagle returns, but this time not to ravage so much as to corrupt by handing over part of his temporal power, in the form of his plumes, to a church that Dante thought should only possess spiritual authority. Coming after the period of persecution and the appearance of heresies in the first few Christian centuries, this is doubtless a reference to the ill-starred Donation of Constantine, which got the church involved in the pursuit of wealth and power.

Fourth, an even more serious threat appears:

> Methought, then, that the earth did yawn between
> > Both wheels, and I saw rise from it a Dragon,
> > Who through the chariot upward fixed his tail,
> And as a wasp that draweth back its sting,
> > Drawing unto himself his tail malign,
> > Drew out the floor, and went his way rejoicing.

Commentators disagree over the meaning of this image, but the best interpretation seems to be that Mohammedanism, here, as in the *Inferno*, regarded as a kind of Christian heresy, has introduced division at a certain historical moment in the very body of Christendom.

At that, further temporal corruptions begin to flourish during what we would call the Dark Ages. Dante's way of presenting a fifth calamity is as follows:

> That which remained behind, even as with grass
> > A fertile region, with the feathers, offered
> > Perhaps with pure intention and benign,
> Reclothed itself, and with them were reclothed
> > The pole and both the wheels so speedily,
> > A sigh doth longer keep the lips apart.

Corruption has taken advantage of a fertile soil on which to breed so that every part of the church is now covered. But a sixth phase deepens these corruptions. With a bizarre series of images drawn from the book of Revelation, Dante seems to suggest that the seven deadly sins in the form of horned heads then sprouted at the key points in the church. And in a final image drawn from the book of Revelation, Dante brings this symbolic account of church history down to his own time by comparing the church to a whore committing fornication with the kings of the Earth in the form of a giant.

Canto 33

It may appear odd that at these altitudes Dante is still so concerned with church and empire. But it accords well with his spirituality, which allows for the individual nature of spiritual insight and progress but is never merely individualistic. In a fallen world, church and state must operate together to help repair the damage done by the Fall. Without their institutional order, not even individual repentance can restore the public order and spiritual atmosphere needed for a good human life. We tend to think either that institutions are unnecessary or that we can achieve perfection by our own power. Dante sees all the truly human things as necessary to one another.

Dante's personal story demonstrates how far short he came of that perfection because "his school," which probably means mere human wisdom, could not reach the divine. Beatrice promises:

>   . . . Truly from this time forward shall my words
>   Be naked, so far as it is befitting
>   To lay them open unto thy rude gaze.

And with this promise which will be fulfilled in *Paradiso,* Dante is led to the pure fountain from which all the other living waters on Earth come forth. Drinking at the original source will restore Dante to his full virtue and prepare him for still greater marvels. Beatrice instructs her nymphs:

>   ". . . Eunoe behold, that yonder rises;
>   Lead him to it, and, as thou art accustomed,
>   Revive again the half-dead virtue in him . . ."

If, Reader, I possessed a longer space
   For writing it, I yet would sing in part
   Of the sweet draught that ne'er would satiate me;
But inasmuch as full are all the leaves
   Made ready for this second canticle,
   The curb of art no farther lets me go.
From the most holy water I returned
   Regenerate, in the manner of new trees
   That are renewed with a new foliage,
 Pure and disposed to mount unto the stars.

Chapter 3

"Everywhere in Heaven
Is Paradise"

Of all the realms of the world beyond, the one that seems to present the fewest and smallest difficulties for a modern person is Heaven. If there is an afterlife, we assume, God must forgive everything or, even if he does not, at least reasonably decent people will get to Heaven and be happy there—somehow. Just to state the common, unanalyzed view reveals how many questions lurk behind this Heaven that so many people, Christians among them, take for granted. But Dante, and all of Christendom before the modern age, took Heaven quite seriously, if that is the right way to speak of the realm of supreme joy and happiness. They were concerned with how to get there, which has made up much of the story of *Inferno* and *Purgatory*. And they sought to understand what such a condition might be like, since it might help them to understand how to live in this world.

Dante feels no shame whatever in speaking of Heaven as similar to things we find excellent in this life, such as piercing light and sound, rich metals and gems, and, above all, supreme joy and love. In this, he also differs from us. Many modern Christians scoff at these material analogies for Heaven, as if the Christian's duty to rise above material wealth and display makes such comparisons juvenile. But the Bible itself is not reluctant to use these same material representations for realities that everyone from St. Paul to Dante to Mother Teresa have known were only weak shadows of the glory to come. If we are unwilling to use these humble earthly signs for what exceeds our experience, we will be forced to remain silent not only about Heaven but also about God, the angels, salvation, and all the things that revelation in God's mercy has wished to communicate to us. An apophatic theology might so refrain; a theological poet cannot.

So our initial problem is that not only the biblical and Dantesque images, but any image of the highest things, embarrasses us. As George Orwell once put it, the only thing Christians could offer at the end of it all was "a choir practice in a jeweler's shop." If truth be told, that childish image of Heaven exists in all of us to a certain extent. It would not be so bad if we retained a child's simple delight in bright colors and sounds, mysteries and laughter, and a host of other things that most adults feel they have outgrown. But most adults do not try to recover that original innocence through the kind of discipline and self-knowledge we have seen emerging up to this point in the poem. Nor do they normally try to work out a vision of Heaven that is more sophisticated, while remaining faithful to the suggestions in the Scriptures.

Another difficulty is that in the modern world in particular we have highly valued the fulfillment of work because it seems to give our lives meaning even on a mundane level. Further, we think respect for all sorts of work is a solid democratic idea, so that the cleaning lady and the lady she cleans for may both be honorable persons doing good in the world. But what will we do when work of the kind with which we are familiar is no longer necessary? Can an authentically *human* existence continue without the spur of things that need doing? The great twentieth-century American architect Frank Lloyd Wright rewrote the words to Bach's hymn "Jesu, Joy of Man's Desiring," to read "Joy in work is man's desiring," and had it sung on Sundays at his art colony Taliesin. There is probably no better measure of the modern belief that a person without work to do is nothing.

Then there is love. Love is Dante's great theme, as it is the great theme of the Bible in both testaments. But how is love to operate in Heaven? Most of us would agree that people in Heaven are "with God," a true but weak affirmation. More speculative persons might venture the opinion that somehow we are all absorbed back into the Love that is God himself. Despite centuries of Christian teaching, we often picture Heaven as a kind of light in which all is one with God. Yet the entire biblical tradition leads us to believe that, even at the height of the beatific vision, individual identity will remain; otherwise there would be no need for love since there would not be two beings present who might exchange such love. So in Heaven, the nature of love itself —where no one has need of anything or need to do anything in the usual meaning of those words—also becomes hard to fathom.

Until now, we have primarily been concerned to learn about evil in order to shun it; to purge the vices that have made the soul limp and crooked so that it can follow its God-given impulses to its proper goal; and we have looked at how the institutions of church and empire help make the pilgrimage to Heaven smoother. But now we have to look at happiness and joy themselves without any cause in temporal actions. Most of us have a vague sense that it is possible to love another person by putting his or her needs ahead of your own. And we all have periods of earthly happiness and perhaps even joy. But the kind of free joy that Heaven entails we can barely understand. As the modern French poet Charles Péguy once said of the kingdom of Christian joy:

> We enter here . . . into an unknown realm, into a foreign realm which is the realm of joy. A hundred times less known, a hundred times stranger, a hundred times less 'us' than the kingdoms of sorrow. A hundred times more profound, I believe, and a hundred times more fecund. Happy are those who some day will have some idea of what it is.

In the final analysis, it is our uncertainty about the very existence of such a degree of happiness and joy that lies at the back of all the other problems with Heaven. When we are full of joy and hope, singing in a jeweler's shop sounds as wonderful as anything. When we are full of joy and hope—and everyone around us is as well—we feel very little need to bolster our own sense of self-worth through work. Not as Wright thought is "Joy in work" man's desiring, but joy and happiness with or without our human work constitute our true desire. It may seem a small difference, but a joy that lasts beyond all efforts into eternity requires no little work to comprehend. That is the realm we are entering now, and we will be happy indeed if Dante enables us to form some idea of it.

Canto 1

The glory of Him who moveth everything
    Doth penetrate the universe, and shine
    In one part more and in another less.
Within that heaven which most his light receives
    Was I, and things beheld which to repeat
    Nor knows, nor can, who from above descends;
Because in drawing near to its desire
    Our intellect ingulphs itself so far,
    That after it the memory cannot go.
Truly whatever of the holy realm
    I had the power to treasure in my mind
    Shall now become the subject of my song.
O good Apollo, for this last emprise
    Make of me such a vessel of thy power
    As giving the beloved laurel asks!
One summit of Parnassus hitherto
    Has been enough for me, but now with both
    I needs must enter the arena left.

In the introduction to the present volume, we looked briefly at the first three lines of this passage as an expression of Dante's syntheses of various truths about the universe. Now that we have traversed the two other eternal realms, the meaning of the whole passage becomes even clearer. As Dante says in his letter to Can Grande, we know that God is everywhere because we can read in many places in Scripture passages such as this one from Psalm 139: "Whither shall I go from thy Spirit? And whither shall I flee from thy presence? If I ascend up into heaven, thou art there; if I descend into hell, thou art there also" (vv. 7–8). In Jeremiah, the Holy Spirit says, "Do I not fill heaven and earth?" (23:24). And the book of Wisdom states, "The Spirit of the Lord has filled the whole world" (1:7). Once we reflect on it, this fact appears a truism, but Dante is about to lead us through an experience by which both he as pilgrim and we as reader can begin to *see and experience* what we may only accept notionally.

That seeing depends on the soul's ability to grow into a greater capacity to absorb the universal light. Both modern cosmology and Genesis agree that the first few instants after the Creation seem to fulfill literally God's command, "Let there be light." To mount again toward that primal light will require an expansion of soul and of vision that, while not exactly painful, since we are now in Paradise, calls for a turning away from past errors, weaknesses, and limitations to a wide range of new human powers.

One of the distinctions that must immediately be drawn, however, is that while God is omnipresent he is not omnipresent, even in heaven, in a uniform way. It has always been difficult for human imagination to conceive of Heaven, and most people today, unfortunately, can only think of it as a kind of blazing light. But that gives us a very empty notion of divinity and would actually make God in Heaven less interesting than the varied world with which we are familiar. The "glory" of God that we encounter in Paradise reveals itself to have two primary dimensions: it is the absolute being that gives relative being to all other creatures, and it is the primary source of all the "essences," or diverse natures, that we see in the world. In his letter commenting on the *Paradise*, Dante specifies that the glory "penetrates, as to essence; shines forth, as to being."

But this glory is difficult to get a grip on. For one thing it transcends simple human experience. And for another, it cannot be told in human speech. As Dante goes on to say: "we see many things by the intellect for which there are no vocal signs, of which Plato gives sufficient hint in his books by having recourse to metaphors; for he saw many things by intellectual light which he could not express in direct speech." For us, this sounds as if "poetry," in the negative sense of made-up stories, is all that we can produce when we turn our minds to such matters. But it will be Dante's constant effort in this cantica to make the poetry point beyond itself to an experience that the mature soul must seek for itself. The invocation to Apollo here, god of poetry and of the sun, is meant to link the two together in our mind for the effort that must now be made. All this will become clearer as both Dante, the pilgrim in the poem and we, as pilgrims journeying by reading him, literally become more accustomed to the elemental light in these realms.

One sign that Dante wants us to find a literal truth behind the metaphors he will need to use is that he immediately turns to the astronomical science of his day for a reference point:

To mortal men by passages diverse
　　Uprises the world's lamp; but by that one
　　Which circles four uniteth with three crosses,
With better course and with a better star
　　Conjoined it issues, and the mundane wax
　　Tempers and stamps more after its own fashion.

It is worth lingering in this opening canto on this technical statement. The sun rises at different points on the horizon at different seasons of the year, but the point at which medieval astronomy thought the first sunrise occurred at the beginning of the world was its position at the vernal equinox, that is, around Easter time. The resurrection into eternal life and the ancient emergence of creatures into the light of being, then, were closely related. And at that time of year in the medieval scheme, four circles—the horizon, the equator, the zodiac, and what they called the colure of the equinox—all intersected (forming three crosses) at the point they held at the moment of creation. Dante probably wants to continue adding meanings to these scientific facts with the notion that these four circles, perfect geometric figures, symbolize the four cardinal virtues, while the three crosses, the Christian symbols, reflect the theological virtues. In short, everything is in position as if a new creation had just occurred, as, indeed, it has with the entry of his soul into Paradise.

Furthermore, he adds that the time is high noon, when the light of the sun is strongest (the descent to Hell began at evening and the ascent of Purgatory at morning) :

When Beatrice towards the left-hand side
　　I saw turned round, and gazing at the sun;
　　Never did eagle fasten so upon it!
And even as a second ray is wont
　　To issue from the first and reascend,
　　Like to a pilgrim who would fain return,
Thus of her action, through the eyes infused
　　In my imagination, mine I made,
　　And sunward fixed mine eyes beyond our wont.
There much is lawful which is here unlawful
　　Unto our powers, by virtue of the place
　　Made for the human species as its own.
Not long I bore it, nor so little while

> But I beheld it sparkle round about
> Like iron that comes molten from the fire;
> And suddenly it seemed that day to day
> Was added, as if He who has the power
> Had with another sun the heaven adorned.

The medievals believed that only an eagle's eye was strong enough to look directly at the sun, and that majestic bird, with its ability to soar off, is first in Dante's mind. Then he immediately thinks of a scientific fact again, how a ray of light striking a mirror reflects back upward and seems to yearn to return from where it came. All creatures are starting to become "mirrors" of the divine for Dante as his vision adjusts to the light. And even at this first encounter with the new reality, he feels as if day had been added to what was already the brightest day on earth.

Since we are not merely describing an objective reality here, but the expanding powers of the soul, Dante turns to another poetical metaphor drawn from classical mythology:

> With eyes upon the everlasting wheels
> Stood Beatrice all intent, and I, on her
> Fixing my vision from above removed,
> Such at her aspect inwardly became
> As Glaucus, tasting of the herb that made him
> Peer of the other gods beneath the sea.

Prior to this, we have not paused much to comment on such poetic flourishes, but this one has particular relevance to the spiritual process occurring within Dante. Glaucus was a fisherman in ancient Greece who laid his catch one day on grass that had magical power to bring them back to life and send them back into the sea. Glaucus himself chewed some of this grass and was changed into a sea god. Given that Dante will shortly refer to the entire universe as a "great sea of being," we cannot help but notice that what he is describing as happening within himself is an expansion of spiritual power into superhuman realms. In fact, he follows this image with the statement:

> To represent transhumanise in words
> Impossible were; the example, then, suffice
> Him for whom Grace the experience reserves.

This is one of Dante's strongest statements that over and above the poetical journey, he hopes to lead us to where we ourselves might experience what cannot be presented merely in words.

He says that, like St. Paul's description of his own rapture in 2 Corinthians, he did not know whether he was still in his body or only a soul now, but he does know that he saw an immense lake of light and heard the "music of the spheres," the harmonious sounds that the ancient world thought emanated from the planets and stars as they moved through space. One of the reasons we are so moved by music, they thought, is that it can transport us back to our origins in this realm of harmonious sound.

But Dante's soul is only beginning to open to reality and his imagination is more of a hindrance than a help in dealing with this spectacle:

> The newness of the sound and the great light
>> Kindled in me a longing for their cause,
>> Never before with such acuteness felt;
> Whence she, who saw me as I saw myself,
>> To quiet in me my perturbed mind,
>> Opened her mouth, ere I did mine to ask,
> And she began: "Thou makest thyself so dull
>> With false imagining, that thou seest not
>> What thou wouldst see if thou hadst shaken it
> Thou art not upon earth, as thou believest;
>> But lightning, fleeing its appropriate site,
>> Ne'er ran as thou, who thitherward returnest."

Imagination itself will have to expand to take in what shall henceforth be encountered. And this faculty of the soul, that seems so capacious, must be exercised properly to measure up to the demand.

Beatrice, with a kind of motherly solicitude, warmly turns toward him to explain:

> "All things whate'er they be
>> Have order among themselves, and this is form,
>> That makes the universe resemble God.
>
> . . . .
>
> And thither now, as to a site decreed,
>> Bears us away the virtue of that cord
>> Which aims its arrows at a joyous mark.

. . . .
So likewise from this course doth deviate
   Sometimes the creature, who the power possesses,
   —Though thus impelled, to swerve some other way,
(In the same wise as one may see the fire
   Fall from a cloud,) if the first impetus
   Earthward is wrested by some false delight.
Thou shouldst not wonder more, if well I judge,
   At thine ascent, than at a rivulet
   From some high mount descending to the lowland.
Marvel it would be in thee, if deprived
   Of hindrance, thou wert seated down below,
   As if on earth the living fire were quiet."
Thereat she heavenward turned again her face.

We already learned some of this lore in canto 17 of the *Purgatory,*
but it is significant that it is repeated here by Beatrice for Dante.
Beatrice was the means by which Dante's spirit was first opened
up to the universe of love. In the personal way of salvation that
Dante is describing, it is only proper that she should be the one
who now encourages him both to see and open up to a world
larger than anything he could conceive of earlier. She reminds
him that souls on earth turn aside from the destination the "bow
of love" shoots them toward. But in the last line quoted, she turns
her own gaze back to heaven, from which she receives the light
that dazzles Dante and toward which they both now will be mak-
ing constantly closer approach. Earlier there has been a correc-
tion of mind and will according to an objective scheme in
preparation for the real ascent. Now intellect, will, and emotion
are being combined in Dante's subjective experience in ways that
suggest much for our own path as well. What we learn after this
is really only learned as it is internalized, acted on, and properly
savored by the soul.

Canto 2

   O ye, who in some pretty little boat,
      Eager to listen, have been following
      Behind my ship, that singing sails along,
   Turn back to look again upon your shores;

> Do not put out to sea, lest peradventure,
>> In losing me, you might yourselves be lost.
> The sea I sail has never yet been passed;
>> Minerva breathes, and pilots me Apollo,
>> And Muses nine point out to me the Bears.
> Ye other few who have the neck uplifted
>> Betimes to th' bread of Angels upon which
>> One liveth here and grows not sated by it,
> Well may you launch upon the deep salt-sea
>> Your vessel, keeping still my wake before you
>> Upon the water that grows smooth again.

This is one of the most curious invocations and invitations to the voyage in all of literature. To begin with, Dante the writer is discouraging a certain type of reader from continuing further. He uses the sea imagery with which we have become familiar at other points in the journey to suggest the immense expanse of the "sea of being" and the "little boat" that is our pilgrim spirit within it. But other than the immensity of the sea, why the warning? A few clues appear in this passage. Dante says he is guided by Minerva, the classical goddess of wisdom, and Apollo, the god of poetry, along with his nine Muses toward the "Bears," the constellations that contain the North Star, the fixed point by which mariners navigate. So Dante is initially counseling prudence: do not foolishly set on this vast expanse unless you have the necessary knowledge and skills; otherwise you will lose yourself.

He continues with a distinction: whoever has already eaten of the Bread of Angels—the rigorous study of philosophy and theology—may follow him into this new realm without fear of getting lost. But at the same time, we need to stick close to him because, as when a ship passes, the wake is visible for a while, but the waters quickly grow smooth and trackless again. Dante is not denying that we all have inborn capacity to reach Heaven. Rather, he is warning that a certain self-formation is necessary as a prerequisite to properly appraising divine things. And with that, he plunges into an illustration.

> Upward gazed Beatrice, and I at her;
>> And in such space perchance as strikes a bolt
>> And flies, and from the notch unlocks itself,

Arrived I saw me where a wondrous thing
    Drew to itself my sight. . . .

In the unfolding of Paradise to which we have come, this passage
represents a kind of spiritual reversal. Beatrice is fixed on God,
Dante on Beatrice, and the result is that the order of events as we
experience them in this world is almost overthrown. Instead of
some act of ours resulting in some consequence, here the connec-
tion with the Almighty is the beginning of everything. So much
is this the case that Dante describes their ascent to the sphere of
the moon, which is swift as the flight of an arrow, from the end
backward. The bolt "strikes," then "flies," then "unnotches" itself
from the bowstring, which is to say that it arrives at its intended
point so immediately that the preceding steps of its motion seem
secondary in retrospect. In this realm, the spiritual end almost
seems to produce the means retroactively.

   They ascend to the moon, and Dante describes the first
extraterrestrial body he encounters in precise details:

It seemed to me a cloud encompassed us,
    Luminous, dense, consolidate and bright
    As adamant on which the sun is striking.
Into itself did the eternal pearl
    Receive us, even as water doth receive
    A ray of light, remaining still unbroken.
If I was body, (and we here conceive not
    How one dimension tolerates another,
    Which needs must be if body enter body,)
More the desire should be enkindled in us
    That essence to behold, wherein is seen
    How God and our own nature were united.
There will be seen what we receive by faith,
    Not demonstrated, but self-evident
    In guise of the first truth that man believes.

This is a complicated passage and confirms that Dante has reason
to warn us about entering onto this part of the journey without
prior preparation. Let us take its points back to front. The "first
truth" referred to in the last line is not some intuition of God, but
what philosophers call the law of non-contradiction, that some-
thing cannot both be and not be in the same way at the same
time. Dante may seem to be saying here that the law of non-

PARADISE

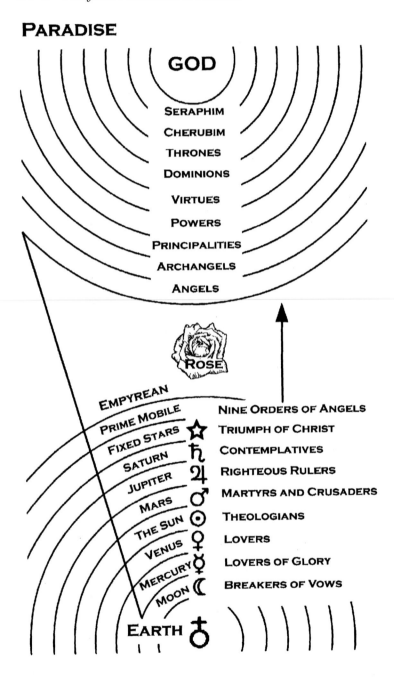

GOD

SERAPHIM
CHERUBIM
THRONES
DOMINIONS
VIRTUES
POWERS
PRINCIPALITIES
ARCHANGELS
ANGELS

ROSE

EMPYREAN — NINE ORDERS OF ANGELS
PRIME MOBILE — TRIUMPH OF CHRIST
FIXED STARS ☆ — CONTEMPLATIVES
SATURN ♄ — CONTEMPLATIVES
JUPITER ♃ — RIGHTEOUS RULERS
MARS ♂ — MARTYRS AND CRUSADERS
THE SUN ☉ — THEOLOGIANS
VENUS ♀ — LOVERS
MERCURY ☿ — LOVERS OF GLORY
MOON ☾ — BREAKERS OF VOWS
EARTH ♁

contradiction will be exploded with notions like the God-man or two bodies occupying the same space. But in fact, he is pointing us toward a truth that will be as self-evident to us in Heaven as the law of non-contradiction is to us on Earth. And a foretaste of that experience is provided in the way the two wayfarers enter this perfect pearl that seems like the stone adamant but also permits them to enter as a ray of light does water, which is to say without disturbance to the medium.

We shall begin to see the spiritual significance of all this shortly. Dante and Beatrice will be penetrating ever more deeply into a reality that is far more substantial than this world and yet at the same time is receptive and unresisting to their desire to move ever deeper. In terms of the human self, this means that we are becoming more our real selves at the very same moment that we are turning away from the superficial self to find our deepest roots in the whole of reality. We enter these high existences like the arrow: rapidly, with force and authority, on the one hand, and like the light in the water on the other, harmlessly, almost statically.

Dante tells Beatrice he is as grateful as he can be to Him "who has removed me from the mortal world," but he has a question: Why do the dark spots on the moon exist? Beatrice welcomes this question because it reminds Dante that the senses and reason have only a limited scope. Dante believes the spots are caused by variations in density, but Beatrice says that this would make the Moon merely the effect of one principle while Dante shall see that, in fact, there are many influences operating in Heaven. She even counsels him to try a scientific experiment, "The fountain to the river of your arts," that will show him that he is mistaken. The recourse to experiment, which might seem to us out of place in Heaven, is really a restatement of Dante's earlier contention that we shall experience truths above that are obscure to us here.

Beatrice uses an interesting image:

> Now, as beneath the touches of warm rays
>   Naked the subject of the snow remains
>   Both of its former colour and its cold,
> Thee thus remaining in thy intellect
>   Will I inform with such a living light
>   That it shall tremble in its aspect to thee.

This "unfreezing" of Dante's intellect is significant, because it will turn the hardened understanding of things as merely variations of matter into a liquid, flowing, and illuminated sense of how all things proceed from a single origin in God, refracted through his deliberate creations so as to manifest the fullness of their source. The canto concludes with Beatrice telling Dante to listen well so that after this he will become himself capable of understanding such things without needing any other guide:

> The power and motion of the holy spheres,
>> As from the artisan the hammer's craft,
>> Forth from the blessed motors must proceed.
> The heaven, which lights so manifold make fair,
>> From the Intelligence profound, which turns it,
>> The image takes and makes of it a seal.
> And even as the soul within your dust
>> Through members different and accommodated
>> To faculties diverse expands itself,
> So likewise this Intelligence diffuses
>> Its virtue multiplied among the stars.
>> Itself revolving on its unity.
>
> . . . .
>
> From this proceeds whatever from light to light
>> Appeareth different, not from dense and rare:
>> This is the formal principle that produces,
> According to its goodness, dark and bright.

As we have seen in other places, our natural tendency to limit our horizons to the interplay of bodies and forces in this world freezes our understanding in a doctrinaire materialism. Dante has purged himself of various faults along the way, but he is now setting out on a sea upon which it is not enough to have left behind faults. We must now have our minds and souls in direct contact with the unity behind the diversity that is the full truth about both ourselves and the universe. It is no accident that Dante compares the universe animated by God to the body animated by the soul at this point. Various theological and philosophical systems have conceived of God as a kind of World Soul. But the force of the comparison here reveals a further spiritual significance because the recognition of the true state of things in the cosmos helps us to understand the true state of things in ourselves. The truth is that we are all derived from the one origin while retaining, even up to the highest degree of contemplation, individuality for all eternity.

Canto 3

Now that we have had a lesson in the basic orientation of heavenly intellect, Dante devotes several cantos to clarifying the nature of heavenly will. That process continues in a two-plied fashion here that reminds us that we not only need to know what is true and right but must also will to remain faithful to it, both when it is easy and when it is difficult.

Dante's attention is drawn to something in the pearl of the moon:

> Such as through polished and transparent glass,
>   Or waters crystalline and undisturbed,
>   But not so deep as that their bed be lost,
> Come back again the outlines of our faces
>   So feeble, that a pearl on forehead white
>   Comes not less speedily unto our eyes;
> Such saw I many faces prompt to speak,
>   So that I ran in error opposite
>   To that which kindled love 'twixt man and fountain.
> As soon as I became aware of them,
>   Esteeming them as mirrored semblances,
>   To see of whom they were, mine eyes I turned,
> And nothing saw, and once more turned them forward
>   Direct into the light of my sweet Guide,
>   Who smiling kindled in her holy eyes.
> "Marvel thou not," she said to me, "because
>   I smile at this thy puerile conceit,
>   Since on the truth it trusts not yet its foot,
> But turns thee, as 'tis wont, on emptiness.
>   True substances are these which thou beholdest."

As we note in the opening image of this passage, the souls in the pearl-like moon are themselves pearl-like, so much so that it is difficult at first to know what they are. The opposite error to that which kindled love "'twixt man and fountain" refers to the well-known classical story of Narcissus, who fell in love with his own image in the water. This classical allusion makes a profound point. Dante has been purged enough of his own self-conceit not to think the reflection is of himself. But he has not yet turned his spirit to trusting in the truth outside him sufficiently to credit what he sees. For us, who have a simple notion of paradise, it may seem odd that even a now naturally perfected soul like Dante's is still subject to turning its gaze toward emptiness. But in the process of moving toward the highest heaven, he will have to penetrate more and more deeply into truth and we see here a common state of our own spirits: we are not in positive error but need to look toward and grip firmly what is real.

Not surprisingly, the reason that the souls of the Moon are in the lowest sphere of the Heavens relates to this introductory material. They were consecrated nuns who allowed themselves to be taken by force from their vows. Dante is not saying here that they have committed a grievous fault, merely that there was an imperfection in their dedication to the truth that, in the most exacting view, resulted in a somewhat lower place in the greater glory. As Beatrice explains immediately, they are wholly trust-worthy now: "For the true light, which giveth peace to them, / Permits them not to turn from it their feet." Dante recognizes the first soul he sees after getting used to her new glory as Piccarda, the sister of his friend Forese Donati. As we might, he wonders whether these sweet souls are not dissatisfied with their relatively low status for a slight fault and receives from her the answer:

> "Brother, our will is quieted by virtue
>   Of charity, that makes us wish alone
>   For what we have, nor gives us thirst for more.
> If to be more exalted we aspired,
>   Discordant would our aspirations be
>   Unto the will of Him who here secludes us;
> Which thou shalt see finds no place in these circles,
>   If being in charity is needful here,
>   And if thou lookest well into its nature;
> Nay, 'tis essential to this blest existence
>   To keep itself within the will divine,
>   Whereby our very wishes are made one;

So that, as we are station above station
    Throughout this realm, to all the realm 'tis pleasing,
    As to the King, who makes his will our will.
And his will is our peace; this is the sea
    To which is moving onward whatsoever
    It doth create, and all that nature makes."
Then it was clear to me how everywhere
    In heaven is Paradise, although the grace
    Of good supreme there rain not in one measure.

This is more than mere resignation and deserves more careful study. To begin with, it reflects back on the previous canto, in which we learned about the diverse effects of the creative impulse of God. Even in Heaven, diversity persists and, while maintaining some connection with worldly history, now forms a God-willed order of charity that neither admits of other desires to the pure soul nor can be other than it is. The original Italian gives a sightly more forceful statement of this spiritual principle, "And *in* his will is our peace." The souls who are placed within that will find that everywhere is perfect Paradise, as we would if we had the same quality of will.

Just before moving on to the next canto, Dante learns from Piccarda that the empress Costanza, whose name ironically means "constancy," is beside her. Constance was the mother of Frederick II, one of the great emperors of Dante's day. As discussion of the perfect dedication of the will continues, the reason for mentioning Costanza will become clear.

Canto 4

Dante begins with what may merely seem a medieval philosophical puzzle, but it has serious import:

Between two viands, equally removed
    And tempting, a free man would die of hunger
    Ere either he could bring unto his teeth.
So would a lamb between the ravenings
    Of two fierce wolves stand fearing both alike;
    And so would stand a dog between two does.
Hence, if I held my peace, myself I blame not,

> Impelled in equal measure by my doubts,
> Since it must be so, nor do I commend.

What Dante is suggesting here under the guise of a mere philosophical problem is a situation in which we often find ourselves. We have two apparently contradictory truths in mind, and desire or fear of one or the other paralyzes us. He is stuck and thus in a state involving neither praise nor blame. But as with all such doubts in a world created by God, perplexity is only the beginning of another phase of wisdom, if we are open to the voice of grace and truth. Beatrice notes that Dante has two difficulties. First, he is wondering how someone who is forced against her will to do something can be anything but blameless. Second, the appearance of these souls reminds him of something he read in Plato about souls existing on the planets and stars and periodically being reincarnated on Earth, a contradiction of Catholic thought. She deals with the second question first. In fact, all the souls in Heaven are in one Heaven above and are merely presented here for the sake of his understanding:

> He of the Seraphim most absorbed in God,
>   Moses, and Samuel, and whichever John
>   Thou mayst select, I say, and even Mary,
> Have not in any other heaven their seats,
>   Than have those spirits that just appeared to thee,
>   Nor of existence more or fewer years;
> But all make beautiful the primal circle,
>   And have sweet life in different degrees,
>   By feeling more or less the eternal breath.
> They showed themselves here, not because allotted
>   This sphere has been to them, but to give sign
>   Of the celestial which is least exalted.
> To speak thus is adapted to your mind,
>   Since only through the sense it apprehendeth
>   What then it worthy makes of intellect.
> On this account the Scripture condescends
>   Unto your faculties, and feet and hands
>   To God attributes, and means something else;
> And Holy Church under an aspect human
>   Gabriel and Michael represent to you,
>   And him who made Tobias whole again.

We have already noticed the intellectual formulation of how God's influence is one and multiple, and here we have further confirmation that the souls, articulated as they must be even in Heaven, if the individuality of their earthly lives is not to be lost, are really united in one place further up. Dante also solves here a question that may have troubled many of his readers, as it still does many today: when the Scriptures speak of God as if he were a material being, the literal sense contains something the ancient Hebrews already knew was merely metaphorical.

Beatrice turns to the question of forced action and what it means for human responsibility:

> If it be violence when he who suffers
>> Co-operates not with him who uses force,
>> These souls were not on that account excused;
> For will is never quenched unless it will,
>> But operates as nature doth in fire
>> If violence a thousand times distort it.
> Hence, if it yieldeth more or less, it seconds
>> The force; and these have done so, having power
>> Of turning back unto the holy place.
>
> . . . .
>
> It would have urged them back along the road
>> Whence they were dragged, as soon as they were free;
>> But such a solid will is all too rare.

Dante had heard Piccarda say that Costanza retained her love for the nun's veil. This would seem to make hers a different case than the one Beatrice is describing. Today, some people would distinguish between the fundamental option of her soul and some of the imperfections she gave in to. But in Dante's system of Heaven, this is not entirely satisfactory. He knows of an absolute will, which stayed firm for Costanza. But Beatrice points out:

> At this point I desire thee to remember
>> That force with will commingles, and they cause
>> That the offences cannot be excused.
> Will absolute consenteth not to evil;
>> But in so far consenteth as it fears,
>> If it refrain, to fall into more harm.

The situation is common; we have the basic will, but not the fortitude to do all and suffer all that the basic will requires. This may seem a highly subtle point, but we are still at the first steps in Heaven, and both mind and will must now wholly dedicate themselves to the true and the good to continue the journey. Dante is satisfied with this resolution of the two ways in which he was torn earlier in the canto; and by that assent, he is becoming a more integrated spirit himself, as each of these difficulties dissolves. In fact, he speaks in terms that underscore this fact:

> Such was the flowing of the holy river
>> That issued from the fount whence springs all truth;
>> This put to rest my wishes one and all.
>
> "O love of the first lover, O divine,"
>> Said I forthwith, "whose speech inundates me
>> And warms me so, it more and more revives me,
>
> My own affection is not so profound
>> As to suffice in rendering grace for grace;
>> Let Him, who sees and can, thereto respond.
>
> Well I perceive that never sated is
>> Our intellect unless the Truth illume it,
>> Beyond which nothing true expands itself.
>
> It rests therein, as wild beast in his lair,
>> When it attains it; and it can attain it;
>> If not, then each desire would frustrate be.
>
> Therefore springs up, in fashion of a shoot,
>> Doubt at the foot of truth; and this is nature,
>> Which to the top from height to height impels us.

There are several powerful arguments in this passage. Dante is being sated with the flowing waters of truth and warmed by them as if they are also light. He for the first time allows God to thank Beatrice for him, since it is beyond Dante's own powers. The mind, if unsatisfied, is both like a beast in a lair and a plant that shoots up from truth to truth as the need to resolve doubt impels it toward its fulfillment. In other words, Dante feels in himself every lower form—mineral (water), animal, vegetable—moving the mind toward God, a further confirmation of a total integration of everything within him toward a single goal. He is experiencing truth, as he tells us you must in Heaven, because there is no other way to be in Heaven.

Canto 8

We jump to the heaven of the planet Venus, the star that governs love and gave rise to dangerous cults, as can be seen both in classical mythology and in the Old Testament. The vision of Venus's influence that Dante, however, comes to is quite different from the mistaken assumptions about erotic love. There will be a progressive intermingling of souls and minds in this canto, but within the order of the real love, which is to say the eternal love that gave birth to the universe. Yet this divine love does not remove the reality of love for specific persons; rather, as we know at rare moments in our life, the divine spark or voice that we detect in another is the normal state of affairs in Heaven where the two dimensions are seen without being completely separated or simply folded into one another.

The souls here tell Dante:

> We turn around with the celestial Princes,
>   One gyre and one gyration and one thirst,
>   To whom thou in the world of old didst say,
> "Ye who, intelligent the third heaven are moving";
>   And are so full of love, to pleasure thee
>   A little quiet will not be less sweet.

In the original Italian, there is a quotation here from the first line of one of Dante's poems addressed to the angels that move the third sphere of Heaven and who will understand a conflict in his soul living on Earth. But in this world there is no conflict, and we see that the growth into eternal love makes souls ready to serve one another without reservation. Indeed, when Dante asks one of the souls to identify himself, he swells with love at the opportunity to do so. We learn that Dante and this spirit knew each other in life, and the soul says he would have shown Dante even greater love while still living, had he survived longer. This is Charles Martel, once king of Hungary, and his descendants would have been ruler over other lands if his father-in-law, the emperor Rudolph, had not misruled and caused chaos. Dante is delighted at this discovery of an old friend and the mode of love they now enjoy.

Canto 9

The next canto completes the reflection on the influence of heavenly love. Another soul approaches, and Dante greets it with a request that, since it can see all in the mind of God, it read his mind—which it promptly does. This degree of intimacy surpasses anything ever experienced on Earth. He finds that this soul is Cunizza, a noblewoman who had many love affairs and multiple marriages, but who was quite generous. Dante may have met her in Florence as a young boy. In passing, we discover also that the shadow of the Earth extends only as far as this sphere, which also contains the spirit of the harlot Rahab, who helped the Israelites conquer the Promised Land:

> Into this heaven, where ends the shadowy cone
>   Cast by your world, before all other souls
>   First of Christ's triumph was she taken up.

This means that Rahab was the first to be released to this sphere, not the first of all souls to be released from Limbo. Nonetheless, hers is a singular honor and reinforces the close connection between righteousness in the abstract and the order of Providence in sacred history.

This recollection of the conquest of the Holy Land in Old Testament times gives Dante a chance to denounce the popes and political leaders of his time who have allowed the Holy Land to pass into Muslim hands. They are so occupied with making money through the manipulation of church regulations that they have forgotten the weightier matters of the law:

> . . . the Evangel and the mighty Doctors
>   Are derelict, and only the Decretals
>   So studied that it shows upon their margins.
> On this are Pope and Cardinals intent;
>   Their meditations reach not Nazareth,
>   There where his pinions Gabriel unfolded
> But Vatican and the other parts elect
>   Of Rome, which have a cemetery been
>   Unto the soldiery that followed Peter
> Shall soon be free from this adultery.

This last line may be meant to remind us of how often in the Bible

Israel's espousal with the land and the marriage between God and his people are human images of a historical reality. The adultery here, as so often in the Bible, is a metaphor for profound infidelity to God.

Canto 10

As we move to the next Heaven, all shadow of the Earth is left behind. And Dante makes this clear by invoking an image of the Trinity and how it looks with love on the order it has created:

Looking into his Son with all the Love
   Which each of them eternally breathes forth
   The Primal and unutterable Power
Whate'er before the mind or eye revolves
   With so much order made, there can be none
   Who this beholds without enjoying Him.
Lift up then, Reader, to the lofty wheels
   With me thy vision straight unto that part
   Where the one motion on the other strikes,
And there begin to contemplate with joy
   That Master's art, who in himself so loves it
   That never doth his eye depart therefrom.

He goes on in an elaborate astronomical passage to show how a slight deviation from the divine order of the world would have resulted in great disorder for us. As modern cosmology has confirmed, this is true in an exact scientific sense, so much so that human life might have been impossible if slight variations in conditions after the Big Bang had been different. But Dante's astronomy always has a spiritual point for us. And the thrust of this passage seems to be that at a certain point in our spiritual growth, we too begin to be absorbed into this loving contemplation of the cosmos and its Creator.

Dante is now in the sphere of the Sun, and he tells us that this further reinforces the growing unity between his spirit and the universe:

And I was with him; but of the ascending
   I was not conscious, saving as a man
   Of a first thought is conscious ere it come.

This is the first time that we have encountered explicitly a state in which the very spontaneous motion of the mind seems coordinated with pilgrimage toward God. And words, always inadequate for superhuman things, are beginning to become still more so:

> And what was in the sun, wherein I entered,
>> Apparent not by colour but by light,
> I, though I call on genius, art, and practice,
>> Cannot so tell that it could be imagined;
>> Believe one can, and let him long to see it.
> And if our fantasies too lowly are
>> For altitude so great, it is no marvel,
>> Since o'er the sun was never eye could go.

The only fit reaction to such marvels is praise, and Beatrice urges Dante to thank God for this experience and concentrate upon the spectacle. Beatrice represents many things, not least a kind of personal channel of grace for Dante. But now that we have passed beyond all earthly attachment, Dante's act has an effect on what must be thought of as his attachment to Beatrice the woman:

> As at those words did I myself become;
>> And all my love was so absorbed in Him,
>> That in oblivion Beatrice was eclipsed.
> Nor this displeased her; but she smiled at it
>> So that the splendour of her laughing eyes
>> My single mind on many things divided.
> Lights many saw I, vivid and triumphant,
>> Make us a centre and themselves a circle,
>> More sweet in voice than luminous in aspect.

Dante's shift of attention away from Beatrice to the multiple lights not only does not displease her, but is a great step toward a new mode of contemplation. As he becomes more fixed on the sources of what he first came to know through Beatrice, he will fulfill his relationship to her and transcend it without abandoning her: Heaven permits many such paradoxes, the basis of all of them being that as we draw closer to the primal unity, the multiplicity of the cosmos becomes truer also, truer in that both we and our relationships with each other become more authentic.

But for now, Dante has some lessons to learn from these new
lights:

> As soon as singing thus those burning suns
> > Had round about us whirled themselves three times,
> > Like unto stars neighbouring the steadfast poles,
> Ladies they seemed, not from the dance released,
> > But who stop short, in silence listening
> > Till they have gathered the new melody.

All the souls in this circle are men. But Dante uses the image of
ladies in a dance since it implies a kind of receptivity to the
divine words and music often associated in the Christian tradi-
tion with holy women, especially the Blessed Virgin. These souls,
fittingly, are those who drank deep of wisdom, figured in the Old
Testament as a woman. And the soul who points out the others
to him is no less than the greatest theologian of the thirteenth
century, Thomas Aquinas. Thomas introduces himself as a mem-
ber of one of the two great religious orders founded just prior to
Dante's time: the Dominicans, his order, and the Franciscans.
These were sometimes regarded as rivals to each other, but it will
be the whole thrust of St. Thomas's address to Dante that, though
different, they were engaged in a single work.

Canto 11

In the way of courtesy that marks Heaven, Thomas, a Domini-
can, begins to praise St. Francis. Like a sun rising on his native
Assisi, Francis embraced Lady Poverty as a troubadour might
have pursued some beauty. Thomas says that not since Christ
himself had anyone so heartily embraced poverty and the purest
Christian life. People flocked to follow him, and Francis's zeal
one day in the mountainous regions of Laverna won him the stig-
mata:

> On the rude rock 'twixt Tiber and the Arno
> > From Christ did he receive the final seal,
> > Which during two whole years his members bore.
> When He, who chose him unto so much good,
> > Was pleased to draw him up to the reward
> > That he had merited by being lowly,

> Unto his friars, as to the rightful heirs,
>   His most dear Lady did he recommend,
>   And bade that they should love her faithfully.

Canto 12

But to complete the second half of the great story of these religious orders, Dante now sees a second circle of lights join the first in a double rainbow. Their flashings and song are thereby increased, and soon one of the light speaks:

> The love that makes me fair
> Draws me to speak about the other leader,
> By whom so well is spoken here of mine.
> 'Tis right, where one is, to bring in the other,
>   That, as they were united in their warfare,
>   Together likewise may their glory shine.

We learn later that this is St. Bonaventure, the great theologian and general of the Franciscans. He returns St. Thomas's courtesy by recounting the birth of St. Dominic, which was attended by signs and visions that promised the great work to which he was called. Bonaventure speaks in martial terms at first about the combat to which Dominic was called, but then compares the growth of the Dominicans to the fresh breath of wind that comes from the west and gives new birth to the vegetation of Europe. Since Dominic was born in Spain not far from the Atlantic Ocean, the image is apt; and it was appropriate that this great soul was named after our Lord—in Latin *dominus*. Dominic too embraced poverty and from the first did not study those subjects that are the means to advancement in the world and the church, but the fresh truth of God. Dominic and Francis were thus like the two wheels of a cart that came to move the church back to its pristine purity and evangelical fervor.

Canto 14

But there is still one more lesson to be drawn from these sages, and it has to do with the future glory of the human body. We have just heard how the primal virtue of God could perfectly impress itself on certain figures in the history of our race. The question now arises, however, in the afterlife, will the transcendent joy and wisdom that Dante is gradually being led into not overwhelm the weaknesses of mortal flesh? We know that Adam and Christ's human nature was perfect, but can our earthly bodies endure the heights of heavenly contemplation?

Dante says his mind at this point was like the water in a vase that, shaken, has circular ripples that converge toward the center and then back out again in an exchange of the great and the small. In the midst of the glorious song of the Trinity and Unity of God in Heaven, he hears "a modest voice, such as perhaps the Angel's was to Mary," which we know spoke of the coming of the divine second person of the Trinity into human flesh. The voice is Solomon's:

> "As long as the festivity
> Of Paradise shall be, so long our love
> Shall radiate round about us such a vesture.
> Its brightness is proportioned to the ardour,
> The ardour to the vision; and the vision
> Equals what grace it has above its worth.
> When, glorious and sanctified, our flesh
> Is reassumed, then shall our persons be
> More pleasing by their being all complete;
> For will increase whate'er bestows on us
> Of light gratuitous the Good Supreme,
> Light which enables us to look on Him;
> Therefore the vision must perforce increase,
> Increase the ardour which from that is kindled,
> Increase the radiance which from this proceeds.
> But even as a coal that sends forth flame,
> And by its vivid whiteness overpowers it
> So that its own appearance it maintains,
> Thus the effulgence that surrounds us now
> Shall be o'erpowered in aspect by the flesh,
> Which still to-day the earth doth cover up;
> Nor can so great a splendour weary us,
> For strong will be the organs of the body
> To everything which hath the power to please us."
> So sudden and alert appeared to me

> Both one and the other choir to say Amen,
> That well they showed desire for their dead bodies;
> Nor sole for them perhaps, but for the mothers,
> The fathers, and the rest who had been dear
> Or ever they became eternal flames.

So Dante's answer is that glorified bodies will be strong enough not only to support the added glory but will themselves add to it by restoring the human race to the original completeness God intended in creating Adam. The reunion of earth and heaven in this return will be the completion of the desire of the ages, not only for each of us as individuals but also for all those who long to be reunited with one another in body as we once existed on earth, as well as in spirit.

Significantly, in this same canto, Dante is transported to the next Heaven, that of Mars. As is always the case with Dante's structure, this suggests that this recovery of the body leads us deeper into a living embodiment of all truth and goodness. He sees against the red backdrop of the planet a white cross bearing Christ. In other words, we see the body of the perfect man courageously consenting to what is necessary to redemption and perfection:

> Here doth my memory overcome my genius;
> For on that cross as levin gleamed forth Christ,
> So that I cannot find ensample worthy;
> But he who takes his cross and follows Christ
> Again will pardon me what I omit,
> Seeing in that aurora lighten Christ.

The souls in the Heaven of Mars are represented as particles that pass singing a heavenly hymn before the brightness of the cross. We shall soon learn that these are the souls of the courageous in this life:

> So from the lights that there to me appeared
> Upgathered through the cross a melody,
> Which rapt me, not distinguishing the hymn.
> Well was I ware it was of lofty laud,
> Because there came to me, "Arise and conquer!"

Dante is working simultaneously in two directions here. He is reminding us that the virtues that bodily life demands are, properly understood, exalted beyond anything we can currently conceive. But in the other direction, at least for the present in the imperfect bodies we are weighted down with, the very brightness of future glory limits what we can currently understand.

Canto 15

But it is fitting, since we have been talking of the body and its glorified future, that Dante now has the experience that many of us hope for in the future life: a reunion with one of his own relatives in eternity. One of the lights from the right arm of the cross detaches itself and trails a ribbon of light behind it, still connecting it with the cross, as it sails down toward Dante. The soul's first words are in Latin, as if such a serious occasion required quasi-liturgical language:

> O sanguis meus, O super infusa
> Gratia Dei, sicut tibi, cui
> Bis unquam Coeli janua reclusa?

> O my blood! O Grace of God,
> superinfused upon thee, to whom
> ever have the gates of Heaven twice opened?

This soul goes on, but in a way that exceeds Dante's ability to apprehend. Little by little, however, he graciously comes down to the level of Dante's understanding. But instead of merely reading Dante's reactions in God, this figure wishes him to speak directly to him, presumably because it is part of the joy of this family reunion that we speak to one another just as we once did in this world. Dante does, and the first person he hears about is the first of the Alighieri, who lived a century earlier:

> "O leaf of mine, in whom I pleasure took
> E'en while awaiting, I was thine own root!"
> Such a beginning he in answer made me
> Then said to me: "That one from whom is named
> Thy race, and who a hundred years and more
> Has circled round the mount on the first cornice,
> A son of mine and thy great-grandsire was;
> Well it behoves thee that the long fatigue
> Thou shouldst for him make shorter with thy works.

Having reminded Dante that prayer for our departed ancestors always remains a primary duty, this soul laments the tribulations of Florence. And he identifies himself as Cacciaguida, Dante's great-great-grandfather. Cacciaguida, we know, fought in the Second Crusade under the leadership of the emperor Conrad III, was knighted, and died around 1147 in battle against the infidels. Canto 16 is a long reflection on the former virtues of Florence before wealth had corrupted the ancient Roman qualities that the city had inherited historically.

In the sequel to this canto, we see the paternal care that Cacciaguida wishes to offer from this courageous height to a son who will soon endure much back in the world. As the following canto unfolds, as is always the case with Dante, that personal history, which we are so quick to assume has relevance only to ourselves privately, is shown to have a public importance as well.

Canto 17

Dante recalls that other great father to him, Vergil, with whom he journeyed through the other two realms and who, as dark forebodings were expressed about Dante's future, counseled him to ask this very ancestor, Cacciaguida, for enlightenment. Within the action of the story, this may point us toward the fact that we must all get to know and draw strength from the particular families that God has placed us within, especially as we venture out into an unforgiving world. Cacciaguida in Heaven shows that this parental care extends beyond the grave and is a place to which we may look in this life, through prayer and careful reflection, for answers to the problems that our immediate circumstances throw up to us. Dante makes a special point of describing the clarity of Cacciaguida's prophecies and advice compared with the soothsayers of the classical world:

> Not in vague phrase, in which the foolish folk
>   Ensnared themselves of old, ere yet was slain
>   The Lamb of God who taketh sins away,
> But with clear words and unambiguous
>   Language responded that paternal love.

Cacciaguida reminds Dante that he can see everything in the

divine Mind, which though it knows the future does not deter-
mine it and therefore leaves open free will—an aside that places
the blame on the human actors and sets up Dante's own need to
resist evildoers courageously.

> . . . thou from Florence must perforce depart.
> Already this is willed, and this is sought for;
>> And soon it shall be done by him who thinks it,
>> Where every day the Christ is bought and sold.
> The blame shall follow the offended party
>> In outcry as is usual; but the vengeance
>> Shall witness to the truth that doth dispense it.
> Thou shalt abandon everything beloved
>> Most tenderly, and this the arrow is
>> Which first the bow of banishment shoots forth.
> Thou shalt have proof how savoureth of salt
>> The bread of others, and how hard a road
>> The going down and up another's stairs.
> And that which most shall weigh upon thy shoulders
>> Will be the bad and foolish company
>> With which into this valley thou shalt fall;
> For all ingrate, all mad and impious
>> Will they become against thee; but soon after
>> They, and not thou, shall have the forehead scarlet
> Of their bestiality their own proceedings
>> Shall furnish proof; so 'twill be well for thee
>> A party to have made thee by thyself.

These are hard truths. The pope shall be involved in Dante's
exile, as will evil men already beginning to plan it. Conditions
will be harsh. Dante's fellow exiles will themselves be beasts, and
he will have to become a party of one to maintain his honor. But
Cacciaguida also tells of the people of virtue Dante shall meet in
exile, first among them Can Grande della Scala, a man stamped
by the martial virtues associated with the planet Mars at his
birth. Can Grande will even show some of the same promptness
of understanding and reciprocity in love that characterize rela-
tions between spirits in the Heavens:

> Thine earliest refuge and thine earliest inn
>> Shall be the mighty Lombard's courtesy,
>> Who on the Ladder bears the holy bird,

> Who such benign regard shall have for thee
> > That 'twixt you twain, in doing and in asking,
> > That shall be first which is with others last.
> With him shalt thou see one who at his birth
> > Has by this star of strength been so impressed,
> > That notable shall his achievements be.

Cacciaguida warns Dante not to envy his enemies, because he will outlive them. But this raises another question for Dante:

> Began I, even as he who yearneth after,
> > Being in doubt, some counsel from a person
> > Who seeth, and uprightly wills, and loves:
> "Well see I, father mine, how spurreth on
> > The time towards me such a blow to deal me
> > As heaviest is to him who most gives way.
> Therefore with foresight it is well I arm me,
> > That, if the dearest place be taken from me,
> > I may not lose the others by my songs.
> Down through the world of infinite bitterness,
> > And o'er the mountain, from whose beauteous summit
> > The eyes of my own Lady lifted me,
> And afterward through heaven from light to light,
> > I have learned that which, if I tell again,
> > Will be a savour of strong herbs to many.
> And if I am a timid friend to truth,
> > I fear lest I may lose my life with those
> > Who will hereafter call this time the olden."

Dante's fear here is that by telling everything he has seen in this journey, he will anger many. It reminds us of his fear, as expressed to the fatherly Vergil as they first set out. Few will believe he has been granted such privilege and knowledge, and even fewer will like what he has to say. Cacciaguida, like a good father, tells him to take courage and, though his words will sting the guilty, to speak the truth and disregard the consequences. For if he has been granted special favors, they are not only for him—heavenly experience never is individualistic—but for the education of others who shall someday read him:

> "A conscience overcast
> Or with its own or with another's shame,
> Will taste forsooth the tartness of thy word;

But ne'ertheless, all falsehood laid aside,
   Make manifest thy vision utterly,
   And let them scratch wherever is the itch;
For if thine utterance shall offensive be
   At the first taste, a vital nutriment
   'Twill leave thereafter, when it is digested.
This cry of thine shall do as doth the wind,
   Which smiteth most the most exalted summits,
   And that is no slight argument of honour.
Therefore are shown to thee within these wheels,
   Upon the mount and in the dolorous valley,
   Only the souls that unto fame are known;
Because the spirit of the hearer rests not,
   Nor doth confirm its faith by an example
   Which has the root of it unknown and hidden,
Or other reason that is not apparent."

Canto 18

And to complete this thought, Cacciaguida points out the great courageous figures from Joshua and Judas Maccabeus in the Old Testament, through the great Christian warriors Charlemagne and Roland, down to people nearer Dante's own time who are now shining spirits in the Heaven of Mars. But after this catalogue and another flash of light from Beatrice, Dante is being moved yet higher and wider:

And as, by feeling greater delectation,
   A man in doing good from day to day
   Becomes aware his virtue is increasing,
So I became aware that my gyration
   With heaven together had increased its arc,
   That miracle beholding more adorned.

He has come to the Heaven of Jupiter, king of the classical gods, the sphere of those rulers who, as the Bible repeatedly tells us, have their authority from above, as God's champions of justice.

These souls fly about like great eagles spelling out the message, "Love justice, O you who judge the earth." Many more stars form the head and neck of an eagle, the traditional symbol of kingship. And this moves Dante, who has just heard of the injus-

tice he will suffer, to a prayer that the influence of justice will off-
set the situation on Earth, largely caused by papal corruption and
greed:

> O gentle star! what and how many gems
>   Did demonstrate to me, that all our justice
>   Effect is of that heaven which thou ingemmest!
> Wherefore I pray the Mind, in which begin
>   Thy motion and thy virtue, to regard
>   Whence comes the smoke that vitiates thy rays;
> So that a second time it now be wroth
>   With buying and with selling in the temple
>   Whose walls were built with signs and martyrdoms!
> O soldiery of heaven, whom I contemplate,
>   Implore for those who are upon the earth
>   All gone astray after the bad example!
> Once 'twas the custom to make war with swords;
>   But now 'tis made by taking here and there
>   The bread the pitying Father shuts from none.
> Yet thou, who writest but to cancel, think
>   That Peter and that Paul, who for this vineyard
>   Which thou art spoiling died, are still alive!

Canto 20

It is also good to look upon those who practiced justice, and the
eagle directs Dante's attention to the six spirits that form its eye.
In medieval bestiaries, it was thought that the eagle was the only
animal able to look directly at the sun. And in many ways there
are hints throughout the *Paradise* that Dante is acquiring, little by
little, this eagle vision so that he can look on the intense source of
the light of existence. He names six figures here who themselves
stared hard into the sun of justice, and did right on Earth. But
first, they all fall silent, and Dante, clearly inspired by the biblical
notion of justice, says he notes a sound like a flowing river. That
flow issues in descriptions of the six figures, the first of whom is
King David:

> He who is shining in the midst as pupil
>   Was once the singer of the Holy Spirit,
>   Who bore the ark from city unto city;

> Now knoweth he the merit of his song,
>> In so far as effect of his own counsel,
>> By the reward which is commensurate.

This is the pattern by which the others will be introduced: first, three lines describing their good qualities, then three lines showing the knowledge of their acts, necessarily incomplete in the world that they now have. The other figures named are the Roman emperor Trajan, whom in Purgatory we have already seen doing justice to a widow, the good king Hezekiah from the Old Testament, the emperor Constantine (whose unfortunate legacy of political power to the church does not invalidate the good he did), a good king William of Sicily, and finally Ripheus, a just Trojan ruler.

The surprising names here are the emperor Trajan, who died in the second century A.D. and the Trojan Ripheus, who lived almost a thousand years before Christ. These names give the eagle the opportunity to explain further a few points to Dante. Both, it says, were Christians when they died, one by anticipation of what was to follow, the other by the grace of what had already happened in the crucifixion and redemption, even though neither was formally and explicitly a Christian. Trajan received graces, an old story says, through the prayers of Pope Gregory the Great, who lived more than five hundred years after him but heard during prayer for Trajan that he had been saved. Obviously, this does not mean that prayer changes God's mind, but that the pope's prayers for a man he thought virtuous released him from some position in Purgatory.

The other case is equally striking. Ripheus received what might be called a kind of baptism of desire, with the three theological virtues themselves, which we saw alongside the chariot at the top of Purgatory, receiving baptism for him:

> The other one, through grace, that from so deep
>> A fountain wells that never hath the eye
>> Of any creature reached its primal wave,
> Set all his love below on righteousness;
>> Wherefore from grace to grace did God unclose
>> His eye to our redemption yet to be,
> Whence he believed therein, and suffered not
>> From that day forth the stench of paganism,

> And he reproved therefor the folk perverse.
> Those Maidens three, whom at the right-hand wheel
>   Thou didst behold, were unto him for baptism
>   More than a thousand years before baptizing.

Such results show that the notion of predestination to one final end or another, while true in a sense because God knows all things, is not an iron law of harsh judgment. Rather it anticipates problems and reaches back into the past to make sure that justice is done. Yet so deep does the just judgment of human souls always remain that the redeemed spirits, who see all things immediately in their contemplation of God, do not see who all the chosen for Heaven are and rejoice:

> And sweet to us is such a deprivation,
>   Because our good in this good is made perfect,
>   That whatsoe'er God wills, we also will.

In the very midst of what might seem a fully comprehensible earthly justice, then, we are being led deeper into the mystery of God. And though we, along with Dante, are penetrating further and further into that mystery, ultimately it is, for us, fathomless. Yet the attitude of these souls tells us something; it is good and just to live in full recognition that God exceeds our grasp. Far from leading to frustration, the contemplation of what forever will elude us, rightly understood, can be a cause for satisfaction. And as we now move into the heaven of the contemplatives, marked by the planet Saturn in the constellation of Leo, we will see both how much needs to become strengthened in Dante and in us to comprehend even a part of these higher realms and how much will remain forever beyond us.

Canto 21

Dante approaches this theme by turning toward a figure who has been distant for a few cantos: Beatrice. And something unusual occurs:

> . . . she smiled not; but "If I were to smile,"
>   She unto me began, "thou wouldst become
>   Like Semele, when she was turned to ashes.

Because my beauty, that along the stairs
  Of the eternal palace more enkindles,
  As thou hast seen, the farther we ascend,
If it were tempered not, is so resplendent
  That all thy mortal power in its effulgence
  Would seem a leaflet that the thunder crushes.

Semele, of course, was the classical figure who became the lover of Jupiter and was tricked into asking him to show himself in his full splendor, with the result that his overwhelming brilliance as the supreme Olympian god burned her to ashes.

    Similar warnings about the dangers to those who would look upon the face of God appear in the Bible, and as Dante begins to describe the nature of the new Heaven to which he has come, he interweaves classical and biblical sources. In this sphere, the age of Saturn, the golden age before the arrival of the other Olympian gods, is combined with the golden ladder of Jacob, which becomes an image of the interchange between Heaven and Earth in contemplation:

Within the crystal which, around the world
  Revolving, bears the name of its dear leader,
  Under whom every wickedness lay dead,
Coloured like gold, on which the sunshine gleams,
  A stairway I beheld to such a height
  Uplifted, that mine eye pursued it not.
Likewise beheld I down the steps descending
  So many splendours, that I thought each light
  That in the heaven appears was there diffused.

    One of these spirits comes to Dante and, in keeping with traditional teachings of grace and revelation, the poet wishes to receive greater illumination, though he knows he does not merit it:

"No merit of my own
  Renders me worthy of response from thee;
  But for her sake who granteth me the asking,
Thou blessed life that dost remain concealed
  In thy beatitude, make known to me
  The cause which draweth thee so near my side;
And tell me why is silent in this wheel
  The dulcet symphony of Paradise,
  That through the rest below sounds so devoutly.

This may seem a strange request until we realize that, wrapped within it, is a sign that Dante's mind and spirit are expanding. Earlier, he had just wished to know who and what were presented to him. Now, coming fresh from the sphere of justice in which he learned God's intimate and providential involvement in the life of each individual, he has a novel thought: Why then are you in particular coming to help me rather than another? The question also concerns Dante's relationship with Beatrice, since she too was a personal channel of grace for Dante. Is there any good explanation for why certain people come to have significance in our lives rather than others?

The answer to this question is complicated. First, this spirit tells Dante that the music of the spheres has not ceased in this new sphere, but exceeds his power to hear:

> "Thou hast thy hearing mortal as thy sight,"
>   It answer made to me; "they sing not here,
>   For the same cause that Beatrice has not smiled."

The higher Dante mounts, therefore, the more what exists will exceed his capacity. And after a brief clarification, Dante learns that this is true not only of the general existences like the Heavens, but of his interaction with particular souls as well. But is it predestined that the spirit before him would have the role he does for Dante, out of all the other people in this sphere? The question sets this spirit spinning like a millstone, grinding out the truth:

> No sooner had I come to the last word,
>   Than of its middle made the light a centre,
>   Whirling itself about like a swift millstone.
> When answer made the love that was therein:
>   "On me directed is a light divine,
>   Piercing through this in which I am embosomed,
> Of which the virtue with my sight conjoined
>   Lifts me above myself so far, I see
>   The supreme essence from which this is drawn.
> Hence comes the joyfulness with which I flame,
>   For to my sight, as far as it is clear,
>   The clearness of the flame I equal make.
> But that soul in the heaven which is most pure,
>   That seraph which his eye on God most fixes,

> Could this demand of thine not satisfy;
> Because so deeply sinks in the abyss
>> Of the eternal statute what thou askest,
>> From all created sight it is cut off.
> And to the mortal world, when thou returnest,
>> This carry back, that it may not presume
>> Longer tow'rd such a goal to move its feet.
> The mind, that shineth here, on earth doth smoke;
>> From this observe how can it do below
>> That which it cannot though the heaven assume it?"

This may seem no answer at all, but it warns us that even in Heaven the depths of the divine counsels will elude us as they do to a much greater degree here on Earth. True wisdom, therefore, resides in recognizing that there is no pursuing this question further than whatever answer the divine ray is willing to give to us, and that is the true nature of contemplation—not something we achieve by effort, but an effort to receive as much as possible what is freely given.

Thus chastened, Dante contents himself with asking who this spirit is rather than why God chose him in particular. The spirit identifies himself as Peter Damiani, a poor contemplative called late in life to be a cardinal. This gives Dante a chance to denounce the corrupt and corpulent princes of the church as the figures of justice in the sphere of Jupiter had denounced the corrupt Christian princes.

Canto 22

A clap of thunder follows that denunciation. And it is no accident that at this stage in his journey Dante describes his reaction as that of a little child, which reminds us of Christ's words about what we must become to enter the kingdom of Heaven. After all the philosophy, all the moral striving and growth of vision, all the serious adult things that we must embrace as a prerequisite, we arrive at a childlike simplicity of contemplation:

> Oppressed with stupor, I unto my guide
>> Turned like a little child who always runs
>> For refuge there where he confideth most;

And she, even as a mother who straightway
　　Gives comfort to her pale and breathless boy
　　With voice whose wont it is to reassure him,
Said to me: "Knowest thou not thou art in heaven,
　　And knowest thou not that heaven is holy all
　　And what is done here cometh from good zeal?
After what wise the singing would have changed thee
　　And I by smiling, thou canst now imagine,
　　Since that the cry has startled thee so much . . .

But Beatrice directs Dante's vision to another figure of contemplation, St. Benedict, the great founder of Western monasticism, who makes the story of building his monastery on top of Monte Cassino a kind of parallel to the heavenly ascent:

And I am he who first up thither bore
　　The name of Him who brought upon the earth
　　The truth that so much sublimateth us.
And such abundant grace upon me shone
　　That all the neighbouring towns I drew away
　　From the impious worship that seduced the world.

Paganism was the idolatry that Benedict's work historically replaced and purified. Dante feels such love and paternal affection in the reply that he says:

Therefore I pray, and thou assure me, father,
　　If I may so much grace receive, that I
　　May thee behold with countenance unveiled.
He thereupon: "Brother, thy high desire
　　In the remotest sphere shall be fulfilled,
　　Where are fulfilled all others and my own.
There perfect is, and ripened, and complete,
　　Every desire; within that one alone
　　Is every part where it has always been;
For it is not in space, nor turns on poles,
　　And unto it our stairway reaches up,
　　Whence thus from out thy sight it steals away.
Up to that height the Patriarch Jacob saw it
　　Extending its supernal part, what time
　　So thronged with angels it appeared to him.
But to ascend it now no one uplifts
　　His feet from off the earth, and now my Rule

Below remaineth for mere waste of paper.
The walls that used of old to be an Abbey
    Are changed to dens of robbers, and the cowls
    Are sacks filled full of miserable flour.

A modern reader coming upon this heaven that is neither in time
nor space is in a much better position than a reader a century ago
to know what St. Benedict is speaking of. Not long ago science
had seemed to make notions of nonspatial or temporal events
mere nonsense. But disciplines such as astrophysics itself now
seem to have made room for what was quite clear in the contem-
plative tradition, that the real Heaven was not up in the sky some-
where but a transcendent realm that must be conceived as
bearing full plenitude prior to and outside of the universe of time
and space.

As Dante approaches this realm, he must pass through the
heaven of the fixed stars that seemed to early astronomers to lie
beyond the wandering motions of the planets. As he rises to that
realm, he recalls the position of the stars when he first felt the air
of Tuscany at his birth. This is one of the places where we sense
that, psychologically and spiritually, the beginning of life and its
consummation are close analogies with one another. Beatrice
underscores this point by telling Dante:

"Thou art so near unto the last salvation,"
    Thus Beatrice began, "thou oughtest now
    To have thine eyes unclouded and acute
And therefore, ere thou enter farther in,
    Look down once more, and see how vast a world
    Thou hast already put beneath thy feet;
So that thy heart, as jocund as it may,
    Present itself to the triumphant throng
    That comes rejoicing through this rounded ether."

So his vision will be purified and strengthened by looking back
one last time at the distance he has traversed. And as Dante does
so he sees all the spheres of Heaven below and, beyond them, the
earth:

The threshing-floor that maketh us so proud,
    To me revolving with the eternal Twins,

> Was all apparent made from hill to harbour!
> Then to the beauteous eyes mine eyes I turned.

And so, we enter upon a wholly different realm even than the heavenly spheres.

Canto 23

The imagery of the poem takes an appropriately tender turn. We just saw Dante as a little child. We now see Beatrice as a mother bird impatient in the dark for the light that will enable her to feed her nestlings:

> Even as a bird, 'mid the beloved leaves
>   Quiet upon the nest of her sweet brood
>   Throughout the night, that hideth all things from us,
> Who, that she may behold their longed-for looks
>   And find the food wherewith to nourish them,
>   In which, to her, grave labours grateful are,
> Anticipates the time on open spray
>   And with an ardent longing waits the sun,
>   Gazing intent as soon as breaks the dawn:
> Even thus my Lady standing was, erect
>   And vigilant, turned round towards the zone
>   Underneath which the sun displays less haste.

And as soon as Dante, too, looks in expectation in the same direction, Beatrice exclaims: "Behold the hosts / Of Christ's triumphal march, and all the fruit / Harvested by the rolling of these spheres!" And indeed he does see a host of lights surmounted by the piercing star of Christ, so bright that his eyes cannot stand it.

We are on the border now of that other Heaven that, unlike the planetary spheres below that catered to Dante's weakness, will mean an entering into a communion with the realm of glory as it exists in itself. Our fallen nature, even when redeemed, becomes accustomed to its reconnection with that realm only step by step. But we know that it is the wisdom and power of Christ that have made the reunion possible:

> O Beatrice, thou gentle guide and dear!
>   To me she said: "What overmasters thee

A virtue is from which naught shields itself
There are the wisdom and the omnipotence
    That oped the thoroughfares 'twixt heaven and earth,
    For which there erst had been so long a yearning."
As fire from out a cloud unlocks itself,
    Dilating so it finds not room therein,
    And down, against its nature, falls to earth,
So did my mind, among those aliments
    Becoming larger, issue from itself,
    And that which it became cannot remember.

It is possible to call this going beyond the human a kind of mysticism, but there is no magical invocation here, merely the encounter with the power and wisdom that cannot be encompassed by the human mind. If Dante's mind seems to "burst," leaving an irrecoverable sense of something we keenly desire to recover, the effects are such as to move us yet further along:

"Open thine eyes, and look at what I am:
    Thou hast beheld such things, that strong enough
    Hast thou become to tolerate my smile."
I was as one who still retains the feeling
    Of a forgotten vision, and endeavours
    In vain to bring it back into his mind,
When I this invitation heard, deserving
    Of so much gratitude, it never fades
    out of the book that chronicles the past.
If at this moment sounded all the tongues
    That Polyhymnia and her sisters made
    Most lubrical with their delicious milk,
To aid me, to a thousandth of the truth
    It would not reach, singing the holy smile
    And how the holy aspect it illumed.
And therefore, representing Paradise,
    The sacred poem must perforce leap over,
    Even as a man who finds his way cut off;
But whoso thinketh of the ponderous theme,
    And of the mortal shoulder laden with it
    Should blame it not, if under this it tremble.
It is no passage for a little boat
    This which goes cleaving the audacious prow,
    Nor for a pilot who would spare himself.

Dante is not sparing himself here in his wrestling to communicate to us something that strains even the semidivine powers of poetry. But Beatrice, his channel of grace, will not allow him to rest content with looking at the face he has loved since his youth. Other wonders are now present:

> Why doth my face so much enamour thee,
>   That to the garden fair thou turnest not,
>   Which under the rays of Christ is blossoming?
> There is the Rose in which the Word Divine
>   Became incarnate; there the lilies are
>   By whose perfume the good way was discovered.

The rose is clearly Mary, and the lilies the apostles. Dante praises the illuminating power for so enabling him to look on these rays that he sees more and more as he does so. Especially the mention of Mary confirms in him a daily desire to see the final vision:

> The name of that fair flower I e'er invoke
>   Morning and evening utterly enthralled
>   My soul to gaze upon the greater fire.

When Dante has Christ and Mary clearly fixed in his sight, a glowing crown comes down on the Virgin's head, representing the angel Gabriel who speaks so sweetly that Dante says:

> Whatever melody most sweetly soundeth
>   On earth, and to itself most draws the soul,
>   Would seem a cloud that, rent asunder, thunders,
> Compared unto the sounding of that lyre
>   Wherewith was crowned the sapphire beautiful,
>   Which gives the clearest heaven its sapphire hue.
> "I am Angelic Love, that circle round
>   The joy sublime which breathes from out the womb
>   That was the hostelry of our Desire;
> And I shall circle, Lady of Heaven, while
>   Thou followest thy Son, and mak'st diviner
>   The sphere supreme, because thou enterest there."

There are no better words for these experiences than Dante's own. But his vision still fails him because the spirits shown ascend to the Primum Mobile, still higher above him. And as a connecting of the end of this episode with the beginning, a certain childlike affection remains among the other souls:

> And as a little child, that towards its mother
> Stretches its arms, when it the milk hath taken,
> Through impulse kindled into outward flame,
> Each of those gleams of whiteness upward reached
> So with its summit, that the deep affection
> They had for Mary was revealed to me.
> Thereafter they remained there in my sight,
> Regina coeli singing with such sweetness,
> That ne'er from me has the delight departed.

Canto 24

To follow all that is happening now, a reader must read all of Dante's words. Here we can only jump, as he says he is forced to by their inadequacy, to the light that now comes to him, none other than the spirit of St. Peter. Beatrice implores him to whom the Lord gave the keys to the kingdom to examine Dante about the faith "By means of which thou on the sea didst walk." And we are reminded of the several places where Dante has pointed out the vastness of the sea of being on which he now moves. Both Beatrice and Peter know from their vision of the divine knowledge that Dante has faith and the other theological virtues, but it is the nature of this realm that Dante himself now begins to speak out the great joy in the redemption that he, and we, have seen the redeemed souls display. Using the familiar image in the medieval world of a university student about to answer inquiries to confirm his degree, Dante says he nervously armed himself with everything he could recall. Peter asks: "Say, thou good Christian; manifest thyself; / What is the Faith?" This request reminds Dante of Peter's brother in Christ, St. Paul:

> "As the truthful pen,
> Father, of thy dear brother wrote of it,
> Who put with thee Rome into the good way,
> Faith is the substance of the things we hope for,
> And evidence of those that are not seen;
> And this appears to me its quiddity."

Then heard I: "Very rightly thou perceivest,
　If well thou understandest why he placed it
　With substances and then with evidences."
And I thereafterward: "The things profound,
　That here vouchsafe to me their apparition,
　Unto all eyes below are so concealed,
That they exist there only in belief,
　Upon the which is founded the high hope,
　And hence it takes the nature of a substance.
And it behoveth us from this belief
　To reason without having other sight,
　And hence it has the nature of evidence."

Dante is expressing how the necessary nature of faith as an unseen premise in this life becomes a visible substance in the next. He confesses that he has this faith, and at Peter's inquiry into how he acquired it, Dante responds with a shining outburst that, in its own way, mimics the effulgence of the heavenly spirits:

"The large outpouring
　Of Holy Spirit, which has been diffused
　Upon the ancient parchments and the new,
A syllogism is, which proved it to me
　With such acuteness, that, compared therewith,
　All demonstration seems to me obtuse."
And then I heard: "The ancient and the new
　Postulates, that to thee are so conclusive,
　Why dost thou take them for the word divine?"
And I: "The proofs, which show the truth to me,
　Are the works subsequent, whereunto Nature
　Ne'er heated iron yet, nor anvil beat."
'Twas answered me: "Say, who assureth thee
　That those works ever were? the thing itself
　That must be proved, nought else to thee affirms it."
"Were the world to Christianity converted,"
　I said, "withouten miracles, this one
　Is such, the rest are not its hundredth part;
Because that poor and fasting thou didst enter
　Into the field to sow there the good plant,
　Which was a vine and has become a thorn!"
This being finished, the high, holy Court
　Resounded through the spheres, "One God we praise!"

In melody that there above is chanted.
And then that Baron, who from branch to branch,
   Examining, had thus conducted me,
   Till the extremest leaves we were approaching,
Again began: "The Grace that dallying
   Plays with thine intellect thy mouth has opened,
   Up to this point, as it should opened be,
So that I do approve what forth emerged;
   But now thou must express what thou believest,
   And whence to thy belief it was presented."
"O holy father, spirit who beholdest
   What thou believedst so that thou o'ercamest,
   Towards the sepulchre, more youthful feet,"
Began I, "thou dost wish me in this place
   The form to manifest of my prompt belief,
   And likewise thou the cause thereof demandest.
And I respond: In one God I believe,
   Sole and eterne, who moveth all the heavens
   With love and with desire, himself unmoved;
And of such faith not only have I proofs
   Physical and metaphysical, but gives them
   Likewise the truth that from this place rains down
Through Moses, through the Prophets and the Psalms,
   Through the Evangel, and through you, who wrote
   After the fiery Spirit sanctified you;
In Persons three eterne believe, and these
   One essence I believe, so one and trine
   They bear conjunction both with sunt and est.
With the profound condition and divine
   Which now I touch upon, doth stamp my mind
   Ofttimes the doctrine evangelical.
This the beginning is, this is the spark
   Which afterwards dilates to vivid flame,
   And, like a star in heaven, is sparkling in me."
Even as a lord who hears what pleaseth him
   His servant straight embraces, gratulating
   For the good news as soon as he is silent;
So, giving me its benediction, singing,
   Three times encircled me, when I was silent,
   The apostolic light, at whose command
I spoken had, in speaking I so pleased him.

In this exchange, what might seem the dull responses of a cate-
chism or a list of proofs from sacred history takes on an eagerness
and delight. Were we in the proper frame of mind, like the apos-
tles and St. Paul, these mere formulas would come to life in us as
well, making our very lives concrete expressions of a reality that
too often we only "believe" with some small part of our brains.

Canto 25

Having manifested the Faith within him, this Dante, who is
becoming part of the celestial realms in his own being, must now
address the second theological virtue, hope. As he turns to that
topic, he first expresses a hope that his great labors in this poem
may someday bring him back to his earthly home, Florence. It is
typical of Dante, as we have come to know him, that even at
these exalted heights he would recall the earthly place wherein
he was baptized and entered the faith:

> If e'er it happen that the Poem Sacred,
>   To which both heaven and earth have set their hand,
>   So that it many a year hath made me lean,
> O'ercome the cruelty that bars me out
>   From the fair sheepfold, where a lamb I slumbered
>   An enemy to the wolves that war upon it,
> With other voice forthwith, with other fleece
>   Poet will I return, and at my font
>   Baptismal will I take the laurel crown;
> Because into the Faith that maketh known
>   All souls to God there entered I, and then
>   Peter for her sake thus my brow encircled.

But so that Dante may now make manifest his hope in full,
another light flutters down as gentle as a dove alongside Peter.
This is the apostle James, one of the "pillars of the church" in the
New Testament. Beatrice, ever solicitous of Dante's advancement,
asks James to evoke Dante's hope. James assures Dante that he
will do fine, "For what comes hither from the mortal world /
Must needs be ripened in our radiance." Dante has been given
this great experience, says James, so that he may strengthen him-
self and others on Earth. But without waiting for Dante's reply,

Beatrice makes a comment about him that we must read as an expression of Dante's own testament:

> "No child whatever the Church Militant
> Of greater hope possesses, as is written
> In that Sun which irradiates all our band;
> Therefore it is conceded him from Egypt
> To come into Jerusalem to see,
> Or ever yet his warfare be completed.

The Egypt and Jerusalem spoken of here are symbolic of the exile on Earth and the homecoming to the true land in the Heavens. Having paid Dante this high compliment, Beatrice knows he will have no difficulty in manifesting these realities he eminently possesses:

> "Hope," said I, "is the certain expectation
> Of future glory, which is the effect
> Of grace divine and merit precedent.
> From many stars this light comes unto me;
> But he instilled it first into my heart
> Who was chief singer unto the chief captain.
> 'Sperent in te,' in the high Theody
> He sayeth, 'those who know thy name;' and who
> Knoweth it not, if he my faith possess?
> Thou didst instil me, then, with this instilling
> In the Epistle, so that I am full,
> And upon others rain again your rain."

Thus, Dante attributes to the psalmist David and St. James himself an influence on him that has enabled him to be full himself and to rain down the grace he has received upon others. James flashes with pleasure at this acknowledgment, and Dante expresses his belief that joy in body and soul shall someday be ours, as is prefigured in the book of Revelation. The Heavens repeat the Psalm "Let them hope in thee who know Thy name" (Ps. 9:10) and then a third light comes on, brighter than the sun:

> This is the one who lay upon the breast
> Of him our Pelican; and this is he
> To the great office from the cross elected.

This is obviously St. John the Evangelist, the disciple whom Jesus loved and who was given as son to Mary by Christ from the cross. John's contemplative gifts were such that some believed he had risen, body and soul, to Heaven. But Dante repudiates that rumor here after gazing to see if John still had his earthly body:

> Even as a man who gazes, and endeavours
>   To see the eclipsing of the sun a little,
>   And who, by seeing, sightless doth become,
> So I became before that latest fire,
>   While it was said, "Why dost thou daze thyself
>   To see a thing which here hath no existence?
> Earth in the earth my body is, and shall be
>   With all the others there, until our number
>   With the eternal proposition tallies.
> With the two garments in the blessed cloister
>   Are the two lights alone that have ascended:
>   And this shalt thou take back into your world."

Christ and Mary alone ascended in the body to the heavens. But this prolonged staring has produced a new situation:

> Ah, how much in my mind was I disturbed,
>   When I turned round to look on Beatrice,
>   That her I could not see, although I was
> Close at her side and in the Happy World!

Canto 26

This strange inability to see Beatrice because of Dante's staring at the brightness of St. John the Evangelist alerts us to the fact that having manifested his beliefs about faith and hope, Dante now must speak of love. Beatrice, of course, he has always maintained was the first motive force toward his discovery of the universal love, but here she is temporarily removed from the discourse so that Dante may speak of the other ways in which his soul expanded into a belief in the reality of the third theological virtue, charity. Beatrice will return for a different purpose later. In the meantime, says John, it is fitting that Dante should speak of love until his sight recovers:

> "Begin then, and declare to what thy soul
>   Is aimed, and count it for a certainty,
>   Sight is in thee bewildered and not dead;

> Because the Lady, who through this divine
>   Region conducteth thee, has in her look
>   The power the hand of Ananias had."
> I said: "As pleaseth her, or soon or late
>   Let the cure come to eyes that portals were
>   When she with fire I ever burn with entered.
> The Good, that gives contentment to this Court,
>   The Alpha and Omega is of all
>   The writing that love reads me low or loud."

Ananias, of course, was the figure who restored St. Paul's sight
after he was blinded by the revelation of God on the road to
Damascus. The parallel here is clear. But Dante's reply under-
scores how totally at one he now is with the fire that entered him
at the sight of Beatrice, so that the Good toward which all things
were initially aimed is not only the beginning and the end, but
every detail along the way, even when it seems, from a human
point of view, to have resulted in a kind of imperfection to be
endured.

But Dante also reviews the other human means through which
the same reality of the Good was brought home to him and
inclined the will to love:

> "By philosophic arguments,
>   And by authority that hence descends,
>   Such love must needs imprint itself in me;
> For Good, so far as good, when comprehended
>   Doth straight enkindle love, and so much greater
>   As more of goodness in itself it holds;
> Then to that Essence (whose is such advantage
>   That every good which out of it is found
>   Is nothing but a ray of its own light)
> More than elsewhither must the mind be moved
>   Of every one, in loving, who discerns
>   The truth in which this evidence is founded.
> Such truth he to my intellect reveals
>   Who demonstrates to me the primal love
>   Of all the sempiternal substances.
> The voice reveals it of the truthful Author,
>   Who says to Moses, speaking of Himself,
>   'I will make all my goodness pass before thee.'
> Thou too revealest it to me, beginning

> The loud Evangel, that proclaims the secret
> Of heaven to earth above all other edict."

John approves of these answers, but in order that Dante may speak out the fullness of the joy and gratitude of his love, prods him to think if there are any other ways he has been "bitten" by the goodness in the world to love:

> "All of those bites
> Which have the power to turn the heart to God
> Unto my charity have been concurrent.
> The being of the world, and my own being,
> The death which He endured that I may live,
> And that which all the faithful hope, as I do,
> With the forementioned vivid consciousness
> Have drawn me from the sea of love perverse,
> And of the right have placed me on the shore.
> The leaves, wherewith embowered is all the garden
> Of the Eternal Gardener, do I love
> As much as he has granted them of good."

And now that Dante has paid full tribute to the universal love, he hears a choir, including Beatrice, singing, "Holy, Holy, Holy," and she restores his vision to him. We are perhaps meant to understand by this that having stated the substance of universal love, Dante now returns to the experience of it in its multiple dimensions.

And having discoursed on the primal love that came to him and all the human race, he also now encounters a fourth light, the soul of the first human being to experience this love, Adam. Beatrice herself instructs him, and the encounter stimulates him into even greater desire. Specifically, Dante wants to know how long ago God placed Adam in the Garden, how long Adam remained there, what was his fault, and what language the first people used? Adam settles the question of the first sin first by laying aside the various speculations that some greater sin must have been concealed symbolically in the eating of the apple. Adam says there was no greater sin other than the turning aside from the divine will. He lays out the number of years since the creation, remarks that he spent only about six hours in Paradise before the Fall, and tells Dante that the original language of the race was already extinct by the time of Nimrod. This may seem of merely historical curiosity to us, but it also suggests that Dante wants to be clear about human origins as he comes to a final knowledge of human ends. For example, he wonders if there was some God-willed language for humanity. Adam points out to him, however, that:

> A natural action is it that man speaks;
>> But whether thus or thus, doth nature leave
>> To your own art, as seemeth best to you.
> Ere I descended to the infernal anguish,
>> "El" was on earth the name of the Chief Good,
>> From whom comes all the joy that wraps me round
> "Eli" he then was called, and that is proper,
>> Because the use of men is like a leaf
>> On bough, which goeth and another cometh.

Canto 27

St. Peter steps forth again as all the heavens assume a red hue. Red, as we know, is the color traditionally associated with charity. But in what seems something of a spiritual reach at this level of perfection, Dante suggests that the heavens are turning red here out of embarrassment for what the times have wrought upon the worship of God. The names in the previous canto changed naturally without affecting seriously the substance of devotion; Peter mentions another kind of change by which "my place"—and he repeats the possessive for emphasis—as good guide for the church has declined to the corruptions of Dante's time:

> "If I my colour change,
>> Marvel not at it; for while I am speaking
>> Thou shalt behold all these their colour change.
> He who usurps upon the earth my place,
>> My place, my place, which vacant has become
>> Before the presence of the Son of God,
> Has of my cemetery made a sewer
>> Of blood and stench, whereby the Perverse One
>> Who fell from here, below there is appeased!"

Blood, too, is red, and the blood of the Lamb and the early martyrs was shed out of love for the human race and on behalf of the church:

> "The spouse of Christ has never nurtured been
>   On blood of mine, of Linus and of Cletus,
>   To be made use of in acquest of gold;
> But in acquest of this delightful life
>   Sixtus and Pius, Urban and Calixtus,
>   After much lamentation, shed their blood.
> Our purpose was not, that on the right hand
>   Of our successors should in part be seated
>   The Christian folk, in part upon the other;
> Nor that the keys which were to me confided
>   Should e'er become the escutcheon on a banner,
>   That should wage war on those who are baptized;
> Nor I be made the figure of a seal
>   To privileges venal and mendacious,
>   Whereat I often redden and flash with fire.
> In garb of shepherds the rapacious wolves
>   Are seen from here above o'er all the pastures!
>   O wrath of God, why dost thou slumber still?"

And Peter predicts that vengeance is coming and tells Dante to speak of it back in the world. But the discourses on charity and its perversion in the church are done. These souls are ready to rise like fiery snowflakes until they escape Dante's sight.

And he himself is rising again, now to the Primum Mobile, or crystalline Heaven, which turns rapidly out of desire to touch the Empyrean and, in its turn, imparts whatever motion there is beneath on all the universe. Its motion is caused by something unmoved and involves other concepts that go beyond everyday understanding:

> "The nature of that motion, which keeps quiet
>   The centre and all the rest about it moves,
>   From hence begins as from its starting point.
> And in this heaven there is no other Where
>   Than in the Mind Divine, wherein is kindled
>   The love that turns it, and the power it rains.
> Within a circle light and love embrace it

> Even as this doth the others, and that precinct
> He who encircles it alone controls."

Beatrice engages in a bit of denunciation herself in this Heaven, observing that from this pure beginning all things get a proper direction, but covetousness and other sins turn aside that impulse, and she laments with Dante that no one governs properly on Earth, not Christian emperor, not pope, as the first motion apparently would wish, so that the whole human family goes astray.

Canto 28

> After the truth against the present life
> Of miserable mortals was unfolded
> By her who doth imparadise my mind,
> As in a looking-glass a taper's flame
> He sees who from behind is lighted by it,
> Before he has it in his sight or thought,
> And turns him round to see if so the glass
> Tell him the truth, and sees that it accords
> Therewith as doth a music with its metre,
> In similar wise my memory recollecteth
> That I did, looking into those fair eyes,
> Of which Love made the springes to ensnare me.

We have here one of the deep turning points of the *Comedy* and of the spiritual life. Although we have not lingered over the many places in the *Paradise* where Beatrice's brilliance overcomes Dante, it is clear that those passages show that he is gradually becoming accustomed to looking on her directly as a glorified being, even as he is becoming adjusted to the heavens. But now Dante does something that no other medieval troubadour ever thought to do. For all the talk in love poetry about seeing God in the beloved's eyes, no one had previously imagined that it might be possible to turn from the reflection in those pupils and look upon the source of that light itself:

> A point beheld I, that was raying out
> Light so acute, the sight which it enkindles
> Must close perforce before such great acuteness.

And whatsoever star seems smallest here
   Would seem to be a moon, if placed beside it,
   As one star with another star is placed.
Perhaps at such a distance as appears
   A halo cincturing the light that paints it,
   When densest is the vapour that sustains it,
Thus distant round the point a circle of fire
   So swiftly whirled, that it would have surpassed
   Whatever motion soonest girds the world;
And this was by another circumcinct,
   That by a third, the third then by a fourth,
   By a fifth the fourth, and then by a sixth the fifth;
The seventh followed thereupon in width
   So ample now, that Juno's messenger
   Entire would be too narrow to contain it.
Even so the eighth and ninth; and every one
   More slowly moved, according as it was
   In number distant farther from the first.
And that one had its flame most crystalline
   From which less distant was the stainless spark,
   I think because more with its truth imbued.

As occurred at the depths of Hell, when seeing all evil finally turned the pilgrimage around into a climb toward the good, so we see here a kind of Christian inversion of the Ptolemaic astronomy available to Dante. When he looks away from Beatrice at the piercing point of light that is the origin of her luminosity and the whole universe, the world is turned inside out. The center now is that light, and all the other spheres we have passed through are more or less distant from it, this earth the most distant of all. In a surprising way, this Copernican Revolution in perspective accords with later discoveries of astrophysics, particularly the theory of the Big Bang, the primal release of light and energy, or the origin of the universe. Spiritually, however, it is after we have learned the true order of the universe both conceptually and experientially that this immediate perception of reality becomes available to us. Beatrice herself tells Dante as he stares that, "From that point / Hangs heaven and all of nature." And she adds of the Empyrean, the circle of fire; that it is swift; "through burning love whereby it is spurred on."

Dante has the experience, but not yet the explanation. Beatrice shows that he now sees the virtue rather than the appearance:

"The circles corporal are wide and narrow
  According to the more or less of virtue
  Which is distributed through all their parts.
The greater goodness works the greater weal,
  The greater weal the greater body holds,
  If perfect equally are all its parts.
Therefore this one which sweeps along with it
  The universe sublime, doth correspond
  Unto the circle which most loves and knows.
On which account, if thou unto the virtue
  Apply thy measure, not to the appearance
  Of substances that unto thee seem round,
Thou wilt behold a marvellous agreement,
  Of more to greater, and of less to smaller,
  In every heaven, with its Intelligence."

These intelligences correspond with the angels who are arranged in hierarchy around God according to the traditional order. Dante's is a vision of the mind ever more closely approaching the whole represented by God, and Beatrice makes sure to say at this point:

From this it may be seen how blessedness
  Is founded in the faculty which sees,
  And not in that which loves, and follows next;
And of this seeing merit is the measure,
  Which is brought forth by grace, and by good will;
  Thus on from grade to grade doth it proceed.

This should not be understood as some cold vision of theological speculation in the mind as superior to the love in the heart. But, as in the opening image of Dante's turn from Beatrice to the piercing star, it is by the apprehension of things that we necessarily first come to love them. Intellect precedes will by discovering the object, but will responds in a series of mutually reinforcing acts that direct the mind deeper and deeper. Dante here sets himself against a notion common in every age that love alone is enough; it is, but only after we have seen clearly enough to distinguish what Love is in its deepest being and manifold manifestations.

Canto 29

This understanding of articulated love is necessary because Love himself, by his very nature, created the world so that new loves in a new order come to exist. As Beatrice explains this orthodox doctrine, Love gives rise to love:

Not to acquire some good unto himself,
    Which is impossible, but that his splendour
    In its resplendency may say, "Subsisto,"
In his eternity outside of time,
    Outside all other limits, as it pleased him,
    Into new Loves the Eternal Love unfolded.
Nor as if torpid did he lie before;
    For neither after nor before proceeded
    The going forth of God upon these waters.

Beatrice uses Aristotle's notions, which were common to the physics and metaphysics of Dante's day, to indicate how the Creator created all things without going out of himself, since in his eternity there is neither before nor after, nor does he need to change to produce change. Some thinkers argued that God first created the angels and the heavens and only much later the world, but Dante, through Beatrice, states the opposite view that the angels, who move the heavens and earth below as intelligences, had to have immediate effects themselves. But we recall that prior to the fall on earth there was a fall in heaven when Lucifer refused the order of love, which now has become a prison for him in Hell. He is stuck forever in his very attempt to flee. The angels now cannot fall, since they were confirmed, in their modesty and obedience, in eternal union with the Almighty. To complete this brief course in angelology, Beatrice says they are wrong on Earth who think that, as creatures, angels must remember and act like us: they look directly in God and have no need of such operations.

This whole discourse connects back with the start of the previous canto, where we were told that we are now seeing the true order of virtue rather than the appearances. Unfortunately, on earth many religious figures indulge in idle and erroneous speculation about things on which they should either be silent or stay, in loving faithfulness, close to the text of the Scriptures. Or as Beatrice puts it:

Christ did not to his first disciples say,
　　"Go forth, and to the world preach idle tales,"
　　But unto them a true foundation gave;
And this so loudly sounded from their lips,
　　That, in the warfare to enkindle Faith,
　　They made of the Evangel shields and lances.
Now men go forth with jests and drolleries
　　To preach, and if but well the people laugh,
　　The hood puffs out, and nothing more is asked.

Since Dante may look directly at reality now, and that looking
and seeing are what kindles love, Beatrice directs him:

Hence, inasmuch as on the act conceptive
　　The affection followeth, of love the sweetness
　　Therein diversely fervid is or tepid.
The height behold now and the amplitude
　　Of the eternal power, since it hath made
　　Itself so many mirrors, where 'tis broken,
One in itself remaining as before.

Canto 30

To carry out this request, Dante will have to leave Beatrice, so
that he may encounter what exceeds even what Beatrice has been
to him in earthly life. She must leave him so that what she
brought him will appear in its own right. Dante pays her one
final, all-encompassing tribute:

If what has hitherto been said of her
　　Were all concluded in a single praise,
　　Scant would it be to serve the present turn.
Not only does the beauty I beheld
　　Transcend ourselves, but truly I believe
　　Its Maker only may enjoy it all.
　.　.　.　.　.　.　.　.　.　.　.
From the first day that I beheld her face
　　In this life, to the moment of this look,
　　The sequence of my song has ne'er been severed;
But now perforce this sequence must desist
　　From following her beauty with my verse,
　　As every artist at his uttermost.

> Such as I leave her to a greater fame
>> Than any of my trumpet, which is bringing
>> Its arduous matter to a final close.

But she has a few last words to impart to this poet who has served her faithfully from their meeting as children in Florence until this culminating vision of the universe. She, this specific woman born at a specific time and place, who lived through certain temporal events with which Dante has been involved, has led him to a place where she must now take her place in the order that is her origin. And Dante will have need of another guide to take him to that final consummation where he and Beatrice and all the redeemed are centered in attention upon Love. Love is the first topic Beatrice turns to as she prepares her departure.

> With voice and gesture of a perfect leader
>> She recommenced: "We from the greatest body
>> Have issued to the heaven that is pure light;
> Light intellectual replete with love,
>> Love of true good replete with ecstasy,
>> Ecstasy that transcendeth every sweetness.
> Here shalt thou see the one host and the other
>> Of Paradise, and one in the same aspects
>> Which at the final judgment thou shalt see."

In this Heaven of pure light, Dante is encompassed by a brightness that admits of no discernment of anything but the light itself. Beatrice says that this is the final preparation for illumination that makes the "candle ready for the flame." And the result is that when it disperses, Dante possesses vision equal to anything he will try to see. In the inversion of the universe caused by the passage out of the appearance of time and space, he will be seeing the redeemed as they actually exist in heaven, not as earlier in a form adapted to human weakness. And this comes about in two ways. First, he sees them recapitulated in a symbolic fashion in the river of time:

> And light I saw in fashion of a river
>> Fulvid with its effulgence, 'twixt two banks
>> Depicted with an admirable Spring.
> Out of this river issued living sparks,
>> And on all sides sank down into the flowers,

> Like unto rubies that are set in gold;
> And then, as if inebriate with the odours,
> They plunged again into the wondrous torrent,
> And as one entered issued forth another.

This is a prefiguring of the even greater vision yet to come. Beatrice tells him that he must drink of this river to pass beyond to the reality. And again Dante speaks of himself in terms of a newborn child entering this kingdom of heaven:

> There is no babe that leaps so suddenly
> With face towards the milk, if he awake
> Much later than his usual custom is,
> As I did, that I might make better mirrors
> Still of mine eyes, down stooping to the wave
> Which flows that we therein be better made.
> And even as the penthouse of mine eyelids
> Drank of it, it forthwith appeared to me
> Out of its length to be transformed to round.
> Then as a folk who have been under masks
> Seem other than before, if they divest
> The semblance not their own they disappeared in.

This unmasking, which reveals true identities, is connected with the nature of the realm. Dante says that a ray of light from God descends to the Primum Mobile, from which it is reflected back up into a flowerlike arrangement of souls centered on God:

> So, ranged aloft all round about the light,
> Mirrored I saw in more ranks than a thousand
> All who above there have from us returned
> And if the lowest row collect within it
> So great a light, how vast the amplitude
> Is of this Rose in its extremest leaves!

Though compared with a rose, in this vision there is no diminishment caused by distance; no shadow intervenes because every part of the eternal realm communicates with every other by means of the Godhead.

Canto 31

> In fashion then as of a snow-white rose
> Displayed itself to me the saintly host,

Whom Christ in his own blood had made his bride,
But the other host, that flying sees and sings
　　The glory of Him who doth enamour it,
　　And the goodness that created it so noble,
Even as a swarm of bees, that sinks in flowers
　　One moment, and the next returns again
　　To where its labour is to sweetness turned,
Sank into the great flower, that is adorned
　　With leaves so many, and thence reascended
　　To where its love abideth evermore.
Their faces had they all of living flame,
　　And wings of gold, and all the rest so white
　　No snow unto that limit doth attain.
From bench to bench, into the flower descending,
　　They carried something of the peace and ardour
　　Which by the fanning of their flanks they won.
Nor did the interposing 'twixt the flower
　　And what was o'er it of such plenitude
　　Of flying shapes impede the sight and splendour;
Because the light divine so penetrates
　　The universe, according to its merit,
　　That naught can be an obstacle against it.
This realm secure and full of gladsomeness,
　　Crowded with ancient people and with modern,
　　Unto one mark had all its look and love.

The angels that fly like bees around this flower communicating
the primal love and the ample blossoming of souls thus form one
thing that Dante first takes in its general form. But when he turns
to Beatrice for further guidance his expectation is fulfilled in a
different way than he thought:

One thing I meant, another answered me;
　　I thought I should see Beatrice, and saw
　　An Old Man habited like the glorious people.
O'erflowing was he in his eyes and cheeks
　　With joy benign, in attitude of pity
　　As to a tender father is becoming.
And "She, where is she?" instantly I said;
　　Whence he: "To put an end to thy desire,
　　Me Beatrice hath sent from mine own place.
And if thou lookest up to the third round

> Of the first rank, again shalt thou behold her
> Upon the throne her merits have assigned her."

And as a final tribute to her Dante intones a prayer:

> O Lady, thou in whom my hope is strong,
> And who for my salvation didst endure
> In Hell to leave the imprint of thy feet,
> Of whatsoever things I have beheld,
> As coming from thy power and from thy goodness
> I recognise the virtue and the grace.
> Thou from a slave hast brought me unto freedom,
> By all those ways, by all the expedients,
> Whereby thou hadst the power of doing it.
> Preserve towards me thy magnificence,
> So that this soul of mine, which thou hast healed,
> Pleasing to thee be loosened from the body.

She and Dante gaze on one another one last time before she turns her eyes toward God and the old man tells Dante to look around the rose as a preparation:

> And she, the Queen of Heaven, for whom I burn
> Wholly with love, will grant us every grace,
> Because that I her faithful Bernard am.

Dante is transfixed at learning that this soul is Bernard of Clairvaux's, the great contemplative and devotee of the Virgin Mary. But we are in the highest Heaven now, where the accomplishments and virtues of individuals are gathered up into a whole of far greater significance. Bernard directs Dante's eyes to their proper place where the Queen of Heaven is surrounded by more than a thousand angels, and he and Bernard both turn to that place for the last touches needed for their vision.

Canto 32

In the perfect wheel, the two gaze upon the various souls redeemed by Christ, on one side those who believed before he came, on the other those who believed after. In addition to his mother, Mary, on the pre-Christ side we see holy women such as Mary Magdalene, Rachel, Sarah, Rebecca, Judith, and Ruth. On the post-Christ side are John the Baptist, Francis, Benedict, and Augustine. Bernard points out many children who died before they had full power of choice. But we are nearing the point where we will leave behind distinctions and classifications because there is only one more being between Dante and God and, as the channel of grace to all humanity, Dante must pass through an encounter with her if he is to meet her Son:

> "... Look now into the face that unto Christ
>   Hath most resemblance; for its brightness only
>   Is able to prepare thee to see Christ."
> On her did I behold so great a gladness
>   Rain down, borne onward in the holy minds
>   Created through that altitude to fly,
> That whatsoever I had seen before
>   Did not suspend me in such admiration,
>   Nor show me such similitude of God.
> And the same Love that first descended there,
>   "Ave Maria, gratia plena," singing,
>   In front of her his wings expanded wide.
> Unto the canticle divine responded
>   From every part the court beatified,
>   So that each sight became serener for it.

This is the angel Gabriel, the one who brought the annunciation of God's full love into the world, and this sets off Bernard on one last pass through the great figures in salvation history before he prepares Dante for the final step:

> "Truly, lest peradventure thou recede,
>   Moving thy wings believing to advance,
>   By prayer behoves it that grace be obtained;
> Grace from that one who has the power to aid thee;
>   And thou shalt follow me with thy affection
>   That from my words thy heart turn not aside."
> And he began this holy orison.

Canto 33

> Thou Virgin Mother, daughter of thy Son
>   Humble and high beyond all other creature,
>   The limit fixed of the eternal counsel,

Thou art the one who such nobility
  To human nature gave, that its Creator
  Did not disdain to make himself its creature.
Within thy womb rekindled was the love,
  By heat of which in the eternal peace
  After such wise this flower has germinated.
Here unto us thou art a noonday torch
  Of charity, and below there among mortals
  Thou art the living fountain-head of hope.
Lady thou art so great, and so prevailing,
  That he who wishes grace, nor runs to thee
  His aspirations without wings would fly.
Not only thy benignity gives succour
  To him who asketh it, but oftentimes
  Forerunneth of its own accord the asking
In thee compassion is, in thee is pity,
  In thee magnificence, in thee unites
  Whate'er of goodness is in any creature.
Now doth this man, who from the lowest depth
  Of the universe as far as here has seen
  One after one the spiritual lives,
Supplicate thee through grace for so much power
  That with his eyes he may uplift himself
  Higher towards the uttermost salvation.
And I, who never burned for my own seeing
  More than I do for his, all of my prayers
  Proffer to thee, and pray they come not short,
That thou wouldst scatter from him every cloud
  Of his mortality so with thy prayers,
  That the Chief Pleasure be to him displayed.
Still farther do I pray thee, Queen, who canst
  Whate'er thou wilt, that sound thou mayst preserve
  After so great a vision his affections.
Let thy protection conquer human movements;
  See Beatrice and all the blessed ones
  My prayers to second clasp their hands to thee!

This remarkable prayer reminds us that just as salvation passed
from God through Mary to the human race, so in the visionary
ascent we must pass individually, aided by all divine love,
through her back to God. This is no light step, and Dante makes
sure to have Bernard pray that this superhuman revelation not

overwhelm Dante's human affections, since he must return to earth to live several years still. And the way she leads him upward is by looking herself, with the perfect vision that said yes to the divine word that came to her:

> The eyes beloved and revered of God,
>> Fastened upon the speaker, showed to us
>> How grateful unto her are prayers devout;
> Then unto the Eternal Light they turned,
>> On which it is not credible could be
>> By any creature bent an eye so clear.
> And I, who to the end of all desires
>> Was now approaching, even as I ought
>> The ardour of desire within me ended.
> Bernard was beckoning unto me, and smiling,
>> That I should upward look; but I already
>> Was of my own accord such as he wished
> Because my sight, becoming purified,
>> Was entering more and more into the ray
>> Of the High Light which of itself is true.

This is a remarkable passage in that it suggests that Dante can see Bernard's gestures even though he is looking upward with the Virgin at God himself, an indirect indication of what has been claimed throughout this *cantica*, that as we become more advanced in the spiritual way, we know all things in God. What Dante can recall and tell of this experience is necessarily little and involves a final unfreezing of something within and dispersal of a mistaken wisdom:

> Even thus the snow is in the sun unsealed,
>> Even thus upon the wind in the light leaves
>> Were the soothsayings of the Sibyl lost.
> O Light Supreme, that dost so far uplift thee
>> From the conceits of mortals, to my mind
>> Of what thou didst appear re-lend a little,
> And make my tongue of so great puissance,
>> That but a single sparkle of thy glory
>> It may bequeath unto the future people;
> For by returning to my memory somewhat,
>> And by a little sounding in these verses,
>> More of thy victory shall be conceived!

Unlike previous points in the poem, where Dante feels he must turn aside in order not to be overcome, at this altitude the opposite is the case—to avert the eye from God is to be lost:

> I think the keenness of the living ray
>> Which I endured would have bewildered me,
>> If but mine eyes had been averted from it;
> And I remember that I was more bold
>> On this account to bear, so that I joined
>> My aspect with the Glory Infinite.
> O grace abundant, by which I presumed
>> To fix my sight upon the Light Eternal,
>> So that the seeing I consumed therein!

In a lovely and graceful passage, Dante ties together all philosophical conceptions and worldly experiences in a primary unity. And his emotions at recalling this confirm to him its reality:

> I saw that in its depth far down is lying
>> Bound up with love together in one volume,
>> What through the universe in leaves is scattered;
> Substance, and accident, and their operations,
>> All interfused together in such wise
>> That what I speak of is one simple light.
> The universal fashion of this knot
>> Methinks I saw, since more abundantly
>> In saying this I feel that I rejoice.

The simplicity of the experience somehow does not negate the fact of the three divine persons eternally reflecting one another:

> Shorter henceforward will my language fall
>> Of what I yet remember, than an infant's
>> Who still his tongue doth moisten at the breast
> Not because more than one unmingled semblance
>> Was in the living light on which I looked,
>> For it is always what it was before;
> But through the sight, that fortified itself
>> In me by looking, one appearance only
>> To me was ever changing as I changed.
> Within the deep and luminous subsistence
>> Of the High Light appeared to me three circles,
>> Of threefold colour and of one dimension
> And by the second seemed the first reflected

> As Iris is by Iris, and the third
> Seemed fire that equally from both is breathed.

In addition to this mystery of the Holy Trinity, in which the Three are One and unite all the good of the universe in one Good, Dante addresses God himself as he contemplates what is beyond all human grasp, because "our effigy"—which is to say, human nature as it existed in Christ—is in some incalculable fashion eternally joined with the simplicity of the Godhead as well. Here all poetry reaches its end, and all commentary on that poetry must also fall silent before the words that point beyond all words. Reality itself carries Dante to all that can be known, loved, and said:

> As the geometrician, who endeavours
>   To square the circle, and discovers not,
>   By taking thought, the principle he wants,
> Even such was I at that new apparition;
>   I wished to see how the image to the circle
>   Conformed itself, and how it there finds place;
> But my own wings were not enough for this,
>   Had it not been that then my mind there smote
>   A flash of lightning, wherein came its wish.
> Here vigour failed the lofty fantasy:
>   But now was turning my desire and will,
>   Even as a wheel that equally is moved,
> The Love which moves the sun and the other stars.

A Brief Bibliography

The only way to appreciate Dante fully is to read the *Divine Comedy* and *Vita Nuova* in their entirety, and to become familiar with at least parts of the other works. The most beautiful translation of the *Vita Nuova* is by the Victorian poet Dante Gabriel Rossetti in his *Dante and His Circle*, which includes other poems by Dante and his contemporaries. The more modern translations by Barbara Reynolds and Mark Musa provide good explanatory notes. We are fortunate to have good English verse translations with notes of the *Divine Comedy* by John Ciardi, Dorothy Sayers, Allen Mandelbaum, and Mark Musa (available with his translation of the *Vita Nuova* in *The Portable Dante*). The *Inferno* by Robert Pinsky may be the most poetically rich version of that *cantica*. Charles Singleton's prose translation of the *Comedy* and his extensive commentary remain the most useful tools in English for an in-depth study of Dante. All translations of great poets leave much to be desired, however, and the reader who really wishes to know Dante must eventually become familiar with the original Italian text.

The best brief introduction to Dante and his times is George Holmes's *Dante* in the Past Masters series. *Dante: A Collection of Critical Essays* (edited by John Freccero) and the *Cambridge Companion to Dante* assemble several of the most important readings of the poet in this century. Erich Auerbach's *Dante, Poet of the Secular World* examines Dante's importance to our modern self-understanding. Robert Hollander thoroughly explains Dante's method in *Allegory in Dante's Comedy* and in his commentary on Dante's letter to Can Grande della Scala. *Dante and Philosophy* by

Etienne Gilson provides a careful reading of this subject. Antonio C. Mastrobuono's *Dante's Journey of Sanctification* introduces important theological qualifications regarding Singleton's influential school of interpretation. Finally, no English reader should neglect the remarkable little book by Charles Williams, *The Figure of Beatrice*.